THE PRAIRIE SCHOOL

UNIVERSITY OF TORONTO PRESS

H. ALLEN BROOKS

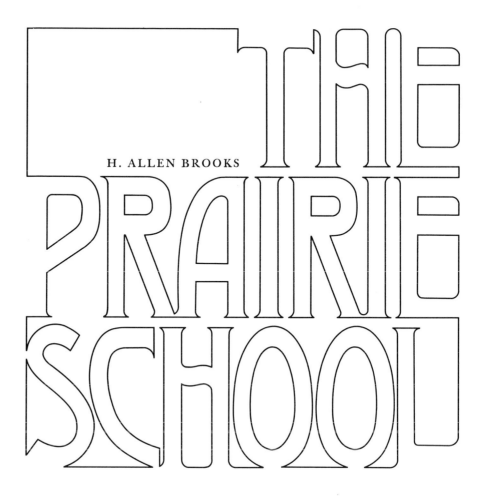

THE PRAIRIE SCHOOL

FRANK LLOYD WRIGHT AND HIS MIDWEST CONTEMPORARIES

© University of Toronto Press 1972
Manufactured in the United States of America for
University of Toronto Press, Toronto and Buffalo
ISBN 0-8020-5251-7
Microfiche ISBN 0-8020-0039-8
LC 72-151363

IN MEMORY OF MY PARENTS

CONTENTS

ILLUS
TRATIONS

PREFACE

This is a study of several men who sought to achieve a fresh and original architectural expression in the American Midwest during the early twentieth century. As a movement it owed much to the inspiration and guidance of Louis H. Sullivan and Frank Lloyd Wright, men whose work has often been subject to inquiry while their contemporaries – their circle – have until recently been largely ignored. And what is known about specific individuals has been presented out of context with the movement of which they were a part. Yet their achievement, which at times matches and occasionally surpasses that of their mentors, is only part of the story. Equally important is an assessment of each architect's contribution to the work of the others and to the movement as a whole, and an analysis of the movement itself – how and why it came into existence, what it achieved, and what caused its abrupt termination at the time of the First World War.

I have not included a detailed discussion of Wright's well known early work, assuming that the reader brings to this more specialized study a general knowledge of Wright's designs. Except for brief references, therefore, the material on Wright is limited to that which is either previously unpublished or not generally known. Since most of his buildings are familiar, the Wright material – and there is a considerable amount – deals primarily with other aspects of his life and career; such considerations will ultimately broaden and deepen our understanding of Wright as man and as architect. Concerning Sullivan, similar criteria were applied, except that a more detailed account, and more illustrations, are devoted to his less familiar post-1900 career. This study, which presents the work of so many men, cannot presume to be all-inclusive. Every building could not be discussed, and architects working outside the American Midwest – and therefore more or less peripherally connected with the movement – have often received only footnote recognition. Much remains to be done.

The book would not have taken its present form without the generous assistance of many of the architects themselves – all of whom are now dead. Frank Lloyd Wright was always most gracious and helpful, obviously enjoying a chance to reminisce about his earlier days and the men and the school of which he was such an essential part. Barry Byrne for twelve years supplied the author with information and, having been an employee at Wright's Studio from 1902 to 1908, kindly read my chapter 4, 'The Studio,' and offered a valuable critique. William G. Purcell, a tireless correspondent, was ever helpful, and Hugh M.G. Garden supplied much useful knowledge about the early days of the movement. John S. Van Bergen and Percy D. Bentley also contributed much. I made the acquaintance of Marion Mahony Griffin and Richard E. Schmidt too late in their lives to make full use of their vast information. Relatives – brothers, sisters, wives, and children, too numerous to mention individually – of Griffin, Maher, Spencer, Drummond, and others have been unstinting in their help.

I am deeply indebted to David Gebhard for generously supplying a wealth of information, and many photographs, concerning Purcell and Elmslie; to David T. Van Zanten for his studies of Marion Mahony; to Grant C. Manson for his work on early Wright; to Mark L. Peisch, William Rudd, and Donald L. Hoffmann for their work on Griffin, Maher, and Berry respectively; and to W.R. Hasbrouck, who has done much to stimulate interest in, and reassess the contribution of, these architects through his quarterly, *The Prairie School Review*, and through the issuance of reprints of previously unavailable articles and books by his Prairie School

Press. The Burnham Library of Architecture and the Avery Memorial Library, where much of the original documentation is now housed, merit special thanks as do their librarians, the late Dorothy Hofmeester and Adolf K. Placzek. Likewise useful was the valuable recording work of the Historic American Building Survey, made readily available to me through the kindness of James C. Massey. These reports are preserved in the Library of Congress. Support, of a financial nature, is gratefully acknowledged from the Canada Council for a fellowship, the American Council of Learned Societies for a grant-in-aid, and the University of Toronto for repeated summer research grants to help make this study possible. Publication was assisted by a grant from the Humanities Research Council of Canada, using funds provided by the Canada Council, and supported by the Publications Fund of the University of Toronto Press. To John M. Robson, who read the manuscript, and John Glover, who prepared many of the photographs, go a special appreciation. Many others, too numerous to list individually, deserve my thanks, some of whom, at least, are recognized in the footnotes.

Yet no enumeration would be complete without mention of teachers and mentors; thanks to Hugh Morrison, who first fired my interest in architectural history and over thirty years ago wrote his timeless study of Louis Sullivan, to the late Carroll L.V. Meeks, who supplied me with the tools and methods of research, to Vincent J. Scully, who originally suggested the subject of this book and has always been a source of inspiration, and to Carson Webster and Hayden Huntley, who initially guided my exploits through this material as a dissertation. Henry-Russell Hitchcock has never – officially – been my teacher, but in many respects I owe him the most of all.

H A B
Toronto, 25 November 1968

THE PRAIRIE SCHOOL

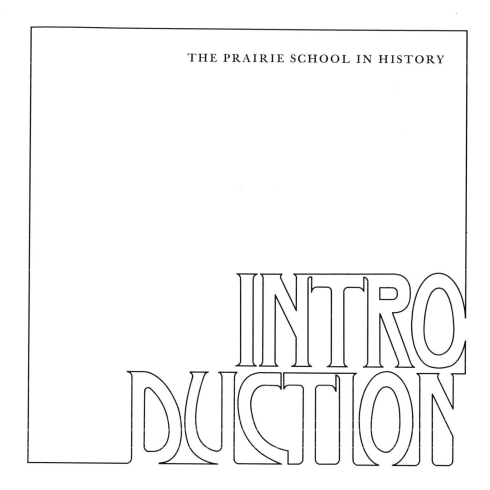

INTRODUCTION

The history of the Prairie School encompasses the period from 1900 until the First World War, yet its seeds were sown years earlier and its life continued, undernourished and without substantial growth, into the nineteen-twenties and thirties. The climacteric year was 1914. The heartland of the movement was the American Midwest, with the focus on suburban Chicago during the formative years and the vast reaches of rural Illinois, Minnesota, Iowa, and Wisconsin during the school's epic period; it was a regional manifestation of the international revolt and reform then occurring in the visual arts.

Irving K. Pond, writing in 1918, characterized the school as follows: 'In imitation of a certain broad and horizontal disposition of lines individually employed, a school of design has sprung up, for which its authors claim the title "American." The horizontal lines of the new expression appeal to the

FIG. 1 The prairie in central (Urbana) Illinois. Photo by H.A. Brooks

1 Irving K. Pond, *The Meaning of Architecture*, Boston, 1918, p. 174

disciples of this school as echoing the spirit of the prairies of the great Middle West, which to them embodies the essence of democracy.'[1] Pond's use of the word 'line,' however, must be interpreted in its broadest possible sense since it affected virtually every aspect of the residential design – the disposition of the single mass or composite massing, the shape of the low, long hipped or gable roof, the horizontal banding of windows, the emphatic belt course or shelf roof between the storeys – which often continued on one side as a lateral porch – and the broad, often forward-set foundation upon which the building was securely placed. The continuity of line, edge, and surface – an inheritance from the earlier Shingle Style – lent horizontal unity to the design, and against these horizontals a spirited interplay was established with short vertical accents, such as piers, mullions, and subsidiary masses.

Every feature of the building – from the basic mass to the smallest detail – was clear, precise, and angular. Ornament, per se, was a rarity; enrichment was dependent on the textural expression of materials and the often lively juxtaposition of various shapes and forms. Only in the stylized or abstract patterns of the leaded glass (or zinc strip) windows did one find consistent ornament. The historical styles, as commonly known, were rejected.

The materials employed were generally brick, or wood and plaster. A light tinted sand plaster (or stucco as it was also called) was used in combination with rough-sawn, stained wood which either suggested the building's structure or served as trim. Brick was never interspersed with these materials, being used alone, or on the first storey of a building when wood and plaster were combined above. Stone, or stone veneer, was rarely used, as was wood sheathing, except perhaps as horizontal boards and battens.

The innovation of new engineering skills or development of materials is not generally associated with residential design and only rarely were these matters the concern of the prairie architects. Steel beams were sometimes incorporated in the fabric of a house – as at Sullivan's Bradley house of 1909 (fig. 82) or Wright's Robie house of the previous year – but no attempt was made to give them a unique expression in design. Small commercial structures usually had load-bearing walls, with steel employed – if at all – only for the roof. Occasionally skeletal construction determined the design, as at Purcell and Elmslie's Merchants Bank of Winona (fig. 130) where the vertical and horizontal rhythm of brick-faced piers and spandrels directly articulated the steel frame.

Concrete was a more appropriate and natural material for small buildings than steel, and Wright's Unity Church of 1906 was a well known early instance of its use. But the form-work for small buildings was often too expensive and plaster over a wood frame was a ready substitute. Wright had proposed concrete for his *Ladies' Home Journal* project of 1906 (fig. 62), yet his executed versions of this design were of wood and plaster (fig. 63). Fortunately the design could be executed in alternate materials, but the broad, plain surfaces were obviously intended for casting in concrete. Only later, in his California houses, did Wright explore the less costly substitute of concrete blocks, but by that date Walter Burley Griffin had built at least two houses in America of concrete (Page and Blythe houses, Mason City, Iowa, 1912–13, figs. 177–8) and patented (1917) in Australia a system of Knitlock concrete blocks. Thus the architects of the Prairie School were aware of new materials and the latest engineering techniques, and in certain instances made notable contributions to the technology. But these matters were not central to their design requirements and had no sustained effect on their work.

In the early years of the movement the appearance of a building was often typified by a low rectangular shape against which were placed, asymmetrically, opposing features such as a forward projecting wing, a laterally extending porch, and an entrance opening. This compositional theme, not new to American architecture, had been seen in the work of H.H. Richardson, as in his libraries or the Potter house in St Louis. The Barrett house in Kenilworth (fig. 3) exemplifies this type, but it stands at that moment before the new vocabulary of form, particular combination of materials, and more expressive unity between plan and exterior shape, had transformed the type into the typical prairie house. This often asymmetrical massing of the early period was gradually modified toward a more symmetrical, formal, and compact disposition of forms in later years; meanwhile the sharp, crisp definition of the individual features continued. Typical of these later designs were the Decker house (by Purcell and Elmslie, fig. 138), the Baker house (by Guenzel and Drummond, fig. 189), or the Blythe house (by Griffin, fig. 179); the desire for a compact, solid form is also seen in most of the small-town banks.[2]

But these easily definable visual characteristics of the prairie house should not obscure our appreciation of how effectively these buildings worked. The plans were often highly sophisticated spatial arrangements which not only were intended to enhance the human experience for those within but also were devised to maximize the sense of space in a restricted

2 The cantilevered forms of Wright's later prairie houses, such as the Thomas Gale house of 1909, had little impact on his contemporaries, who were moving in the direction of more solid, compact forms – as Wright himself was to do after about 1915.

area. This has had immense significance in our time when land and building costs, and the absence of domestic help, have necessitated the construction of smaller and smaller homes, homes which can have a sense of spaciousness that belies their actual size. Wright's genius lay in his uncanny ability to manipulate space for the enrichment of the living experience – something that can be appreciated only by those who have intimately known his buildings. Yet other architects helped to interpret this manner of defining space, and make it available to a larger public. Nor was Wright the sole originator. In contrast to his horizontal extensions of overlapping space, Griffin manipulated space through a series of vertically interpenetrating levels, thereby foreshadowing similar mid-century developments in the United States. Such sophistications obviously eluded the speculative builder when he endeavored to recapitulate certain mannerisms of the prairie house.

Louis H. Sullivan was the spiritual leader of the school. To him the younger men turned for inspiration and instruction – yet Sullivan was the philosopher, the teacher who offered a manner of thinking rather than specific means to achieve an end. The 'Kindergarten Chats,' not actual designs, comprised his system of education, but for the young, impatient residential architect this was not enough. It remained for Sullivan's most gifted pupil, Frank Lloyd Wright, to devise new forms and to assume a master's mantle. Wright's proved ability, unquestioned genius, and aristocratic presence soon brought matters into focus and caused a reorientation and consolidation within the group. Uniformity of expression temporarily superseded experimentation, as many sought guidance or training from Wright; for some, his briefly became the dominant mode. However, the road to independence lay not, as Wright hoped, in separating his concept of an organic architecture from his vocabulary of form; rather it lay in accepting his forms as a consequence of his process, and then applying Sullivan's manner of thinking to gain independence and a more individual, personal expression in design.

In the earliest years, about 1900, less impetus went into designing than into discussion and debate, the forum being the Chicago Architectural Club, the Architectural League of America, or merely the communal drafting rooms shared by several architects in Steinway Hall. In the next period productivity somewhat increased, although fewer architects were concerned – some were working full-time for Wright, while others left the fold, preferring to pursue a safer, more traditional course. The final period, particularly after 1910, was the greatest for the school: the participants increased in number, productivity was at a peak, and the most brilliant designs were then produced.

Among the architects who constituted the Prairie School, and whose work was entirely, or for a period of time, identified with the movement, were Louis H. Sullivan, Frank Lloyd Wright, Walter Burley Griffin, George Grant Elmslie, William Gray Purcell, Barry Byrne, Hugh M.G. Garden, Richard E. Schmidt, Robert C. Spenser, Jr, William E. Drummond, Marion Mahony, Thomas E. Tallmadge, Vernon Watson, Dwight H. Perkins, John S. Van Bergen, Percy Dwight Bentley, Francis C. Sullivan, Parker N. Berry, and, more peripherally, George W. Maher, Arthur Heun, George Dean, and many others.

The Prairie School is related to an earlier development in Chicago, that which is now commonly called the Chicago School.[3] The line of continuity is largely through Sullivan, whose words and work expressed something more fundamental than the simplification and elimination which characterized most of Chicago's tall commercial buildings. Yet Sullivan and the other early skyscraper architects failed to develop an architecture indiscriminately applicable to residential, ecclesiastical, and civic design; theirs was a limited commercial style. This, indeed, was the great achievement of the Prairie School – they devised a mode universally applicable to every building type. And it is one which is distinctive from its predecessor even where commercial buildings are concerned. While the impetus of the earlier group was largely spent by 1900, such buildings as the Champlain (1903) and Republic (1905, 1909) by Holabird and Roche, the Chicago Business College (1910) by D.H. Burnham & Co., and the Lemoyne (1914–15) by Mundie, Jensen and McClurg, perpetuated the characteristics of the 1890s.[4] Stylistically they differ – in their rhythms, forms, and materials – from such contemporary Prairie School designs as the Schoenhofen Brewery Building (1902) by Garden for Schmidt (figs. 10–12), the Larkin Company Administration Building (1904) by Wright, the Carl Schurz High School (1908) by Perkins (fig. 53), or the Chicago Edison Shop (1912) by Purcell and Elmslie (fig. 155). The architects of the earlier group, with one exception, did not participate in the work of the Prairie School. That exception, of course, was Sullivan, whose work, after 1900, is predominantly associated with that of the younger men.

Historical interest in the Prairie School has fluctuated in accordance with our appreciation of the buildings themselves. The school was early recog-

3 To refer to the earlier group, the skyscraper builders, as a school may be of questionable usage. Certainly it is less appropriate in that context than it is in regard to the later group, i.e., the Prairie School.

4 Illustrations of these buildings will be found in Carl W. Condit, *The Chicago School of Architecture*, Chicago & London, 1964, figures 131, 136, 141, and 143 respectively.

5 Arthur C. David, 'The Architecture of Ideas,' *Architectural Record*, *15*, 1904, 363–4

6 F.W. Fitzpatrick, 'Chicago,' *Inland Architect and News Record*, *45*, 1905, 46

7 Ibid., p. 47

nized, and enjoyed national publicity until about the time of the First World War. With the nineteen-twenties it was all but forgotten. The thirties and forties saw two developments, both antipathetic to an appreciation of the school. One was the preference for monographs – such as those concerning Sullivan and Wright – studies which by their very nature de-emphasized the contribution of other men. Secondly there was a rising interest in technology and in the machine-age sources for modern architecture, which focused attention on the steel-frame commercial buildings of the 1890s in Chicago rather than the later residential designs and which, ultimately, led to a curious perversion of the term that long had denoted the Prairie School. The term 'Chicago School' had, by the nineteen-forties and fifties, come to designate those Chicago architects primarily concerned with commercial architecture during the 1890s – rather than the school which is our immediate concern. The later group had so nearly been forgotten that its designation was usurped for another cause. By the time interest revived in Wright's contemporaries (during the nineteen-fifties and sixties), the exclusiveness of the term was lost. Thus 'Prairie School' was substituted in its stead. This sequence of events is traced in greater detail below.

Writing for the *Architectural Record* in 1904, Arthur C. David was quick to observe the beginnings of a movement. The participants he called architectural 'protestants.' 'Their work,' he noted, 'derives its momentum and inspiration chiefly from the work of Mr Louis Sullivan, and from a very able architect, who issued from Mr Sullivan's office, Mr Frank Lloyd Wright. But it is too young to have a history, and probably ten years must pass before a very intelligent estimate can be placed upon its value.'[5] Later authors were more specific.

By 1905 F.W. Fitzpatrick could speak of a school. He said, 'Chicago has even created a new school, virtually a new style,' and went on to elaborate: 'Louis Sullivan was the first man – in Chicago or anywhere else – who boldly cast off the thralldom of precedent and treated the new condition of structure in a frank and artistic manner. ... Others, and younger men have followed in his wake. Wright, Maher, Long, Drummond, Shaw, Schmidt, and a dozen others, most of them in Chicago, and, if I am not mistaken, many of them pupils of Sullivan, have given us much ... , particularly in domestic architecture, of which we may well be proud.'[6]

While he applied no name, Fitzpatrick did juxtapose the words Chicago and school: 'So, with our Chicago school.'[7] Three years passed before

Thomas E. Tallmadge actually coined the phrase by entitling an article, 'The "Chicago School." ' In 1908 he wrote:

In regard to the workers individually ... a pretty story could be written descriptive of the early struggles and aspirations and ultimate success of the little band of enthusiasts who had raised their standard of revolt against the disciplined ranks and array of custom. An ideal artistic atmosphere pervaded the colony in the old lofts of Steinway Hall. There were Perkins, Wright, Spencer, Myron Hunt, George Dean, Birch Long, and with them – associated in spirit if not in person – was the gifted but irresponsible genius Harvey Ellis, poet-architect, whose pencil Death stopped ere it had traced more than a few soft lines of his dream of beauty.[8]

To Tallmadge and others the 'Chicago School' meant the work of Wright and his contemporaries as manifest primarily in residential architecture after the turn of the century. Nowhere in his essay did Tallmadge mention Jenney, Burnham, Root, Holabird, Roche, Warren, or other architects of tall commercial buildings. On this point he was absolutely clear: 'The most prominent architects who have furthered the movement, and whose work in some instances illustrates the context, are, Frank Lloyd Wright, Dean and Dean, Richard E. Schmidt, Garden and Martin, George Maher ... , Perkins and Hamilton, Nimmons and Fellows, Spencer and Powers, Arthur Heun, Max Dunning, Walter Griffin, Howard Shaw, and many others.'[9]

Tallmadge's title was not without its rivals. Frank Lloyd Wright also described the emergence of the school in his famous paper 'In the Cause of Architecture' (1908). He noted that 'the "New School of the Middle West" is beginning to be talked about and perhaps some day is to be.'[10] He elaborated no further, other than to prophesy that 'some of the young men and women who have given themselves up to me so faithfully these past years will some day contribute rounded individualities of their own, and forms of their own devising to the new school.'[11]

Wright's term, the 'New School of the Middle West,' which presupposes the existence of an earlier school, was eminently appropriate yet failed to win acceptance. Only Wright and his English admirer C.R. Ashbee repeatedly used the phrase. Brevity was certainly a controlling factor, Tallmadge's two words being more succinct than the six used by Wright.

Other terms were proposed but fared no better than Wright's. Peter B. Wight (1915) wrote 'of what might be called the Sullivan school of design in honor of its foremost exponent.'[12] And the same year Wilhelm Miller

8 Thomas E. Tallmadge, 'The "Chicago School," ' *Architectural Review* (Boston), *15*, 1908, 73

9 Ibid.

10 Frank Lloyd Wright, 'In the Cause of Architecture,' *Architectural Record*, *23*, 1908, 156

11 Ibid., p. 164

12 Peter B. Wight, 'Country House Architecture in the Middle West,' *Architectural Record*, *38*, 1915, 390

13 Wilhelm Miller, *The Prairie Spirit in Landscape Gardening*, Urbana, 1915, p. 5

14 J.J.P. Oud, 'The Influence of Frank Lloyd Wright on the Architecture of Europe,' *The Life-Work of the American Architect Frank Lloyd Wright* (H.T. Wijdeveld, ed.), Santpoort, Holland, 1925, p. 86

15 The quotation continues: 'Perhaps the best of them were Frank Lloyd Wright, George Elmslie, George W. Maher, and Walter Burley Griffin. Others who received Sullivan's impress to a greater or less degree were: William Gray Purcell, who worked in partnership with Elmslie for several years; Hugh Garden; Dwight Perkins; Robert C. Spencer; George Dean; Richard E. Schmidt, for several years in partnership with Hugh Garden; William Drummond; and Claude Bragdon. Until the work of the Chicago School is better known than it is at present, however, it will be impossible to estimate correctly the real force and character of Sullivan's direct practical influence in this country.' (Hugh Morrison, *Louis Sullivan, Prophet of Modern Architecture*, New York, 1935, pp. 269–70).

suggested the 'definition of the "Prairie Style" ' because of the dominant horizontality of the houses which was derived from the prairies.[13] In 1925 the Dutch architect J.J.P. Oud mentioned 'the rise of a "Wright-school" in the West of America.'[14] But the term 'Chicago School' was the one that stuck.

In sum, therefore, it was generally accepted that a school of architects existed in the American Midwest; the school comprised certain architects whose particular concern was residential design in the early twentieth century; and the designation most often used to describe these architects was 'Chicago School.' This term, however, ultimately underwent a metamorphic change in meaning in accordance with history's changing attitude toward our architectural past – which was that the residential achievement came to be considered less significant than the commercial work of the 1890s. This change in meaning, as 'Chicago School' increasingly designated the architects of tall commercial buildings, began late in the 1920s and was sanctified by Sigfried Giedion's highly influential, technological interpretation of modern architecture, *Space, Time and Architecture* (1941). In either usage Louis Sullivan was cast in a key role, yet the emphasis shifted from his place as progenitor of the movement which developed after 1900, to his dominant position among the skyscraper builders of the nineties.

Hugh S. Morrison, in his splendid study, *Louis Sullivan, Prophet of Modern Architecture* (1935), was the last to maintain the term 'Chicago School' in its original meaning as well as to comprehend Sullivan's true relation to the group:

there were a few hardy spirits who admired him immensely as a prophet and as a man, and these came to be known as the "Chicago School." Sullivan wanted no one to be an imitator, not even of himself, and his success as a teacher may be indicated by the way in which his followers for the most part acquired his manner of thinking rather than his specific stylisms. Some of them, armed with this start, progressed into individual styles only remotely resembling Sullivan's. From the middle nineties up to the time of the War, and even after, there was a small but vital current of fine work produced by these men, forceful and individual in character and always fundamentally sound.[15]

In the decade prior to Morrison's book the term 'Chicago School' had been neglected. In the spate of books devoted to American architecture which appeared between 1924 and 1928 only Tallmadge (*The Story of Architecture in America*, London, 1927) used the phrase. Other authors –

Mumford, Bragdon, Hamlin, Edgell, and Kimball – did not use the term, and so eased the way for a redefinition. The first book to suggest the now commonly accepted meaning was Henry-Russell Hitchcock's *Modern Architecture: Romanticism and Reintegration*, published in 1929. There the author juxtaposed two words – 'the masterpieces of the Chicago school: skyscrapers ... '[16]

However one book, more than any other, was responsible for recasting the image of the Chicago School. This was Sigfried Giedion's extraordinarily influential *Space, Time and Architecture* (1941). Giedion constantly reiterated the phrase and always with the same meaning – the tall commercial buildings of Chicago and the architects who designed them. Thereafter it was necessary for the historian to differentiate between two schools. Hitchcock, in his 1942 monograph on Wright, mentioned 'the new "Chicago school" ' in reference to the second of the two successive schools,[17] explaining the difference more fully in 1963 – 'the two "Chicago Schools," the earlier concerned chiefly with big business buildings and the latter with domestic work ... '[18] This usage, however, created some doubt when the term was used, as to which Chicago School was intended.

Vincent Scully's brilliant discussion of the Shingle Style made precise the distinction between the schools. He called the latter the 'Second Chicago School.'[19] This phrase is clear and indicates the close relation between the two schools. Yet journalistic practice contravened; periodicals referred to the mid-twentieth-century revival of skyscraper building in Chicago as 'the Second Chicago School.' The *Architectural Forum*, in a special issue devoted to Chicago architecture (May 1962), said 'The Second Chicago School [was] led by Mies van de Rohe and many of his former students.'[20] Thus the phrase 'Second Chicago School,' like 'Chicago School,' was being applied to two different historical periods, and to different types of work.

An alternate title was proposed by William H. Jordy who, instead of 'second,' suggested 'suburban Chicago School.'[21] This term dispelled any mid-city connotation and correctly placed the emphasis on residential design, but did not recognize the role played by small-town clients. Jordy's term, however, failed to win acceptance.

Confusion reached a peak in 1964 when two books were published with identical titles, each dealing with a different subject. Carl W. Condit, in *The Chicago School of Architecture*, discussed tall commercial buildings in Chicago, while Mark L. Peisch, under the same title, dealt primarily with the career of Griffin in Australia and America, and with Griffin's midwest contemporaries.

16 Henry-Russell Hitchcock, *Modern Architecture: Romanticism and Reintegration*, New York, 1929, p. 108

17 Henry-Russell Hitchcock, *In the Nature of Materials*, New York, 1942, p. 31

18 Henry-Russell Hitchcock, *Architecture of Skidmore Owings and Merrill, 1950-1962*, New York, 1963, p. 9

19 Vincent J. Scully, Jr, *The Shingle Style*, New Haven, 1955, pp. 146, 158

20 *Architectural Forum*, 116, 1962, 89

21 William H. Jordy and Ralph Coe, eds., *American Architecture and Other Writings by Montgomery Schuyler*, Cambridge, Mass., 1961, p. 1

22 For a more complete discussion of these two terms see my '*Chicago School*: Metamorphosis of a Term,' *Journal of the Society of Architectural Historians*, 25, 1966, 115–18. And for a rebuttal of my post-Giedion definition of 'Chicago School' (as being too restrictive) see Titus M. Karlowicz, 'The Term Chicago School: Hallmark of a Growing Tradition,' *Prairie School Review, 4, 3*, 1967, 26–30.

23 *Architect's Journal*, London, 1936, reprinted in *The Natural House*, New York, 1954, p. 27. The dates listed in this quotation should be noted. Wright fostered the view, still erroneously held by many historians, that the school's existence coincided with his Oak Park career – and therefore terminated in 1910 when he left for Europe. What Wright did not wish to admit, or to have others know, was that the movement thrived without him and – most irritating of all – achieved its greatest success after 1910.

Chicago School means many things to many people; generally it now refers to the early skyscrapers of Chicago and to the architects who designed them.[22] Probably it is too late to re-establish the original meaning of that term, and in any case it is not necessary. An alternate phrase was introduced by Wright in 1936 while discussing his early colleagues: 'Among these contemporaries the more ambitious began to call the new buildings that appeared upon the prairies from 1893 to 1910 "the prairie school." '[23] This term was reintroduced in the 1950s,[24] and in 1964 (at the very moment when critics failed to agree on the meaning of 'Chicago School') it gained confirmation and currency with the advent of the quarterly journal *The Prairie School Review*. 'Prairie house' and 'prairie style' had long been accepted in our nomenclature, and 'Prairie School' – by emphasizing the prairies of the Midwest rather than the city of Chicago – is a more faithfully descriptive term.

24 A revival of interest in Wright's contemporaries began during the 1950s when three PHD dissertations were simultaneously in preparation – my own on 'The Prairie School: The American Spirit in Midwest Residential Architecture, 1893–1916' (1957), which was entirely researched, restructured, and rewritten in the preparation of this volume; a monograph by David Gebhard concerning the work of Purcell and Elmslie (1957); and Mark L. Peisch's study of Walter Burley Griffin (1959), which was published verbatim as *The Chicago School of Architecture* (1964). During the 1960s there has been an ever increasing number of master's and doctoral theses devoted to individual architects of the Prairie School.

Any attempt to deal with such basic issues as why the Prairie School came to exist, why it achieved widespread acceptance, and why, after 1914–16, it no longer was sustained, must take into account the cultural milieu. Yet political, economic, and social histories of the Midwest abound, and specific facets of intellectual history have been considered by the architectural historian.[1] Certain factors, however, have not been the subject of previous inquiry and of these, three are of special significance: the Arts and Crafts Movement, the vogue for bungalows, and the influence of homemaker magazines.

Literature must also be considered, not because of its influence, but because of the splendid insight it offers into prevailing attitudes and standards of taste. And thanks to the renaissance in American letters then occurring in Chicago, there is a wealth of material upon which to draw.[2]

1 Wayne Andrews in *Architecture, Ambition and Americans, A Social History of American Architecture* (London, 1964) promulgates the theory that conspicuous display of wealth underscores the design vitality of much American architecture. Clay Lancaster treats a specific stylistic influence in *The Japanese Influence in America* (New York, 1963).

2 For a useful background study see Bernard Duffey, *The Chicago Renaissance in American Letters*, Michigan State University Press, East Lansing, 1954.

3 Emily Wheaton, 'The Russells in Chicago,' *Ladies' Home Journal, 19,* 1901, 1 ff.

4 *Atlantic Monthly, 80,* 1897, 541

5 Sinclair Lewis, *Babbitt* (first published 1922), Signet Classic, New York and Toronto, 1961, p. 5

6 Ibid., p. 14

7 Colin Rowe, 'Chicago Frame,' *Architectural Review, 120,* 1956, 289. Carl W. Condit, in *The Chicago School of Architecture* (Chicago and London, 1964), presents enlightening new documentation from clients' letters stipulating that economy and efficiency, not aesthetics, must determine the skyscraper design. See especially pp. 52–4 and p. 120.

In 1901–2 the *Ladies' Home Journal* published a serial which set forth the turn-of-the-century social values of the upper middle-class Chicagoan. Entitled 'The Russells in Chicago, the Experiences of a Young Boston Couple who Moved to the West,' the story contrasts the social attitudes prevalent in Chicago with those of the East.[3] Notably absent are the values established by tradition and convention. The Russells discover to their amazement that people are judged as individuals rather than according to family and background. Whom you like is an equally valid criterion as whom you *should* like. And by extending these values to architecture, it implies that greater freedom from tradition and convention prevails, and that choice may be governed solely by reason and practicality.

This freedom from architectural conformity was repugnant to Henry B. Fuller who, in 1897, chronicled 'The Upward Movement in Chicago.' He lauded certain civic, institutional, and cultural groups for what he called their sophisticated taste, but reproached commercial architecture for failing to respond to values higher than those of the businessman. 'Nowhere,' Fuller observed, 'is the naïf belief that a man may do as he likes with his own held more contentiously than in our astounding and repelling region of "sky-scrapers," where abuse of private initiative, the peculiar evil of the time and place, has reached its most monumental development.'[4] The conventional values which Fuller sought were wanting, and yet others found beauty in these forms, as did Babbitt, the middle-class salesman in Sinclair Lewis' novel of that name: 'The towers of Zenith [i.e., Chicago] aspired above the morning mist; austere towers of steel and cement and limestone, sturdy as cliffs and delicate as silver rods. They were neither citadels nor churches, but frankly and beautifully office buildings.'[5] From his window Babbitt could see a thirty-five storey office building:

Its shining walls rose against April sky to a simple cornice like a streak of white fire. Integrity was in the tower, and decision. It bore its strength lightly as a tall soldier. As Babbitt stared, the nervousness was soothed from his face, his slack chin lifted in reverence.[6]

Babbitt responded spontaneously to these buildings, and the entrepreneur found them a good investment. As Colin Rowe has since remarked, 'They were factual rather than idealistic; and for the taste of the time they were equipment rather than architecture.'[7]

When the businessman built a home, however, he was somewhat more conservative: Babbitt, for example, lived in 'a Dutch Colonial house.' Even so, the midwest businessman was not as bound by tradition as his eastern counterpart. Wright, for instance, said of his early clients: 'I found them chiefly among American men of business with unspoiled instincts and ideals. A man of this type usually has the faculty of judging for himself. He has rather liked the "idea" and much of the encouragement this work receives comes straight from him because the "common sense" of the thing appeals to him.'[8] This attitude was noted as early as 1904 by Arthur C. David, who said of the Prairie School, 'their clients, the well-to-do western gentlemen for whom the houses are built, do not seem to demand the use of European styles and remnants to the same extent as do the eastern owners of expensive buildings.'[9]

In this respect one is reminded of Marshall Field, the Chicago merchandise king, who many years before had instructed his architect to design a home so that it would express 'dignity, simplicity, and common sense.'[10] After a quarter century, in 1900, these same characteristics were being sought by certain clients, but no longer by the families of great wealth. The latter had become increasingly conservative as they came to represent the establishment and lived by inherited wealth. The early tycoons were rapidly passing from the scene – Pullman died in 1897, Armour in 1901, Palmer in 1902, Swift in 1903, Yerkes in 1905, and Marshall Field in 1906. As the social order became more stabilized, which occurred somewhat sooner among the very rich than among the well-to-do, conservatism increased, and acquired social values began to supersede more spontaneous ones. Conformity, and especially conformity to imported values, became increasingly prevalent as insecurity and a subconscious inferiority complex with regard to things and institutions 'back east' increased.

It was a younger generation, of a different social stratum (such as the fictional Russells or Babbitt) who, after 1900, were more apt to champion simplicity and common sense as their architectural ideals. These were the people who read the *House Beautiful* magazine, Gustav Stickley's *Craftsman*, and Henry Saylor's articles and books about bungalows. These were the people who identified themselves with the Arts and Crafts Movement.

Arts and crafts was a movement and not a style. It was an attitude, an approach to a problem, that advocated no specific vocabulary of forms. It pleaded for simplicity, elimination, and respect for materials. Its most salutary effect, in retrospect, was the purification of public taste. The Prairie School, as we shall see, was extremely close to the arts and crafts, much closer than was the designer who practised in the historical styles.

8 *Architectural Record*, 23, 1908, 158
9 Ibid., *15*, 1904, 362–3
10 John Drury, *Old Chicago Homes*, Chicago, 1941, p. 36

11 Mabel T. Priestman, 'History of the Arts and Crafts Movement in America,' *House Beautiful*, 20, 6, 1906, 14. This short but useful article appeared in two parts in October (pp. 15–16) and November (pp. 14–16), 1906.

12 *House Beautiful*, 3, 1897, 29

13 Ibid.

14 Jane Addams, *Forty Years at Hull House*, New York, 1935, p. 375

15 The *Catalogue of the Eleventh Annual Exhibition of the Chicago Architectural Club* (Chicago, 1898) printed membership lists showing 103 active members of the CAC and 128 members of the Chicago Arts and Crafts Society. The Society's constitution, which was adopted at Hull House on 31 October 1897, was also published.

16 At the previous meeting in the series, on 17 November, Wright's uncle, Rev. Jenkin Lloyd Jones, had spoken, thus increasing the possibility that Wright, at least, was aware of the lectures. (Program published in the *Inland Architect and News Record*, 18, 1891, 54; my thanks to William Forsey for this reference.) Crane's oft-repeated lecture appears in his *The Claims of Decorative Art* (Boston, New York, Cambridge [Mass.], 1892), the preface of which is signed and dated 'Edgewater, Illinois, January, 1892.' Crane also addressed the Twentieth Century Club on 'Art and Modern Life,' a topic not among those collected in the above mentioned book.

17 While on a nine-month tour of America with his family, Crane spent some five weeks in Chicago (mid-December 1891 till mid- or late January 1892), during which time an exhibition of his work opened at the Art Institute (pamphlet, entitled *Exhibition of Designs by Walter Crane*, dated 1892). The exhibit then traveled to St Louis, Philadelphia, and Brooklyn, NY; previously it had been seen in Boston. See Walter Crane, *An Artist's Reminiscences*, London, 1907, pp. 362–409.

This closeness furnished a basis of mutual understanding with the potential client – both spoke the same language and shared the same ideals.

The Arts and Crafts Movement began in England as a reform movement dedicated to the improvement of standards in design. William Morris was the founder and chief protagonist; others, notably Walter Crane, C.R. Ashbee, Baillie Scott, and C.F.A. Voysey, played a more subordinate part. The movement began in the sixties and was most popular in the eighteen-eighties and nineties. In the United States its most enthusiastic public support was achieved only after Morris' death in 1896.

Chicago was among the earliest and most important centers of arts and crafts activity in America,[11] a factor not insignificant for the future of architecture. It was at Jane Addams' famed Hull House where the local movement got its start.[12] This comes as no surprise, because the settlement was patterned after Toynbee Hall in London, where C.R. Ashbee's Guild School of Handicraft, later known as Essex House, had begun.[13] At the art gallery and studio, which were incorporated into the first building erected at Hull House, Miss Addams observed how 'the work of the studio almost imperceptibly merged into the crafts.'[14] Thus by the mid-nineties the arts and crafts came into existence at Hull House, and it was there that, on 22 October 1897, the Chicago Arts and Crafts Society was founded. Among the charter members were those architects of the Prairie School who had their offices in Steinway Hall – Hunt, Perkins, Spencer, and Wright, as well as Irving and Allen Pond – and within a few months the Society was participating in the 1898 annual exhibition of the Chicago Architectural Club, where it had more exhibits than did its host.[15]

Communications between England and the American Midwest were numerous and direct, making it possible for Chicagoans to have a first-hand knowledge of the English arts and crafts. On 29 December 1891, Walter Crane lectured at the Art Institute on 'Design in Relation to Use and Materials,' a topic of interest to the architect and layman alike.[16] Crane's work was presented at a special exhibition sponsored by the Art Institute in 1892.[17]

C.R. Ashbee was even more familiar to the Chicago scene. He made two visits, gave numerous lectures, and twice had his work exhibited at the Chicago Architectural Club. He visited the United States from October 1900 to February 1901 under the auspices of the British National Trust, and while in Chicago he addressed ten different gatherings where, according to his subsequent report, he received his warmest and most sympathetic welcome.[18] Wright made every effort to oblige the English designer, even volunteering to serve as the local secretary for the British National Trust! Ashbee, in turn, singled out Wright as the only Chicago architect to be specifically mentioned in his final report: 'Several ladies and gentlemen also joined the informal committee, and Mr Frank Lloyd Wright, one of the leading spirits among the younger architects, and of whose work the city may well be proud, was appointed secretary.'[19] Thus Wright's friendship with Ashbee, who later wrote the foreword for Wright's *Ausgeführte Bauten* (Berlin, 1911), was initiated at this early date rather than, as has been usually thought, during Ashbee's visit of 1908.

At the 1898 Chicago Architectural Club exhibition 'several specimens from Essex House, the work of Mr C.R. Ashbee' were on display,[20] and at the annual exhibition of 1900, fourteen of his designs were shown. Work by eighteen other Englishmen, including Walter Crane, was also represented.[21]

Between England and Chicago the most enduring link, except for the highly influential *Studio* magazine, which began publication in 1893, was in the person of Joseph Twyman (1842–1904).[22] Twyman, a native of Ramsgate, England, immigrated to Chicago and undertook a life-long campaign to spread the gospel of William Morris. At the Toby Furniture Co., with which he was associated, he established a Morris showroom where reputedly 'much of [the furniture was] from the Red House itself,' that is from Morris' own home at Bexley Heath.[23] Twyman frequently lectured in Chicago and, although more concerned with furniture design than with architecture, he was an associate member of the Chicago Architectural Club and spoke there on at least two occasions.[24] His 1900 paper emphasized, in the true spirit of the arts and crafts, that a basic principle of design was 'the nature of material,' a phrase closely associated with architecture and a favorite saying of Wright's. Following his death in 1904 the Chicago Architectural Club honored him by preparing a special memorial exhibition of his work, and one reviewer noted that Twyman was the 'foremost in this country in interpreting the art of William Morris.'[25]

18 C.R. Ashbee, *A Report by Mr C.R. Ashbee to the Council of the National Trust for Places of Historic Interest and National Beauty, on His Visit to the United States in the Council's Behalf*. October MDCCCC to February MDCCCCI, Essex House Press, London, 1901, p. 10. Ashbee visited fourteen states on his coast-to-coast tour and observed that 'Chicago is the only American city I have seen where something absolutely distinctive in aesthetic handling of material has been evolved out of the Industrial system' (p. 11). He was referring to the architecture of steel frame buildings and the 'spirit of the prairie.'

19 Ibid., p. 10

20 *House Beautiful*, 3, 1898, 203

21 *Annual of the Chicago Architectural Club, Being the Book of the Thirteenth Annual Exhibition*, Chicago, 1900, p. 131 ff. Tony Garnier of Paris had two entries, a chimney piece and a decorative wall panel design.

22 For biographical material see Frederic E. Dewhurst, 'The Work of Joseph Twyman,' *Architectural Record*, 18, 1905, 453–9, and the obituary in the *American Art Annual*, 5, 1905/6, 124.

23 *House Beautiful*, 13, 1903, 172

24 His paper of 18 February 1900, on 'Furniture,' was published in the *Inland Architect and News Record*, 35, 1900, 19–20, and that of 21 December 1903, on 'The Art and Influence of William Morris,' was printed in the *Inland Architect and News Record*, 42, 1904, 43–5.

25 Ibid., *45*, 1905, 29

26 *House Beautiful, 3*, 1897, 29

27 Oscar Lovell Triggs, *Chapters in the History of the Arts and Crafts Movement*, Chicago, 1902, p. 193. In Appendix II Triggs reprints his 'The Industrial Art League,' which appeared in the *House Beautiful, 11*, 1902, 197–8.

28 *House Beautiful, 20*, 6, 1906, 14

29 Edgar Kaufmann and Ben Raeburn, eds., *Frank Lloyd Wright: Writings and Buildings*, New York, 1960, pp. 56, 64

Direct communications between England and America did not result in the English ideals being accepted on faith. Morris' basic postulation – that machine manufacture must be renounced in favor of a craft system of production – was unpalatable to Americans. This, along with Morris' socialistic tendencies, helps explain why America so long remained aloof.

The constitution of the Chicago Arts and Crafts Society was careful not to disparage the machine, agreeing, although cautiously, 'to consider the relation of the machine to the workingman.'[26] More amazing was the Industrial Art League of Chicago with its positive program for training industrial designers. The League was founded in 1899 by Oscar Lovell Triggs (1865–1930), literary critic and biographer of Walt Whitman. He realized that 'The higher the work [required of the machine and] the more of intelligent design necessary for a product, the greater is the need for skilled craftsmen to initiate and execute a given design.'[27] And to provide for these craftsmen the Industrial Art League established workshops and offered instruction in the industrial arts. The early disbandment of the League reflected the rapidity with which its objectives won acceptance. M.T. Priestman, in her article on the 'History of the Arts and Crafts Movement in America' (1906) observed: 'having accomplished its pioneer work, the League was discontinued in 1904, its interests having been assumed by other organizations. The active interest taken in the movement in Chicago gave opportunity for many small Guilds and Schools to come into existence.'[28]

Among those who advocated acceptance of the machine, no one was more succinct and outspoken in his views than Wright. He comprehended the true value of Morris' message, even in so far as it affected the machine. Speaking (appropriately) at Hull House in 1901, two years after the founding of the Industrial Art League, Wright expressed his thoughts in his justly famous paper, 'The Art and Craft of the Machine.'

That he [William Morris] miscalculated the machine does not matter. He did sublime work for it when he pleaded so well for the process of elimination its abuse had made necessary; when he fought the innate vulgarity of theocratic impulse in art as opposed to democratic; and when he preached the gospel of simplicity ...

William Morris pleaded well for simplicity as the basis of all true art. Let us understand the significance to art of that word – SIMPLICITY – for it is vital to the Art of the Machine.[29]

Wright, however, went beyond mere acceptance of the machine. He extolled the beauty of machine-made materials: the machine 'teaches us that the beauty of wood lies first in its qualities as wood ... as a material having in itself intrinsically artistic properties, of which its beautiful markings is one, its texture another, its color a third,'[30] Wright also compared modern engineering to a machine aesthetic and in doing so anticipated Le Corbusier's more widely publicized remarks by more than twenty years. Wright said: 'The tall modern office building is the machine pure and simple ... the engine, the motor, and the battle-ship [are] the works of art of the century!'[31]

The contrast, therefore, between the English Arts and Crafts Movement and its American counterpart was fundamental; it centered on the question of the machine and the concept of reform. Reform, in England, carried the implication of revival – the revival of certain earlier art forms (as Voysey in reviving the medieval stucco cottage), or the revival of a handcraft means of production. The American movement, coming at a later time, was more positive in its attitude toward the machine. And in its quest for simplicity, it often exalted the art of primitive people or distant lands; interest ranged from Navajo rugs to the bungalow of India.

The vogue for bungalows was characteristic of the age. These low, spreading houses, with their affected lack of pretension, epitomized the desire for a basic, primitive simplicity – though actually, they were neither primitive nor simple. Their character was often determined by the articulation and nature of their materials, so that the stick and board-like quality of beams, planks, and shakes, and the massive ruggedness of stone and brick were emphasized. An openness, freedom of plan, and unassuming scale were also typical; the restriction to one storey, while common, was not universal. Indeed, when the term first gained currency in the 1880s, it usually referred to summer cottages several storeys in height.[32] And for all that was written about the Indian bungalow, it was almost unknown as a visual type. Photographs of it were rarely published, so that people relied almost exclusively upon literary description. A maximum latitude for interpretation resulted.

Regional variations in the bungalow were pronounced and Henry H. Saylor, the authority on the subject, was able to discern ten types of American bungalows in 1911. One of these – and this is central to our theme – he called the 'Chicago type bungalow,' which he described as #8:

It may stand as a certain type of permanent home for the Middle West, developed

30 Ibid., p. 65
31 Ibid., pp. 59, 60
32 For a discussion of bungalows see Clay Lancaster, 'The American Bungalow,' *Art Bulletin*, *40*, 1958, 239–53, and Vincent J. Scully, Jr, *The Shingle Style*, New Haven, 1955, esp. p. 157.

33 Henry H. Saylor, *Bungalows*, New York, 1911, pp. 39, 41

34 Biographical information from the *National Cyclopaedia of American Biography*, New York, 1910, *14*, pp. 290–1. Stoeckel (Americanized to Stickley) was born at Osceola, Wisconsin, attended pioneer schools, and worked as a stonemason under his father from age 12 to 17 when the family moved to Brandt, Pennsylvania, where he got work in a chair factory owned by his uncle which he, and his brothers, took over four years later. At about the age of 17 he began reading the works of John Ruskin. See also John Crosby Freeman, *The Forgotten Rebel, Gustav Stickley and his Craftsman Mission Furniture*, Watkins Glen, New York, 1966.

along the lines of the one-story plan. There is a great deal of character and originality of motive to be found in the work of what has come to be called the "Chicago School" of architects. Their use of the strong horizontal line, as being most in keeping with the flat plains of the Central West, has brought about almost a new style in the architectural types of the world.[33]

Saylor related the work of the Prairie School to the American bungalow, yet recognized its high degree of originality. This was important for the public; it allowed them to believe, as they often did, that the prairie house was not an anomaly but held an approved place in the architectural scene. This was important to a prospective client.

The regional bungalow-type that developed in California enjoyed the greatest popularity, and numerous examples were soon built throughout the nation. In California – but not until after 1907 – Charles and Henry Greene, under renewed Oriental influence, evolved a highly personal and sophisticated bungalow strain, and it was in their work that the local type achieved its finest form. The designs of Greene and Greene were well known, with both the *Inland Architect and News Record* and the *Western Architect* publishing their work in 1908. But by this late date the midwestern architect had established his direction, a direction which was increasingly less sympathetic to the more lightweight, stick-like craftsmanship which typified the best in Greene and Greene.

No discussion of the bungalow and the Arts and Crafts Movement in America could possibly conclude without mention of Gustav Stickley and his *Craftsman* magazine and, by extension, of the tremendous influence in matters of taste that the newly founded magazines exercised during the early years of this century. Among these the *Craftsman* was unique. It was the personal vehicle of Stickley (1858–1942), a native of Wisconsin and a prominent furniture manufacturer. His youthful enthusiasm for John Ruskin and William Morris made him discontented with available furniture designs, so that by 1900 he began fabricating handmade furniture which he designed himself. These items were marketed under the name of Craftsman. The venture was an immediate success and soon he expanded his workshops at Eastwood, New York, where, in 1901 he founded the *Craftsman* magazine to help disseminate his ideas and create a broader public for his wares.[34]

The earliest issues of the *Craftsman* doted on Morris, Ruskin, and the English Arts and Crafts Movement, and with an unusual streak of architectural good sense lauded the residences designed by Wilson Eyre and

E.G.W. Dietrich. Typical of Stickley's erratic editorial policy, however, was his brief encounter with Art Nouveau. In June 1902, Art Nouveau was introduced to the reader as an artistic catastrophe, yet by the following month it was welcomed as a commendable experiment in the best tradition of the arts and crafts! Important articles by S. Bing, A.D.F. Hamlin, and others then followed before Stickley's interest waned in 1905–6.[35] During this interim though, Stickley's robust, angular Craftsman furniture, composed of heavy vertical and horizontal members, gave way to slightly less weighty forms, thinner members, and the occasional curve.

In matters architectural Stickley was a self-appointed authority who found nothing more to his liking than his own inept Craftsman Homes. These designs, published as a regular feature in the *Craftsman* (and later in book form) were boxy and crude in plan and utterly devoid of any artistic sensitivity in design. A sense of proportion was not one of Stickley's attributes. 'My ideal of architecture,' he wrote, 'is beauty through elimination,'[36] and although this statement has certain Miesian overtones Stickley's work proved conclusively that simplification in itself is no sure formula for good design.

Simplicity was the only real loyalty to which Stickley remained forever true. The word permeated his every thought and article; for several years the subtitle of the *Craftsman* was *An Illustrated Monthly Magazine for the Simplification of Life*. This simplification of life Stickley found best exemplified in the lives of the Hopi Indians.

But in spite of Stickley's idiosyncrasies, his readers were devoted, and over the years probably no American did more to support and popularize the Arts and Crafts Movement than he. It is particularly surprising therefore, that Stickley, as a Midwesterner, paid so very little heed to architecture in Chicago. Indeed it remained for Sullivan to seek out Stickley. In a letter to the editor in 1905 Louis Sullivan wrote that 'I like the spirit you are infusing into the *Craftsman*,'[37] and over the next few years he published several articles in its pages. One of these ('What is Architecture,' 1906) resulted in his being commissioned to design the National Farmers' Bank in Owatonna. And this was one of the few midwestern buildings ever illustrated by the *Craftsman*.

Sullivan's interest in the *Craftsman* strikes an almost pathetic note. One senses that he was vainly seeking a means of communication – some way to convey his message. His 'Kindergarten Chats,' a series of 52 articles written as instruction for the layman and young architect in 1901–2, had not had their intended effect, nor had his lectures and papers delivered at the

35 The Secessions experienced similar treatment. Stickley was ecstatic about the German pavilion for the Louisiana Purchase Exposition at St Louis in 1904 and thereafter many pages of the *Craftsman* were devoted to German and Austrian Secessionist art. But disenchantment came in 1907 when he wrote 'Secession Art – Growth, Meaning and Failure' (*Craftsman, 13*, 1907, 36–49).
36 Gustav Stickley, *More Craftsman Homes*, New York, 1912, p. 4
37 *Craftsman, 8*, 1905, 453

38 For an analysis of the architectural designs published in *Godey's Lady's Book* see George L. Hersey, 'Godey's Choice,' *Journal of the Society of Architectural Historians, 18,* 1959, 104–11.

Architectural League of America. His next try was through the *Craftsman,* which did have the positive result of initiating a phase of sporadic bank commissions. He then wrote (1906–8) a book, 'Democracy: A Man Search,' to try and communicate his ideas, but the manuscript remained unpublished at his death.

Ultimately more significant than the *Craftsman* were the new homemaker magazines that were introduced at this time. These periodicals catered to home owners or potential builders of homes and to their various home-related hobbies and activities. Editorial policy was usually directed toward the middle or upper middle-class family and particularly toward women and their role in the home. This, of course, was a reflection of the new place of women in the social order. The first and best known of the homemaker magazines was the *House Beautiful,* which began publication in 1896. The others, except for the relatively late *Better Homes and Gardens* (1922), appeared during the following decade.

Women's magazines were not new. The *Ladies' Home Journal* had existed since 1883, and *Godey's Lady's Book* had been published between 1846 and 1892. However, these were not homemaker magazines; the word 'Lady' in both titles was significant. The social life, customs, and etiquette of the lady of the house, as well as her interest in cuisine, clothing, clubs, and travel, were the things of importance. Approved architectural designs were illustrated, particularly in *Godey's,* but the house was not the focus of attention.[38] *Country Life in America,* which began publication in 1901, was even more peripheral to our theme since, in contrast to its English counterpart, it rarely mentioned or illustrated home designs and decoration.

The very inception of the homemaker magazine reflected a sociological change wherein taste, particularly the housewife's taste, took increased precedence over building per se. This is pertinently demonstrated by the changed character and changed title of several magazines, each of which was modified from a more technical building magazine to a homemaker publication. The *Scientific American Building Monthly,* for example, became *American Homes and Gardens* in 1905, and *Keith's Magazine on Home Building* was the progenitor of *Beautiful Homes Magazine.* Not all homemaker magazines began as building journals however. The *House Beautiful* had no predecessor (despite its absorption of the *Domestic Science Monthly* in 1902), nor did *House and Garden,* founded in 1901. The latter carried a subtitle which stipulated its missionary field: *An Illustrated Monthly Devoted to Practical Suggestions on Architecture, Gar-*

den Designing and Planting, Decoration, Home Furnishing and Kindred Subjects; a typical, subjective article title was 'The Small House which is Good.' Without doubt the editor was a self-styled arbitrator of household taste.

For the Midwest, and midwestern architecture, the most important homemaker magazine was the *House Beautiful*. It alone was published in Chicago and therefore more directly reflected, and influenced, midwestern taste.[39] Its early date of founding – December 1896 – gave it leadership in what became a highly competitive field, and also gave it a different editorial outlook. Unlike its future competitors, the *House Beautiful* came into existence with the swelling tide of enthusiasm for the Arts and Crafts Movement, upon whose crest it rode for several years. The *Studio* was often quoted, simplicity was the byword, and European arts and crafts designs were often illustrated. Work by Van de Velde and Baillie Scott was published in 1898, by Voysey in 1899, and by Townsend in 1900.

It is no coincidence that the first two articles ever published about Frank Lloyd Wright appeared in the *House Beautiful* (in 1897 and 1899).[40] These well illustrated texts – which thus far have eluded bibliographers – praise Wright's Studio and home in the most glowing arts and crafts terminology, and leave no doubt in the reader's mind but that Wright is among the finest, and most understanding, arts and crafts designers in America – a judgment which of course was true. At that time, while the arts and crafts was so influential for the homemaker, these articles must have aided Wright in securing a sympathetic clientele.

The work of the Prairie School was given much publicity by the *House Beautiful*, especially after Robert C. Spencer, Jr became a contributor in 1905. He wrote more than 20 articles between 1905 and 1909, many of these for a series entitled 'Planning the Home'; for illustrations he drew heavily on the work of the school. This implied, of course, that these designs best fulfilled the practical and aesthetic requirements of a home.

In certain respects the *House Beautiful* was the American counterpart of the *Studio* in England. It served to popularize and spread the gospel of the Arts and Crafts Movement, and in turn attracted people who shared these interests. C.R. Ashbee was one of these. After visiting Chicago in 1908 he contributed several articles including a series on 'Man and the Machine' (1910); therein he revealed his belated acceptance of the machine, an acceptance probably resulting from his visits to America. Of the prairie architects he said, 'The "School of the Middle West" and we architects of the arts and crafts movement in England are working to the same goal ... '[41]

39 Published by Herbert S. Stone and Company, and edited by Eugene Klapp and Henry Blodgett Harvey
40 'Successful Homes III,' *House Beautiful, 1*, 1897, 64–9, and Alfred H. Granger, 'An Architect's Studio,' *House Beautiful, 7*, 1899, 36–45
41 *House Beautiful, 28*, 1910, 56

42 *Illinois Society of Architects Monthly Bulletin*, 24, 1940, 1

This sentiment was shared by many a Midwesterner. George Grant Elmslie later wrote that 'The genesis of the modern movement belongs in the far greater part to England and her men.'[42]

The preceding discussion of arts and crafts, the bungalow, and homemaker magazines suggests reasons why the Prairie School could exist, and why its homeland was the American Midwest. The architect and client shared ideals in common, such as simplicity and respect for materials, which they had learned from the Arts and Crafts Movement, and the vogue for bungalows extended its aura of respectability to the prairie house. The Midwesterner also felt less social pressure to conform to historical styles than did his eastern counterpart, and magazine publicity offered added justification for building this type of house.

This implies, and I think correctly, that the average client of a Prairie School architect was largely unaware of what he was getting in terms of architecture. He accepted the design at face value because it expressed ideals which were reasonable and practical, and because it related to certain qualities which society then held dear – even though the design was different from prevailing standards of architectural taste. When Wright remarked that the 'idea' of his houses appealed to the ordinary man of business, the word was well chosen; the sophistication of many of these designs, particularly the manipulation of interior space, must have passed largely unnoticed. The greater sense of restfulness, relaxation, and repose, and the new richness to be experienced in living, were benefits which the average client assuredly did not foresee and probably never wholly attributed to the architect. He got more than he asked for, but hardly realized it. He 'loved' his house, but didn't know exactly why.

The client, however, should not be deprecated for failing to comprehend the subtleties of his architect's design. After all, the most astute architectural critics of the day were equally, and perhaps more, undiscerning and superficial when writing about the new architecture of the Midwest. They did not understand it for what it was. Such illustrious critics as Montgomery Schuyler and Russell Sturgis, or the architect C.R. Ashbee, were obviously at a loss when describing even Wright's greatest masterpieces, and what they did appreciate was often for the wrong reasons.

Had the client, and the critic, appreciated these houses for what they sometimes were – a new experience in the act of living – the future of the Prairie School might have been quite different. But this was not to be; only the transitory characteristics were usually noticed and these, with a change in taste, became outmoded.

Why the Prairie School came to exist has been touched upon in this chapter. Even more perplexing is the question of why a movement of such vitality should collapse so abruptly after 1914. It is a question which has long puzzled the historian, but I believe the key to its answer, as will be shown later, lies in the factors already discussed.

That Frank Lloyd Wright has figured so prominently in the above, and will in the discussion which immediately follows, is a measure of his involvement rather than an attempt to emphasize his role. It also reflects his constantly increasing prominence as an architect, with the result that his activities more readily found their way into print. It is no coincidence that, although an 'anti-joiner,' Wright belonged to the Chicago Arts and Crafts Society, that his work was so often published in the *House Beautiful*, or that he spent much time designing the marginal decorations and layout for William C. Gannett's essay, *The House Beautiful*, which he and William Winslow – in the best spirit of the arts and crafts – printed on a hand press in 1897. His home and Studio were decorated and furnished in sympathy with arts and crafts ideals, as was his costume. Grant C. Manson has observed that Wright's long hair, flowing bow tie, and smock was a match for Elbert Hubbard (1856–1915) who, even more than Stickley, was the true American counterpart of William Morris.[43] Hubbard, also a Midwesterner (Illinois), met Morris in 1892 and thereafter established his famous Roycroft shops and press at East Aurora, New York.[44] The two men probably met while Wright was working in Buffalo. John Lloyd Wright recalls how 'Elbert Hubbard was almost as picturesque [in costume] as was Father – they talked arts, crafts and philosophy by the hour.'[45]

43 Grant C. Manson, *Frank Lloyd Wright to 1910*, New York, 1958, p. 155
44 Published at the Roycroft Press were Hubbard's abbreviated biographies, called *Little Journeys*, as well as the periodicals *Philistine* and *Fra*. At the peak, his Roycroft Shops employed over 500 people. For a biography of Hubbard see David Arnold Balch, *Elbert Hubbard*, New York, 1940. During Ashbee's American tour of 1900–1 he visited East Aurora, so it could be through Ashbee that Wright became acquainted with Hubbard's work.
45 John Lloyd Wright, *My Father Who is on Earth*, G.P. Putnam's, New York, 1946, p. 32

When the Thirteenth Annual Exhibition of the Chicago Architectural Club opened in mid-March 1900, one jubilant reviewer announced that 'exceptionally fine things from the designing standpoint are so numerous that it would take a week of inspection and a jury's table of values to determine which were most worthy of special comment.'[1] Such lavish praise was hardly justified, but it implies that the exhibition was non-controversial and the model of conservatism, which was absolutely true. The Queen Anne, colonial, and classical styles, to use terminology of the day, reigned supreme, making mockery of such published club objectives as presenting 'new thought in art and design' and, 'while revering the past, yet plac[ing] principle before precedent.'[2]

By 1902, however, the situation had changed. Highly original work was much in prominence. The reviewers were dismayed.

A quiet revolt had occurred within the club, as several protagonists gained control of the executive and the jury of admission. Their ideas were reflected in the exhibition, and they and their friends alone were represented in the catalogue. Sullivan (who prepared a special frontispiece) and Wright were given the most space, the latter having a separate section of 14 plates devoted to his work – even though he was not a member of the club. This favoritism was accorded by a small group of admirers, that coterie of young architects so closely associated with Steinway Hall.

Steinway Hall was an eleven-storey office and theater building by Dwight H. Perkins who, on its completion, rented the loft and part of the topmost floor.[3] These quarters he offered to share with others, and during 1896–7 a small group was formed. First to respond was Robert C. Spencer, Jr, Perkins' acquaintance from student days at MIT. Spencer came from the Schiller Building where Wright was also installed – the latter having moved there with Cecil Corwin, his closest friend. Corwin, however, departed for the East and Wright, always in need of companionship, keenly felt the loss. 'That place in the Schiller Building soon seemed nothing at all without him,' Wright noted in his autobiography.[4] Later Spencer supplanted Corwin as Wright's best friend, and both moved from the Schiller Building (which Wright had helped Sullivan design) to Steinway Hall. Myron Hunt also joined in, making an original group of four.

Of the earliest days at Steinway Hall, only Wright has left a record:

I had met Robert Spencer, Myron Hunt, and Dwight Perkins. Dwight had a loft in his new Steinway Hall building – too large for him. So we formed a group – outer office in common – workrooms screened apart in the loft of Steinway Hall. These young men, newcomers in architectural practice like myself, were my first associates in the so-called profession of architecture.[5]

The office, number 1107, was on the top floor, and on the roof above, reached by a small staircase from the corridor on the 11th floor, was a spacious A-frame loft ideally suited for a drafting room. The secretary, whose services were shared by all, maintained the front office on the floor below. It was a lively association, with all participating in each other's work. Sometimes they formally collaborated, as when Perkins and Spencer designed a church for Wilmette (a competition entry), or when Perkins and Wright designed All Souls for Wright's uncle, Jenkin Lloyd-Jones.[6] The latter building was eventually built, but only after both architects had disassociated themselves from the scheme. And Wright apparently helped Myron

1 *Inland Architect and News Record*, 35, 1900, 18. The reviewer was Robert Craik McLean, editor of the journal.

2 *Annual of the Chicago Architectural Club, Being the Book of the Thirteenth Annual Exhibition*, Chicago, 1900, p. 6. The titles of the Chicago Architectural Club catalogues vary greatly from year to year.

3 Steinway Hall, now demolished, was located at 64 E. Van Buren Street, just east of the Loop, although the original street numbering was 17. Construction was completed in 1896; renaissance in detail (and faced with Roman brick), the design had a bold simplicity hardly to be expected in an architect's first major work.

4 Frank Lloyd Wright, *An Autobiography*, Duell, Sloan and Pearce, New York, 1943, p. 131

5 Ibid.

6 An illustration of the Perkins-Spencer First Congregational Church project may be found in the *Chicago Architectural Club Catalogue Ninth Annual Exhibition* of 1896. The crisp, angular design is original in its massing and combines several Tudor Gothic details. For illustrations of All Souls see Grant C. Manson, *Frank Lloyd Wright to 1910*, New York, 1958, p. 157.

7 Biographical information from *The Book of Chicagoans*, Chicago, 1917, p. 533, and an interview with Miss Eleanor E. Perkins, the architect's daughter. The early death of Dwight's father posed financial problems and it was through the aid of Charles Hitchcock that Perkins attended MIT. Hitchcock was a benefactor of the University of Chicago, where Perkins later designed several buildings including Hitchcock Hall, a men's residence which dates from 1901. Perkins was married in 1891 and had two children, Eleanor Ellis and Lawrence Lincoln, the latter being senior partner in the architectural firm of Perkins and Will.

8 Biographical information from *The Book of Chicagoans*, Chicago, 1917, and the *Brickbuilder*, 24, 1915, 76, where a portrait photograph of Spencer will be found

9 For the factual documentation on Wright's life before 1887 see Thomas S. Hines, Jr, 'Frank Lloyd Wright – The Madison Years: Records versus Recollections,' *Wisconsin Magazine of History*, 50, 1967, 109–19, which was reprinted in the *Journal of the Society of Architectural Historians*, 26, 1967, 227–33.

Hunt with a double house in Evanston for Catherine White. How many times these men worked together cannot be known, yet certainly none worked in isolation.

Three of them had studied at MIT. Dwight Heald Perkins (1867–1941), who was born in Memphis, Tennessee and raised in Chicago, attended the Institute for two years (1885–7) – remaining thereafter as an instructor for an additional year. He had experience in several offices, including some five years with Burnham and Root, where he managed the downtown office during the exigency of the Columbian Exposition. With the ensuing depression, however, Burnham (John Root died in 1891) released Perkins (1894), but not without a prospective commission – the design of Steinway Hall.[7]

Robert Clossen Spencer, Jr (1865–1953) entered MIT the year after Perkins; he was already in possession of a Bachelor of Mechanical Engineering degree from the University of Wisconsin (1886). He left the Institute without completing his studies, worked for Wheelwright and Haven and then Shepley, Rutan and Coolidge in Boston before going to Europe on a Rotch Travelling Scholarship. Upon his return in 1893 he settled in Chicago, starting in the local office of Shepley, Rutan and Coolidge before entering private practice in 1895.[8]

Myron Hunt (1868–1952) was born in Sunderland, Massachusetts, and studied at Northwestern University (1888–90) before attending MIT (1890–2). He then worked in Boston and Chicago, and made an extensive European tour (1894–6), before opening his own office in Chicago. He remained, however, only until 1903 when he moved to Los Angeles and entered partnership with Elmer Grey who, like Spencer, was a native of Milwaukee.

Frank Lloyd Wright (1867–1959) had less formal education than the others. He had left high school before completing his senior year (April 1885), but later attended the University of Wisconsin as a Special Student in civil engineering – apparently for about two semesters – while working for A.D. Conover, who was the Dean of Engineering at the university and also a practicing architect.[9] In the spring of 1887 Wright left Madison for Chicago where he found employment with Joseph Lyman Silsbee, a fashionable residential architect who had helped introduce the Shingle Style into the Middle West. It was at Silsbee's office that Wright met Cecil Corwin. After about five months Wright left Silsbee to work for Louis Sullivan, with whom he stayed until 1893.

Although four men founded the group at Steinway Hall, the situation was not static. By 1898, Henry Webster Tomlinson (1870–1942) had moved into room 1106 and later joined Perkins and the others next door. Meanwhile Wright departed for The Rookery (perhaps he found Steinway Hall too sociable), but later he returned and occupied Tomlinson's former office instead of actually sharing space with the others. About this time, January 1901, Wright and Tomlinson entered into partnership, Wright's only partnership during his long career.[10] The arrangement, as Grant C. Manson has pointed out,[11] was a business convenience with Tomlinson not participating in the work of design, but it is indicative of the close relations that existed among the men at Steinway Hall.

Irving K. Pond (1857–1937) and Allen Bartlit Pond (1858–1929) were older, with a well-established practice when, in 1899, they were first listed as occupying room 1109 Steinway Hall. At first they shared much in common with the younger men, but gradually there developed a widening rift. By 1918 Irving Pond, in *The Meaning of Architecture*, was vehemently to reject the achievements of the Prairie School.[12] He was the real designer for the firm, having graduated from the University of Michigan in civil engineering (1879), and worked first for William Le Baron Jenney and then for Solon S. Beman, the protégé of George Pullman, for whom Beman was then building the town of Pullman, Illinois.[13] In 1886 the brothers founded their partnership, prior to which Allen Pond had had less than a year of training in S.S. Beman's office. He was a civics major at the University of Michigan, had taught high-school Latin for three years, and then studied contract and business law before moving to Chicago. A cheerful, athletic person, Allen always devoted as much time to social work as to the practice of architecture. Both brothers were active at Hull House, where most of the buildings were of their design.

Of all the newcomers at Steinway Hall, Walter Burley Griffin was to be the most auspicious. He arrived fresh from N. Clifford Ricker's architectural course at the University of Illinois and for about two years, from 1899 to 1901, was with the group at 1107 Steinway Hall. Thereafter he worked for Wright at the Oak Park Studio. Others who joined the coterie in 1107 included Adamo Boari, a dynamic Italian whose prize-winning design for the Palace of Fine Arts in Mexico City precipitated his departure,[14] and (by 1901) Birch Burdette Long, a highly talented renderer. At the opening of the new century then, the roster of architects at Steinway Hall read as follows: room 1107 – Perkins, Spencer, Tomlinson, Griffin, and Long; room 1109 – Pond and Pond; room 1106 – Wright.[15]

10 The letterhead on their square stationery comprised four lines and read: 'Studio/Frank Lloyd Wright/ Webster Tomlinson/Architects.' One such letter, dated 30 January 1901, and signed by Wright, is in the Avery Library collection, Columbia University.

11 Manson, *Frank Lloyd Wright to 1910*, p. 137

12 Irving K. Pond, *The Meaning of Architecture*, Boston, 1918, pp. 174–5

13 Irving K. Pond, 'Pullman – America's First Planned Industrial Town,' *Illinois Society of Architects Bulletin, 18–19*, 1934, 6–8. The best, though brief, account of the Ponds will be found in Carl W. Condit, *The Chicago School of Architecture*, Chicago and London, 1964. For illustrations of their early work see the *Architectural Record, 18*, 1905, 148–60.

14 The Palacio de las Bellas Artes was begun in 1905 but not dedicated until the mid nineteen-thirties. Its Tiffany stained glass theater curtain is its most famous feature. Boari also designed the Correo Mayor (Central Post Office) at about the same time (James Norman, *Terry's Guide to Mexico*, Garden City, 1962, p. 236). As a designer Boari seems to have little, if anything, in common with the others in Steinway Hall.

15 Information concerning office addresses (from which approximate dates are obtained) is taken from the Chicago Architectural Club catalogues, which

were published annually between March and May, and the *Lakeside City Directory of Chicago*.

16 Paper prepared by Robert C. Spencer, Jr and read before the Illinois Society of Architects, 28 November 1939. Transcript at the Ricker Library, University of Illinois, p. 3

17 Frank Lloyd Wright, *A Testament*, Horizon Press, New York, 1957, p. 34. Whether they met for lunch or dinner seems to be in question.

18 Information obtained in conversation with Frank Lloyd Wright, 27 October 1956

19 Thomas E. Tallmadge in the *Architectural Record, 60*, 1926, 71

20 *Architectural Review, 15*, 1908, 73

21 *Architectural Record, 23*, 1908, 156

As it was impracticable for all kindred souls to join the group at Steinway Hall, a mealtime club was formed which lasted for several years. Only two accounts, written years later by Spencer and Wright, record these gatherings of the late eighteen-nineties. Spencer, in 1939, said they 'used to meet for some years once a month at the old Bismarck Restaurant for a steak dinner in one of the private rooms. ... At these little informal dinners we could discuss our architectural problems and theories ... '[16] Wright first mentioned the club in 1957: 'Before long a little luncheon club formed, comprised of myself, Bob Spencer, Gamble Rogers, Hardy and Cady, Dick Schmidt, Hugh Garden, Dean, Perkins, and Shaw, several others; eighteen in all. We called the group the "Eighteen". ... The little luncheon round-table broke up after a year or two.'[17]

To the ten participants mentioned by Wright can be added six others, the second Dean brother (George or Arthur), Alfred Granger, Arthur Heun, Myron Hunt, and Irving and Allen Pond.[18] That totals 16. It is also possible that Webster Tomlinson should be included too.

Those not from Steinway Hall were generally the more conservative designers, as became evident in later years. James Gamble Rogers became best known for his collegiate Gothic, while Howard Shaw was once fittingly described as 'the most rebellious of the conservatives, and the most conservative of the rebels.'[19] He never quite abandoned the historical styles. The partners Frank W. Handy and J.K. Cady were closer to the Ponds in age and in artistic temperament, though not their equals as designers. The Deans, Alfred Granger, and Arthur Heun flirted with the new movement for several years, but were unwilling to make a full commitment. Hugh Garden, and indirectly his future partner Richard E. Schmidt, were alone in making a real contribution to the Prairie School.

The environment of Steinway Hall, and the various architects' activities – the Eighteen, the Chicago Architectural Club, the Architectural League of America, and the Chicago Arts and Crafts Society – was undoubtedly highly stimulating. Thomas E. Tallmadge said, 'An ideal artistic atmosphere pervaded the colony in the old lofts of Steinway Hall,'[20] while Frank Lloyd Wright said, 'I well remember how the "message" burned within me, how I longed for comradeship until I began to know the younger men and how welcome was Robert Spencer, and then Myron Hunt, and Dwight Perkins, Arthur Heun, George Dean, and Hugh Garden. Inspiring days they were, I am sure, for us all.'[21]

The 'inspiring days' spent in 'an ideal artistic atmosphere' did not, however, immediately change the character or caliber of designs produced. That awaited the future. Work for the most part recalled the historical styles, with an obvious preference for the so-called Queen Anne or Tudor Gothic modes.

Typical of the period, and interesting as a collaborative design from Steinway Hall, is the duplex house for Catherine M. White at 1313, 1319 Ridge Avenue in Evanston (1899, fig. 2). Hunt was the architect, but he was apparently assisted by Wright.[22] Parallels to the work of both architects exist in the design, as well as to the work of H.H. Richardson. Wright's unpublished George W. Smith house at 404 Home Avenue, Oak Park (1898), has a similar double-pitch roof, three-two window arrangement, and string course merging with the second storey sills, while the crisp, angular quality of the White house, the bold voids for windows, and the rigid symmetry are characteristic of Hunt, as seen in his Frances M. Sweet house in Evanston. The massing of the Catherine M. White house, however, apparently derives from Richardson's Stoughton house at Cambridge, Massachusetts, a similarity more apparent before both

22 Information obtained from Frank Lloyd Wright, 27 October 1956. Wright told the author that Myron Hunt came to him for help in designing this house and that he, Wright, had assisted in preparing the design. One wonders whether it was Wright who suggested using Richardson's Stoughton house as the model.

FIG. 2 Myron Hunt. Catherine M. White house, 1313, 1319 Ridge Avenue, Evanston, Illinois, 1899. Photo by H.A. Brooks

23 An illustration of the Northwestern University Settlement project (dated June 1899), will be found in the Chicago Architectural Club *Catalogue* of 1900, p. 69, and in the *Inland Architect and News Record*, *35*, 3, 1900. A photo of the J.J. Wait house is in the *Inland Architect and News Record*, *30*, 6, 1898, and the *Western Architect*, *2*, 1903, 16. For Spencer's H.N. Kelsey project see the Chicago Architectural Club *Catalogue*, 1898, the *Inland Architect and News Record*, *31*, 5, 1898, or the *Journal of the Society of Architectural Historians*, *19*, 1960, 7.

One of the finest and most original designs of the period was the project for an interior arcade prepared by Spencer for the American Luxfer Prism Company competition of 1898. Illustrated in the *Inland Architect and News Record*, *32*, 2, 1898, and in the *Journal of the Society of Architectural Historians*, *19*, 1960, 6.

NOTE: Plates published by the *Inland Architect and News Record* are not numbered, therefore the issue number (1 through 6) of each volume in which they appear is listed in my reference.

24 Frost and Granger were brothers-in-law. This explains the existence of the firm, as well as why they became renowned as railroad station architects – their father-in-law was Marvin Hughitt, president of the Chicago and North Western Railroad.

Alfred Hoyt Granger (1867–1939) was eleven years junior to Charles S. Frost

houses were remodeled and the open galleries enclosed. This gallery connects the two symmetrical halves of the White house, but the continuity of shingled surface, found in the Stoughton house, is here absent because sharp edges and abrupt changes of plane predominate, and are defined in brick.

Less distinguished, yet sharing with the White house a similar predilection for high roofs, sharp-edged brickwork, and a complex massing, were numerous projects and executed designs by the architects at Steinway Hall, and the Eighteen. These included the buildings at Hull House by Pond and Pond, the project for a Northwestern University Settlement exhibited (1900) by Perkins, his somewhat earlier J.J. Wait House in Chicago, and the projected home for H.N. Kelsey at Wilmette of 1898 by Spencer.[23] Spencer was particularly prone to English antecedents and the Tudor half-timbering which Wright used only in his Nathan G. Moore house was often found in Spencer's work. Also typical are many of the suburban stations for the Chicago and North Western Railroad (often earlier in date) built by Frost and Granger, and their Frederick Bartlett house (1901) on Prairie Avenue, Chicago, a design which derives directly from Norman Shaw's 180 Queen's Gate in London.[24]

Only one residential architect in Chicago had developed a consistent, personal mode at this time, and he was not at Steinway Hall or among the

(b. 1856). He was from Zanesville, Ohio, and studied at Kenyon College, MIT, and the Ecole des Beaux-Arts (Atelier Pascal). He was in H.H. Richardson's office at the time of the latter's death in 1886, and in 1898 he went into partnership with Frost. (Obituary: *Monthly Bulletin, Illinois Society of Architects*, *24*, 1940, 8.) Granger, but apparently not Frost, was a member of the Eighteen. Granger authored an early article concerning the work of Frank Lloyd Wright – 'An Architect's Studio,' *House Beautiful*, *7*, 1899, 36–45.

For a discussion, but particularly the illustrations, see Harry W. Desmond,

'The Work of Frost and Granger,' *Architectural Record*, *18*, 1905, 115–45. Also Alfred Hoyt Granger, 'The Designing and Planning of Railway Stations,' *Brickbuilder*, *9*, 1900, 142–4, 201–2.

Eighteen. This was George W. Maher (1864–1926).[25] Maher, with some 10 years of experience behind him, entered private practice in 1888 at the age of 23 – by which time his views on architecture were well established. A paper on 'Originality in American Architecture,' read before the Chicago Architectural Sketch Club in 1887, outlined Maher's architectural values. He believed that 'the right idea of a residence [is] to have it speak its function,'[26] which for him meant a psychological rather than a purely utilitarian function. He sought 'the idea of' massiveness, centralization, and substantiality in residential architecture, and Richardson he lauded for best achieving these goals.

Maher's apprenticeship was with Bauer and Hill, and then with J.L. Silsbee. The latter – simultaneously – had Maher, Frank Lloyd Wright, and George Grant Elmslie as his draftsmen, a fact which testifies to his status as a teacher, and to his influence on the Midwest scene.[27] Wright as late as 1894 occasionally worked in Silsbee's mode, while Maher's designs, after he entered practice in 1888, showed a profound indebtedness to Silsbee until the mid-nineties.[28] By then Maher was assimilating other experiences, which culminated in the John Farson house of 1897.

A preference for symmetrical, blocky masses, and slick but solid masonry walls, soon predominated in Maher's designs. An early instance is the Charles V.L. Peters house (1895),[29] which was built for J.L. Cochran, a real estate developer and a former client of Silsbee's. Although built of brick, the cube shape, pointed hip roof, three symmetrical windows on the second floor, and broad veranda across the front, were characteristic of houses found on Main Street in almost every town.[30]

25 George Washington Maher was born in Mill Creek, West Virginia, attended public school in New Albany, Indiana, and (according to *The Book of Chicagoans*, Chicago, 1911) in 1878, at age 13, began working under the Chicago architects August Bauer and Henry Hill. About 1891 Maher spent some three months traveling in Europe; in 1894 he married Elizabeth Brooks and had one son, Philip Brooks Maher, who joined his father's firm in 1914. Maher's home, built just prior to his marriage, is at 424 Warwick Road, Kenilworth, Illinois, the picturesque design being characteristic of his early work.

Maher was briefly, between late 1889 and early 1890, in partnership with Charles Corwin. The firm was called Maher and Corwin, but the experience does not seem to have affected Maher's development as a designer.

26 Maher's talk, 'Originality in American Architecture,' was published in the *Inland Architect and News Record*, 10, 1887, 34–5; the quotation is from page 34. An abridgment is printed in the *Prairie School Review*, 1, 1, 1964, 12–15. The next most important among his numerous papers is 'Art Democracy' (*Western Architect*, 15, 1910, 28–30), which gives an excellent insight into his personal philosophy.

27 The situation in Silsbee's office in 1887 recalls that of Peter Behrens' office in Berlin about 1910 when Mies, Gropius, and Le Corbusier were present.

28 For a discussion of the Silsbee, Wright, Maher relationship see my 'The Early Work of the Prairie Architects,' *Journal of the Society of Architectural Historians*, 19, 1960, 2–10.

29 The Peters house is illustrated in the *Inland Architect and News Record*, 27, 4, 1896. Maher's projects and executed works were assiduously published by the *Inland Architect and News Record* beginning in 1888.

30 Such houses are described in Sinclair Lewis' *Main Street*: 'It proved that what he [Will Kennicott] wanted was a house exactly like Sam Clark's, which was exactly like every third new house in every town in the country: a square, yellow stolidity with immaculate clapboards, a broad screened porch, tidy grassplots, and concrete walks; a house resembling the mind of a merchant who votes the party ticket straight and goes to church once a month and owns a good car.' (*Main Street*, Signet Classic, New York, 1963, p. 288.)

31 Maher called the Farson house a 'Colonial residence' (*Inland Architect and News Record*, *30*, 1897, 54). The parallel with contemporary 'colonial' work (and perhaps even the design source) may be seen in the S.W. Stevens house, Lowell, Massachusetts, which was illustrated in the *Inland Architect and News Record* (*26*, 6, 1896) and, therefore, readily available to Maher. The Stevens house, although less earthbound and pyramidal than Maher's design, had a veranda across the front, three symmetrical window groupings, and a low hip roof with a central dormer. The overtly classical details – Doric columns, dentils – of the Stevens house, however, are absent in the Maher design. Instead there is an austerity worthy of German nineteenth-century classicism, perhaps intentional since the cornice of the Farson house is strikingly similar to many Schinkel designs.

32 *Inland Architect and News Record*, *34*, 1899, 32

More significant is the Edgar G. Barrett house (1896) at 255 Melrose Avenue, Kenilworth (fig. 3), with its broad hip roof (and shelf-roof at the front), central tower, and long projecting porch, all characteristic of Richardson's shingled Potter house in St Louis. Maher's design, however, is more solid and substantial, more plastic, and more emphatically horizontal.

A synthesis occurred in Maher's 1897 design for the John Farson house at 217 Home Avenue, Oak Park (fig. 4). Here the idea of massiveness, centralization, and substantiality, which he sought, was achieved. The symmetry of the Peters house is combined with the breadth and horizontality of the Barrett house, as well as with the formality and Roman brick of Wright's Winslow house; also important for Maher was the colonial revival.[31]

The Farson house was published with the comment that 'The architect submits this design as a type for an American style,'[32] which points out Maher's greatest weakness as a designer. He thought in terms of 'types,' and throughout his career he exploited first one type and then another. As a result his oeuvre falls naturally into several distinct periods, the earliest being a Silsbee phase, the next based on the Farson type (this lasted until about 1902–5), and a third and shorter period (c. 1905–8) inspired by the

FIG. 3 George W. Maher. Edgar G. Barrett house, 255 Melrose Avenue, Kenilworth, Illinois, 1896. *Inland Architect* 1897

modern movements in England and Austria. Designing was difficult for Maher, as attested to by the awkwardness of many of his houses. Thus he repeatedly fell back on the expedient of a formula, which, once arrived at, was frequently repeated for several years – until a new type was substituted in its place.

Our aesthetic judgment of Maher's work may not be high, yet we cannot overlook his real contribution. He did create, where others failed, a consistent and occasionally highly personal series of ahistorical designs,

FIG. 4 George W. Maher. John Farson house, 217 Home Avenue, Oak Park, Illinois, 1897. Photo Brooks collection

33 *Twelfth Annual Exhibition of the Chicago Architectural Club, Catalogue,* Chicago, 1899, pp. 27–8

34 *American Architect and Building News, 64,* 1899, 42, and *Inland Architect and News Record, 33,* 1899, 30

35 *Brickbuilder, 8,* 1899, 109

36 *Inland Architect and News Record, 33,* 1899, 41

designs which enjoyed great public favor and had a profound influence on other architects as well.

A word, in closing, should be said of the Chicago Architectural Club, for it was here that Maher and others exhibited their work, and here that the group from Steinway Hall, and the Eighteen, ultimately found a most useful and effective forum for expression. The club, with its membership of draftsmen and young architects, was avowedly an educational organization which sponsored talks, demonstrations, and design competitions, which were held in the club rooms at the Art Institute of Chicago. During the 1898–9 year, for example, there were 32 scheduled meetings, including a lecture by Sullivan on 'The Principles of Architectural Design,' and one by Wright on 'The Practical Nature of the Artistic.'[33] The most significant event was the annual exhibition held in the galleries of the Art Institute each spring. Members and non-members could submit, and entries often numbered between five and six hundred items. An elaborate, illustrated catalogue was prepared, this dating back to 1894. From the late nineties until 1902 the architects from Steinway Hall and the Eighteen were increasingly active in the club's affairs. A year did not pass without their holding important administrative posts, and occasionally they represented the controlling majority. Spencer, Garden, Perkins, Schmidt, and George Dean were particularly active in this regard, but also Irving Pond, Hunt, Granger, and Shaw. The year 1902 saw Spencer as president, and a jury of admissions to the annual exhibition consisting of Spencer, Dean, and Schmidt; Dean was also the catalogue editor. With these men in charge it is small wonder that the Chicago Architectural Club, with its 120 members, seemed to express a single point of view.

Equally important as a forum of expression was the Architectural League of America, an organization established largely through the initiative of the Chicago Architectural Club. The latter had called for a founding convention to be held in Cleveland, Ohio, 2–3 June 1899, with delegates from all architectural societies in the United States. The stated purpose was to increase co-operation between the various clubs, especially in matters of education and exhibitions.[34] Ten clubs and three chapters of the American Institute of Architects responded to the call by sending 97 representatives to Cleveland, 'averaging about 32 years of age and being about evenly divided between practising architects and prominent draftsmen.'[35] The Chicago delegation included George Dean, Long, Perkins, Tomlinson, and Wright.[36] Wright, although not a member of the Chicago club, apparently attended as a delegate through the good will of his friends. He was an active participant, however, and went to meetings, read papers, and took part in discussions – although he held no administrative post.

Sullivan, the idol of the younger generation, did not attend the Cleveland meeting, but sent a paper that was read by Tomlinson. 'It was the event of the convention,' reported the *Inland Architect and News Record*, 'so thoroughly did it embody the thoughts and feelings of every draftsman present.'[37] Immediately it established the tenor of the League's proceedings. The *Brickbuilder* called it 'a ringing paper';[38] under the title, 'The Modern Phase of Architecture,' Sullivan confidently stated his faith in the younger generation and in their ability to regenerate the art of architecture as 'the noblest, the most intimate, the most expressive, the most eloquent of all.'[39] Other papers presented at the convention, as those by Tomlinson and Dean, dealt with more specific matters, such as exhibitions and education.

The founding convention of 1899 was a resounding success. The architectural journals outdid themselves in reporting on the proceedings, and the enthusiasm which marked the event suggested an auspicious beginning. Albert Kelsey of Philadelphia was elected president and Tomlinson of Chicago secretary. The choices indicate a cautious compromise between East and Midwest as, indeed, was the choice of Cleveland for the site of the founding convention. Chicago, however, was selected for the next meeting with the Chicago Architectural Club to serve as host.

The Chicago convention of 7, 8, and 9 June 1900 was the most notable in the annals of the League. It consisted of three parts – sessions devoted to the reading and discussing of papers, a business meeting, and a banquet at which Sullivan was the guest speaker. The latter event, appropriately held in the Auditorium Building, was the occasion of Sullivan's celebrated address, 'The Young Man in Architecture,' a subject that he later expanded upon in 'Kindergarten Chats.'[40] His theme was architectural education, and specifically the means of developing a 'well rounded and perfected personal style.'[41] He rejected both books and buildings and insisted that 'the human mind in operation is the original document.'[42] Mental logic, he contended, was comparable to the logic of natural growth and, therefore, the study of nature best trained the mind to think in a logical and rhythmical pattern.

Sullivan sought to take the pupil to school to nature, there to observe the organic creation of form – the natural growth process as forms unfold from an inner core and develop into that which is at once functional and aesthetic, structural and beautiful, with each part inseparable from and

37 Ibid., p. 43

38 *Brickbuilder*, 8, 1899, 111

39 Sullivan's paper, 'The Modern Phase of Architecture,' was published in *The Architectural Annual*, Albert Kelsey, ed., Philadelphia, 1900, p. 27. The *Annual* was published under the auspices of the League.

40 Sullivan's talk was published in its entirety by the *Inland Architect and News Record*, 35, 1900, 38–40 (this entire June issue was devoted to the League convention), and the *Brickbuilder*, 9, 1900, 115–19. The paper was reprinted in Louis H. Sullivan, *Kindergarten Chats and Other Writings*, George Wittenborn, New York, 1947, pp. 214–23, which is the source used here.

41 Ibid., p. 220

42 Ibid., p. 217

43 Ibid.

44 Ibid., p. 219

45 *American Architect and Building News*, 68, 1900, 87

46 *Architecture*, *1*, 1900, 224. For an excellent account of Sullivan's interest in the League see Sherman Paul, *Louis Sullivan, An Architect in American Thought*, Englewood Cliffs, 1962.

47 *Inland Architect and News Record*, *37*, 1901, 33. Emil Lorch (b. 1870) was a non-resident member of the Chicago Architectural Club, giving his address as Detroit, Michigan. His professional education had been obtained in Paris and at MIT (1890–2). In 1901 he attended the League's Philadelphia convention as a delegate from the Chicago club, and was elected corresponding secretary. Much of his later life was devoted to architectural education.

48 For a discussion of pure design, including extracts from the papers read, see *Inland Architect and News Record*, *37*, 1901, 33–5.

necessary to the other. This, Sullivan insisted, should be the first phase of an architectural education. Above all else education must engender 'the basis of organized thinking'[43] because only 'a logical mind will beget a logical building.'[44]

Sullivan also attended the working sessions of the League, and there his presence caused quite a stir. The *American Architect and Building News*, in reporting on the opening proceedings, said that 'The feature of the morning, however, was the ovation to Mr Sullivan, who was present in the audience as a spectator and called upon to address the convention. He was evidently the master, and, as one of the later speakers (Wright) expressed it, they the disciples, and he was greeted with continued and continued applause, which only stopped as he began his extemporaneous remarks. ... His English, as usual, was charming, albeit at times quite unintelligible.'[45] Sullivan's manner of speaking also provoked comment in *Architecture*: 'Mr Sullivan's delivery is most pleasing. He sings his song into your ears and, as by the cadence of a lullaby, objection is disarmed and opposition stilled.'[46]

While many papers, as well as the banquet address, dealt with education, no theory aroused greater interest than that set forth by Emil Lorch. 'Under the influence,' reported the *Inland Architect and News Record* in 1901, 'and it does not seem improper to say under the leadership of Mr Emil Lorch, for the past two years, the League has devoted much attention to the discussion of the necessity for the study of pure design in architectural education in place of the time-honored practice of training the student along classical and historical lines. The clubs of the League have endorsed the movement for which the Chicago Club gave initiative, and it has already grown so strong and developed such practical and feasible characteristics as to compel the attention of architectural educators everywhere.'[47]

The fundamental idea behind pure design was that all architecture is based upon an abstract, geometric order. To design a building, therefore, the architect must first analyze the component parts – each of which could be expressed by one or more geometric shapes – and then 'compose' these parts so as to establish the basic massing of the building. This initial process was similar to a child's use of building blocks. Once the basic massing was established all subsequent aspects of the design would evolve from the abstract order of the unified parts. The detailing and decoration would be inspired by the abstract shapes that constituted the basis of the design.[48]

The concept of pure design, like so many theories for architectural design in the nineteenth century, might well have come to naught but for one listener at the League convention. Upon Wright they made a deep impression and through his subsequent work the essence of pure design was transmitted to the world. These discussions helped Wright apply his early Froebel kindergarten experiences to the practical requirements of building. The radical modification in his mode of design is exemplified by Unity Church, a building created with the idea of pure design in mind. In *An Autobiography*, Wright recalls his thoughts as he developed the design: 'Meanwhile glancing side reflections are passing in the mind – "design in abstraction of nature-elements in purely geometric terms" – that is what we ought to call pure design? This cube – this square – proportion.'[49]

Wright's choice of words and use of quotation marks suggest that he was mulling over the deliberations of pure design (sometimes also called abstract design) that he heard at the League. Although Grant C. Manson has convincingly demonstrated how the Froebel kindergarten toys influenced Wright's architectural design,[50] it is worth noting that Wright did not apply the Froebel lesson to buildings until after he learned of pure design. In 1900 Spencer had noted the Froebel influence on Wright's decorative work, but did not associate it with his architecture.[51] Not until after Wright's earliest prairie houses were designed did the abstract geometric forms common to both the toys and pure design appear in his work. The League discussions, it seems, served as the catalyst which helped Wright to realize the potential of the Froebel lesson.

What he learned at the League was far more significant than what he said. 'Mr Frank Wright,' reported the *American Architect and Building News*, (*sic*), 'in his long paper on "Architects" (*sic*), belabored every existing condition and every ordinary practitioner, right and left, up and down, back and front, without any exception either as to practice or design.'[52] The comment is rather harsh, yet truthfully Wright's talk was not particularly constructive. He merely reiterated Sullivan's plea for the study of nature, while broadly condemning contemporary architecture, the evils of which he attributed to the architects' quest for money. He made no specific proposals, and expounded no theory of his own – thus indicating that his concept of organic architecture was still unformulated in his mind.

The local *Inland Architect and News Record* was more patronizing regarding Wright's talk yet, contrary to general practice, it did not summarize, or publish, the text: 'Frank Wright read a paper on "The Architect." He prefaced his excellent paper by the remark that "after listening to the master (Sullivan) it hardly seemed proper to listen to the disciple." '[53]

49 Wright, *An Autobiography*, p. 157

50 Manson, *Frank Lloyd Wright to 1910*, pp. 5–10

51 Robert C. Spencer, Jr, 'The Work of Frank Lloyd Wright,' *Architectural Review* (Boston), 7, 1900, 69

52 *American Architect and Building News*, 68, 1900, 87. The *Brickbuilder*, 9, 1900, 124–8, published the text of Wright's paper 'The Architect' and a rearranged and edited version appears in Frederick Gutheim, *Frank Lloyd Wright on Architecture*, New York, 1941, pp. 6–21.

53 *Inland Architect and News Record*, 35, 1900, 43

54 *Architecture*, *1*, 1900, 224

55 *American Architect and Building News*, *68*, 1900, 87

56 *Architecture*, *1*, 1900, 225

57 The proposals were that *The Architectural Annual* become the official organ of the League and that 'Progress before Precedent' be adopted as a motto. (*American Architect and Building News*, *68*, 1900, 87.)

58 The telegram read: 'Greetings to the convention. I regret not to be with you. I hope that your deliberations will result in a firmer stand than ever for a rational conception and working ideal of the architectural art. Push on in the good work; I am with you in spirit. s/ Louis H. Sullivan' (*Brickbuilder*, *10*, 1901, 112).

'Education' was published in the *Inland Architect and News Record*, *39*, 1902, 41–2, and in Sullivan, *Kindergarten Chats*, pp. 224–6.

According to one account 'The best paper of the convention was delivered by Mr Elmer Grey of Milwaukee. It was upon the subject of "Indigenous and Inventive Architecture," and while the subject is kind of a scare crow the paper was a delightful surprise. It was a good exposition of searching analyses and sound reasoning.'[54] At its conclusion Sullivan, to whom Grey had paid homage in his opening remarks, spoke out enthusiastically in support of Grey's views.

In some quarters there were strong feelings that the Architectural League of America had been founded as a protest against conservative elements in the profession, especially as exemplified by the American Institute of Architects. So current was this impression that the president felt obliged publicly to disavow the fact and urge 'that the League's attitude toward that association should be one of deference and respect ... '[55] Sullivan was in the opposing camp, however, and took pains to say so in the opening sentence of his banquet address: 'It is my premise that the Architectural League of America has its being in a sense of discontent with conditions now prevailing in the American malpractice of the architectural art [and] in a deep and wide sense of conviction that no aid is to be expected from the generation now representing that malpractice ... '[56]

The existence of two factions inevitably enlivened the proceedings but did nothing to facilitate the work of the League. East was pitted against Midwest and, although the New York delegation vetoed two proposals favored by Chicago,[57] the host club finally won the day. The by-laws were amended to allow the executive to serve a two-year term instead of one, and to provide that all officers represent a single geographic area. The immediate past-president of the Chicago Architectural Club, Joseph C. Llewellyn, was then elected president of the League with Schmidt, Lorch, Garden, and Spencer in supporting roles. For the moment it seemed that Chicago was in control, but two years later the leadership had shifted to New York.

The next two conventions were the last to excite much interest among Chicagoans. In 1901 Sullivan dispatched a telegram of encouragement to Philadelphia, and in 1902 he sent a short paper on 'Education' to Toronto.[58] Spencer read papers on both occasions and Perkins spoke at Toronto, but thereafter their participation was nil. The spirit and enthusiasm that had marked the early conventions was gone and in its stead a staid conservatism prevailed. If, in fact, the League had been founded in dissent, its voice was quickly calmed and ere long the League was absorbed by its erstwhile enemy – the American Institute of Architects.

Among the League's most active protagonists were those from Steinway Hall and the Eighteen, the same men who played such a decisive part in the Chicago Architectural Club. Their greatest involvement was prior to 1902, a year that marked their domination of the club's annual exhibition and their effective usurping of the illustrated catalogue to promote their special interests. Thereafter, however, the club's general membership regained control and never again was the exhibition so expressive of so few. This, in retrospect, was an early, highly vocal phase of the new movement, one of close comradeship which marked a period when design maturity had not yet been gained and no clear course was established. Once this was achieved – after 1902 – the emphasis shifted from debate to designing; this, ultimately, was more rewarding. The earliest designs, as discussed in the following chapter, were not always intrinsically exciting or of special merit; they reflect a period of searching for a valid, independent, and often highly personal means of expression.

Before turning to these early designs, however, a postscript seems warranted concerning Wright's changing attitude toward his comrades. Many readers, and historians as well, have been preconditioned by Wright's late-in-life assessment of his early contemporaries – a judgment which bears no relation to what Wright himself said, and apparently believed, at the time these events were closest to him. On three occasions, in 1908, 1932, and 1957, Wright wrote about the group at Steinway Hall or the Eighteen, and with each account – separated by approximately 25 years – his attitude changed. The change was from one of friendship, indebtedness, and personal need to one of blatant hostility and condemnation. During the period in question he wrote: 'how I longed for comradeship until I began to know the younger men and how welcome was Robert Spencer, and then Myron Hunt, and Dwight Perkins, Arthur Heun, George Dean, and Hugh Garden. Inspiring days they were, I am sure, for us all.'[59]

Wright was then 40 and at the crest of his career. He had no rivals and the future promised only prosperity and prestige. Yet the next 24 years were filled with disillusionment. His 'New School of the Middle West' had flourished and then disintegrated, and his own work had tapered off drastically while several of his former pupils were more active and honored than he. These were also years scarred deeply by personal tragedy. It is perhaps understandable that bitterness crept into his writing and maybe a characteristic human failing that, while trying to reestablish his own image in the public eye, he would malign his contemporaries.[60] In *An Autobiography*, published in 1932, he began by telling how the group was formed:

59 *Architectural Record*, 23, 1908, 156

60 It must be pointed out, however, that Wright's bitterness developed *prior* to the series of tragedies which affected his personal life. C.R. Ashbee, who stayed with the Wrights during his 1908 visit to America (and had not seen his host since 1900), made the following entry in his Journal for December 1908: 'Lloyd Wright who 8 years ago was with his school full of fire and belief, and meantime has become famous and practically made "the school of the Middle West" has grown bitter, he has drawn in upon himself, it is the bitterness of an anarchic socialism.' (Quoted with the kind permission of Felicity Ashbee.) For part of the correspondence between Wright and Ashbee see Alan Crawford, 'Ten Letters from Frank Lloyd Wright to Charles Robert Ashbee,' *Architectural History*, 13, 1970, 64–76. I am indebted to Mr Crawford for apprising me of, and furnishing me with, the complete correspondence.

61 George Dean and Hugh Garden did not, as implied here, have their offices in Steinway Hall. They were in the Eighteen.

62 Wright, *An Autobiography*, p. 131. In 1914 Wright vented his emotions against many of these architects, yet at that time he did not specifically discuss the group at Steinway Hall. See 'In the Cause of Architecture; Second Paper,' *Architectural Record*, 35, 1914, 405–13.

63 Ibid., p. 132

64 Frank Lloyd Wright, *A Testament*, Horizon Press, New York, 1957, pp. 34–5

65 Ibid., p. 33. Wright, as noted in the introduction, was well aware of the school; in 1908 he coined for it the name, 'The New School of the Middle West,' and in 1936 referred to it as 'the Prairie School.'

None of the original group but Wright has left an account of the early days at Steinway Hall. Thomas Eddy Tallmadge, the group's most ardent historian and coiner of the term 'Chicago School,' joined the Chicago Architectural Club in 1900 but apparently had little first-hand knowledge of the group prior to 1905 when he entered partnership with Vernon Watson.

That place in the Schiller Building soon seemed nothing at all without him [Cecil Corwin]. I had met Robert Spencer, Myron Hunt, and Dwight Perkins. Dwight had a loft in his new Steinway Hall building – too large for him. So we formed a group – outer office in common – workrooms screened apart in the loft of Steinway Hall. These young men, newcomers in architectural practice like myself, were my first associates in the so-called profession of architecture. George Dean was another and Hugh Garden.[61] Birch Long was a young and talented "renderer" at this time and we took him into the Steinway loft with us.[62]

Following this matter-of-fact statement concerning the founding of the group, Wright then re-evaluated his contemporaries in a manner quite contrary to his earlier assessment.

Never having known Sullivan much themselves, at this time these young architects were all getting the gospel modified through me. And I should have liked to be allowed to work out the thing I felt in me as architecture with no reflections or refractions from them or libelous compliments until I had it all where I felt it really ought to be. But that was not possible. I was out in the open to stay. Premature though it might be.[63]

The bitterness of this attack bears little relation to the account of 1908. Any hint of loneliness and need is gone and instead there is only animosity. Although the account of how the group was formed is essentially unbiased, this tone too was to change with Wright's last published version in *A Testament* (1957). Now he assumed the role of absolute supremacy:

Because I was, so far as they were concerned, Sullivan's "alter ego," a small clique soon formed about me, myself naturally enough the leader ...

I with those nearest me rented a vacant loft in Steinway Hall: a building Dwight Perkins had built. But Spencer, Perkins, Hunt and Birch Long (clever boy renderer) moved in with me. Together we subdivided the big attic into studio-like draughting rooms.[64]

Here fact and fiction mingle with equal freedom and Wright's crusade to discredit his contemporaries seems almost complete. Even the school which emerged, and of which he had once spoken so fondly, was now disclaimed as something he had never known: 'until the phrase "Chicago School" appeared so many years later, I was not aware that anything like a "school" had existed.'[65]

Wright's retrospective attitude is to be regretted, especially since he, perhaps more than any other, benefited from this environment. Probably it is no coincidence that his two most brilliant and productive periods followed closely his intimate involvement with a group of young architects, the first commencing in the late eighteen-nineties at Steinway Hall and continuing in the Studio, and the second beginning after the Taliesin Fellowship was formed in 1932. The Fellowship, in effect, re-created the group milieu that existed about 1900 – except that it was an autocracy. And it is precisely this autocratic system that Wright, late in life, wished to think had existed at Steinway Hall.

The exhibition sponsored by the Chicago Architectural Club in 1902 was dominated by the group from Steinway Hall and the Eighteen, their designs prompting one conservative reviewer to pen these hasty lines:

When one sees the seriously beautiful work, even in domestic architecture, that is being done in other parts of the country, notably in the East, one is ashamed of the trivial spirit that is abroad here among us. There is a set of younger men here in Chicago who foster all this sort of thing. They have among them men with artistic spirit and feeling but their aim seems to be always to strive for the semi-grotesque, the catchy. Their compositions lack the best principles of honest design. Their aim seems to be to impress upon the beholder the belief that they are so filled with artistic inspirations and ideas that the flood cannot be held back for a minute, but must be dashed down onto paper as fast as ink or lead can carry it. There *is* a certain dash about it [however], but how will these things look, say, even twenty years from now?[1]

The critic's own bias was perfectly clear: 'two notably fine houses (were) finished ... in Chicago this year, one a beautiful Colonial on Wellington Avenue, the other an equally good French Renaissance on North State ... '[2]

FIG. 5 Hugh M.G. Garden. Robert Herrick house, 5726 University Avenue, Chicago, Illinois, 1900. *Inland Architect* 1902

1 *American Architect and Building News*, 76, 1902, 29

2 Ibid.

The 'set of younger men' were certainly well represented at the exhibition, but the catalogue carried the situation to an extreme – it was a monograph dedicated to their work.[3] Sullivan designed the special frontispiece,[4] and between Sullivan and the original four from Steinway Hall were divided some 60 per cent of the plates[5] – these being placed in the most prominent locations. First, after an introductory plate, came Perkins' work, followed by the designs of Hunt and Spencer. Wright was honored in a special section at the end, with its own frontispiece announcing 'The Work of Frank Lloyd Wright.' This included 14 plates, or nearly one-quarter of the illustrations – and in the exhibition itself where an entire section of the gallery was set aside for his work, there were 65 exhibits (one-eighth of the total exhibition), including models, drawings, photographs, and many designs for ornament and furnishings.[6] Of the remaining plates, 16 were allotted to 8 other members of the Eighteen,[7] and 5 went to sympathetic friends, Maher, Drummond, and Grey. The introductory plate, significantly, illustrated a Beacon of Progress by Désiré Despradelle, the Ecole-trained Frenchman who had taught many of these architects at MIT; his inclusion was an obvious act of homage.[8]

The group from Steinway Hall and the Eighteen had undoubtedly won the day, so far as the Chicago Architectural Club and its annual exhibition were concerned. Nevertheless, their unity was hardly apparent in their architectural designs – only in their mutual idealization of simplicity did their work display a common bond. Some accepted the historical styles, desiring only to simplify them and thereby achieve a contemporary freshness. Others sought consciously to create a new style – by evolving new forms from old, or by applying some theory or system of design. Thus the discussions of pure design, of organic design, and of rhythm in design, each of which, it was thought, would aid the architect in arriving at a more viable architectural expression. But not until after the exhibit of 1902 did

3 The 1902 catalogue was entitled *The Chicago Architectural Annual*, and in addition to 57 plates contained a list of patrons, members, and officials. This was bound in a hard cover and imprinted 'CAC 1902.' A separate eight-page list of exhibits (477 in number) was called the *Catalogue of Exhibits Chicago Architectural Club* (1902, Art Institute, Chicago). Most years the exhibits were listed in the illustrated catalogue rather than being published separately.

4 A richly interlaced floral ornament entwined the stanza of a poem which read:

Science moving swiftly
calls to the Art that sleeps
with heavy eyes, the while, her
   sister-arts
lead those who, toiling, seek the
   truth.
This Art, dreaming brings forth here
   and there a Man
who ardent, stretches out his hands
   and prays that
Nature show him God and
Truth and Love: so teaching
him to Build.

5 Of the 57 plates, 14 were allocated to Wright, 8 to Sullivan, 6 to Spencer, 4 to Perkins, and 1 to Hunt.

6 Some 30 of the 65 items that Wright exhibited were decorative designs, including copper bowls, table scarfs, lamps, chairs, glass designs, and sculpture with each embroiderer, coppersmith, and electroglazier listed by name

– a practice common throughout the Arts and Crafts Movement.

7 The eight being Howard Shaw, George Dean, Hugh Garden, Arthur Heun, Pond and Pond, Richard Schmidt, and Birch Long

8 Désiré Despradelle, a graduate of the Ecole des Beaux-Arts and the atelier Pascal, came to the Institute following the death of Eugène Létang in 1892, the latter having taught there since 1871. For a history of the school at MIT see Caroline Shillaber, *Massachusetts Institute of Technology School of Architecture and Planning 1861-1961: A Chronicle* [no city], 1963.

a consistent, systematic approach to the problem emerge, and leading ultimately to a reorganization and consolidation within the group.

Hugh Garden (1873–1961)[9] created some of the finest designs of the period, these often sharing Sullivan's concern for a strong, positive massing, simplification of basic forms, and careful attention to the relation between solid and void. His house in 1900 for the novelist and teacher, Robert Herrick, was notable for its severely rectangular façade, precisely incised windows, and stark, unrelieved surfaces of brick (fig. 5). Order and clarity prevailed. The hard, almost machine-like precision of the walls recalls the double house for Catherine White (fig. 2) or other works of the period; absent were the varied massing and picturesque roofs so typical of the time. This building, later remodeled internally by Barry Byrne for the Newman Club at the University of Chicago, still stands at 5726 University Avenue, in Chicago.

Similar characteristics prevail in Garden's theater project for Marion, Indiana, a work exhibited at the Chicago Architectural Club in 1901 (fig. 6). The repetitive rhythm of the open loggia, combined with the strong

9 Hugh Mackie Gordon Garden was born (1873) in Toronto where the family lived until moving to Minneapolis in 1887, and shortly thereafter to Chicago. The early death of his father posed financial problems, and curtailed Hugh's education. In Minneapolis he began working as a draftsman/renderer and the move to Chicago was prompted by the promise of greater opportunity. Most of his experience was gained in the Chicago offices of Flanders and Zimmerman, Henry Ives Cobb (where he met Louis C. Mullgardt), and Shepley, Rutan and Coolidge, prior to 1893 when he began free-lance designing. In 1892 he joined the Chicago Architectural Club and for many years served as an officer or on various committees and juries.

FIG. 6 Hugh M.G. Garden. Project: Theater for Marion, Indiana, 1901. Chicago Architectural Club *Catalogue* 1901

horizontal of the shelf roof, lent unity and an air of monumentality to this splendid little design.

Garden also designed the Third Church of Christ, Scientist, in Chicago, completed in 1901 and, of related design, the First Church of Christ,

FIG. 7 Hugh M.G. Garden. First Church of Christ, Scientist, Marshalltown, Iowa, 1902–3. Photo by K.L. Henderson, courtesy Wesley I. Shank

Scientist, in Marshalltown, Iowa.[10] The latter was constructed during 1902–3 of wood frame covered with stucco. It was a Greek cross in plan with short arms which emphasized the unity of the single, auditorium-like space within; its capacity was approximately 400 persons. Cross gables, steep in pitch, composed the roof and made possible the placement of large triangular windows, divided by vertical mullions within the gable ends (fig. 7). The glass was executed by Giannini and Hilgart of Chicago. These windows were made particularly distinctive by the strut-like brackets linking the mullions to the broadly overhanging gable roof. In contrast to this colorful and highly plastic treatment was the simplicity of the lower walls with their finish of smooth stucco – except where there were apertures for the entrance and lower windows.

Garden was particularly apt at designing commercial architecture, and a splendid example is his Grommes and Ullrich Building (1901) at 108 W. Illinois Street in Chicago (fig. 8). Brick, rather than stone or terra cotta, is the principal material, with an emphatic horizontality achieved by interspersing broad, uninterrupted spandrels with large 'Chicago windows' separated by slightly recessed piers – piers de-emphasized by the abstract pattern of their brickwork. An area of smooth brick frames the building, while a simple coping caps the cornice. The ground storey is now remodeled, but the character of the building remains unchanged.[11]

Garden was a gifted designer. He possessed a fine sense of proportions, and was a most talented renderer. Yet the business and technical side of architecture concerned him little, and resulted in his distaste for private practice; for many years he prepared designs and presentation drawings for others.[12] Richard E. Schmidt (1865–1958)[13] frequently sought his services, a fact which was finally acknowledged in 1906 when the firm of

Coolidge, and Frank Lloyd Wright. Garden informed the author (31 October 1955) that he also did some drawings for Sullivan.

The perspective of Wright's Cheltenham Beach project, signed by Corwin and Garden, is universally given an enormous date of 1899. Actually it was designed some five years earlier, in 1895 or late 1894. It seems that Wright's only entry in the 1895 Chicago Architectural Club exhibition has escaped notice: 'Study for a Pleasure Resort at Cheltenham.' This date is corroborated by Corwin's name on the drawing, because Corwin left Chicago about 1896. [13] Schmidt, who was Garden's senior by eight years, was born in Ebern, Germany, and came to America the following year. He was educated in Chicago's public schools and studied architecture at MIT for two years (1883–5). In 1887 he entered practice, and the following year joined the Chicago Architectural Club; about 1894 he was briefly in partnership with T.O. Fraenkel (Fraenkel and Schmidt, Architects) with whom he shared an office for several years. Birch Burdette Long, before moving to Steinway Hall, was in Schmidt's office (no. 1013, the Teutonic Building, 172 Washington Street, Chicago) for over two years (1898–1900), and beginning in 1899 Frank Garden, one of Hugh's brothers, and Adolph Stander were also there.

---

10 For information concerning these churches I am indebted to Wesley I. Shank. See his 'Hugh Garden in Iowa,' *Prairie School Review*, 5, 3, 1968, 43–47.

11 Of heavy timber construction, the building was designed so that four additional stories could be added later (Frank A. Randall, *History of the Development of Building Construction in Chicago*, Urbana, 1949, pp. 218–19). An

early photograph of the building (originally a warehouse) was published in the *Architectural Record* for April 1905, p. 341, under the name of 'Richard E. Schmidt, Architect.'

12 Garden is listed in the Chicago Architectural Club catalogues as doing work for Henry Ives Cobb, Flanders and Zimmerman, William R. Gibb, Alfred H. Granger, Richard E. Schmidt, Howard V.D. Shaw, Shepley, Rutan and

FIG. 8 Hugh M.G. Garden (for Richard E. Schmidt). Grommes and Ullrich Building, 108 W. Illinois Street, Chicago, Illinois, 1901. Photo courtesy B.C. Greengard

Richard E. Schmidt, Garden and Martin was founded.[14] Indeed, most of the early, well-publicized Schmidt buildings are precisely those which were designed by Garden. The Grommes and Ullrich Building is one of these; another is the Albert F. Madlener house (1902) at 4 W. Burton Place, Chicago.

The Madlener house has the dignity of a renaissance palazzo – it is stately without being grandiose (fig. 9).[15] Horizontal bands of buff Indiana limestone bind the lower and topmost windows to the cubic mass, while the middle windows seemingly hover on a broad surface of carefully laid Roman brick. An assertive, forward-set foundation, virtually a podium of stone, relates the building to the ground, while a rich Sullivanesque (though more geometric) ornamental band frames the entrance. The

FIG. 9 Hugh M.G. Garden (for Richard E. Schmidt). Albert F. Madlener house, 4 W. Burton Place, Chicago, before March 1902. Historic American Building Survey photo by Harold Allen

14 In 1925 the name was changed to Schmidt, Garden and Erikson, thus eliminating Schmidt's first name from the title. Edgar D. Martin, an engineer, left the firm in order to work for Pond and Pond.

15 The Madlener house, with many illustrations and a critique by Russell Sturgis, was published in the *Architectural Record*, *17*, 1905, 491–8. The building is located at the corner of N. State Street and W. Burton Place and is now occupied by the Graham Foundation for Advanced Studies in the Fine Arts.

clarity of the mass and sense of order are the most striking characteristics of this splendid design. Yet the emphasis accorded the several storeys is inconsistent with their use. The impressive *piano nobile* contains only bedrooms while the de-emphasized ground floor serves as the principal living area of the house; the seemingly insignificant attic shelters an imposing ballroom.

The concrete and steel frame Schoenhofen Brewing Company Building which Garden designed in 1902 for Schmidt was, as the Madlener house, faced with brick and limestone. But the brick was common rather than

FIG. 10 Hugh M.G. Garden (for Richard E. Schmidt). Schoenhofen Brewing Company Building, 1770 Canalport Avenue at 18th Street, Chicago, 1902. *Architectural Record* 1905

FIG. 11 Hugh M.G. Garden (for Richard E. Schmidt). Schoenhofen Brewing Company Building. Seward Street and 18th Street façades. Schmidt, Garden and Erikson archives, courtesy Mrs Garden Mitchell

FIG. 12 Hugh M.G. Garden (for Richard E. Schmidt). Schoenhofen Brewing Company Building. Plan. *Architectural Record* 1905

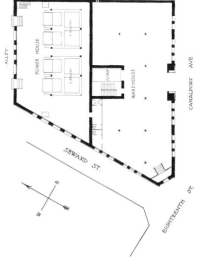

16 Russell Sturgis wrote an illustrated review of the building in the *Architectural Record*, *17*, 1905, 201–7. The working drawings, which list Schmidt as architect, are dated in November and December 1902.

17 George C. Nimmons (1865–1947) obtained his early training with Burnham and Root, and William K. Fellows (1870–1948) studied architecture at Columbia University. The firm, which was founded during the late nineties, specialized in commercial and industrial design until 1910 when Fellows entered partnership with Dwight Perkins and John Hamilton.

Illustrations and a descriptive text of the Rosenwald house will be found in the *Architectural Record*, *18*, 1905, 27–32.

Roman and the Bedford stone was cool in tone. The trapezoidal building (see plan fig. 12) served two functions: as a warehouse for the storage of hops (seen in the familiar Canalport Avenue elevation, fig. 10) and, on the backside, as a powerhouse, which had its own distinctive fenestration (fig. 11).[16]

The main elevation brilliantly solves the vexing and age-old problem of designing a long, rectangular façade (fig. 10). The five bays are divided by smooth brick panels, and each bay is then subdivided by slender piers. Vertically the motif embraces three storeys, thus adding unity and dignity to the design. In spite of its fine proportions, however, the building lacks the robustness which seems implicit in its design, and this sense of two-dimensionality is heightened by the lack of visual unity between the three façades.

Nimmons and Fellows[17] were renowned as industrial architects, and one of their rare residential designs demonstrates their attempt at evolving

FIG. 13 Nimmons and Fellows. Julius Rosenwald house, 4901 Ellis Avenue, Chicago, 1903. *Architectural Record* 1905

something new. For the head of Sears Roebuck and Company, Julius Rosenwald, they built the house (1903) at 4901 Ellis Avenue, corner of 49th Street, in Chicago – but the intellectual process proves to be more fascinating than the design (fig. 13). The mass is uncompromising. It is capped by a hipped roof; the basement and attic are clearly separated from the main floors – where size and location of windows is determined by interior need. 'Chicago-windows' are interspersed with conventional casements, but their variety in size, and random placement, suggests disorder. The result leaves much to be desired.

Sullivan, meanwhile, although actively concerned with the current state of 'the architectural art,' provided no leadership through his work. The singularly fine Carson Pirie Scott Store dates from 1899, but there is no other work of equal distinction prior to his National Farmers' Bank at Owatonna of 1906–8. Tall commercial buildings, and ornament, were his strength, otherwise he seemed ill at ease in design, as the entries in the 1902 annual exhibition made clear. Marked by variety, they ranged from sentimental photographs of his rose gardens at Ocean Springs, Mississippi, to numerous designs for ornament. Projects for residences were also included, houses for Arthur Henry Lloyd of Chicago, Ellis Wainwright of St Louis, and Mrs Nettie F. McCormick of Lake Forest, Illinois. The latter was

FIG. 14 Louis H. Sullivan (and George G. Elmslie). Project: Nettie F. McCormick house, Lake Forest, Illinois, before March 1902. Chicago Architectural Club *Catalogue* 1902

illustrated in the catalogue and showed a substantial, well-proportioned building with decisively handled bands of fenestration (fig. 14). The broad porch and hipped roof emphasized the horizontality of the rectangular mass, as did the laterally extending pergola and octagonal summer house. Although masterfully handled, the design was not highly original. It owed much to the midwest vernacular, to Wright, and perhaps to Maher. Comparison with Wright's *rendering* of the William Winslow house, published in the *Architectural Review* of 1900, is striking due to the similarity of the long arbor terminating in an octagonal pavilion, both being set in association with a strongly rectangular, hipped-roof house. Perhaps the veranda implies knowledge of Maher's work (Farson house), although this feature was also common in the vernacular. The open plan is axial with rooms so arranged as to focus on the semi-circular conservatory at the far left – which in turn leads toward the arbor and pavilion beyond.

Sullivan had little interest in residential design and Wright earlier had spared him this chore. It is possible, therefore, that he still deferred such responsibility when willing assistance was at hand – as was available in the

FIG. 15 Robert C. Spencer, Jr. Project: 'A Southern Farmhouse Costing $3000,' 1900. *Ladies' Home Journal* January 1901

person of George Elmslie (1871–1952).[18] But Elmslie's uninspired contemporary design for W.G.A. Millar of Pittsburgh,[19] his brother-in-law, lacks the quality of the McCormick project to which it is related – a closer resemblance is to Maher's more boxy Peters house. This suggests that the breadth and pleasant proportions of the McCormick design derive from Sullivan; that it is possible to isolate the sources is perhaps a measure of Sullivan's disinterest in the problem, and his willingness to permit Elmslie to advance suggestions.

Wright's own work, based on a decade-long search for appropriate architectural forms, and augmented, perhaps, by the stimulation he received from his colleagues at Steinway Hall, came rapidly to maturity after 1900.[20] Most notable were his projects for the *Ladies' Home Journal*, published in February and July 1901, and called 'A Home in a Prairie Town' and 'A Small House with "Lots of Room in It," ' designs which were realized in the Warren Hickox house at Kankakee and the Ward Willits house at Highland Park. Concurrently, seven Model Farmhouses by Robert Spencer were published in the same journal, and one of these, 'A Southern Farmhouse Costing $3000,' appeared in January 1901 (fig. 15). It was long and

FIG. 16 Robert C. Spencer, Jr. Project: 'A Shingled Farmhouse for $2700,' 1900. Plan of first storey. *Ladies' Home Journal* April 1901

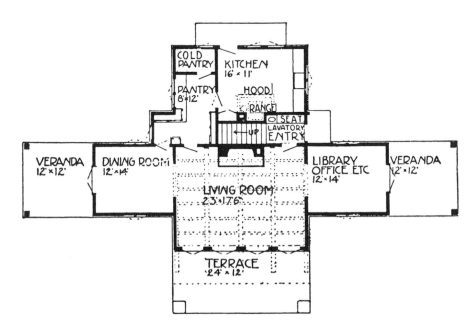

18 George Grant Elmslie was born (1871) near Huntley, Scotland, and immigrated to the United States in 1884 with his parents. In 1887, when about 16, he began his architectural training in the office of J.L. Silsbee, where he met Maher and Wright. Two years later Wright recommended him to Sullivan, and for nearly 20 years Elmslie stayed with Sullivan before entering into partnership (1909) with William Gray Purcell, a firm which subsequently became the most active and productive within the Prairie School. For a discussion of the role of Elmslie in Sullivan's office see David Gebhard, 'Louis Sullivan and George Grant Elmslie,' *Journal of the Society of Architectural Historians, 19*, 1960, 62–8.

19 Illustrated in David Gebhard, 'William Gray Purcell and George Grant Elmslie and the Early Progressive Movement in American Architecture from 1900 to 1920,' unpublished doctoral dissertation presented to the University of Minnesota, August 1957, figure 5

20 A discussion of this search, and the various controlling influences, will be found in my 'Frank Lloyd Wright,' *Encyclopedia of World Art, 14*, 1967, pp. 858–60.

21 Robert C. Spencer designed many projects for farmhouses. See his 'American Farmhouses,' *Brickbuilder*, 9, 1900, 179–86, 'The Farmhouse Problem,' *Annual of the Chicago Architectural Club*, Chicago, 1900, pp. 38–40, and 'Attractive Farmhouses for Real Farmers,' *Country Life in America*, 6, 1904, 546–8. His seven farmhouses for the *Ladies' Home Journal* were published in the issues of October and December 1900, and January, February, April, May, and June 1901.

22 Illustrations of Wright's projects will be found in Hitchcock, *In the Nature of Materials*, figs. 58–63, and Manson, *Frank Lloyd Wright to 1910*, pp. 104–7. Wright's Ward Willits house of 1902 also has some affinity with Spencer's earlier Southern Farmhouse project (fig. 15).

low with hipped roofs terminating over open lateral porches. The two-storey living room established an assertive cross-axis, with light entering through the clerestorey. Another project in the series was 'A Shingled Farmhouse for $2700'; it was distinguished by its open, cruciform plan and uninterrupted flow of space along the horizontal axis (fig. 16).[21]

These Spencer projects are crude and unsophisticated compared to Wright's masterpieces, yet the similarity of concept is striking.[22] Wright was the superior designer, and one initially assumes that Spencer utilized Wright's idea for the massing and organization of interior space – while rejecting Wright's vocabulary of form. However, in terms of competence, it seems unlikely that Spencer did so. An alternative response is that Wright assisted Spencer, yet there is no evidence of Wright's superior skill in these designs (as, for example, was apparent in the Catherine M. White house). A third and unanticipated possibility exists, therefore, that Spencer's designs came first and acted as a catalyst for Wright, helping him achieve a synthesis in his own designs – it is almost as if Wright were showing Spencer how he, Spencer, should have designed them. This is possible, as Spencer's 'A Shingled Farmhouse' (fig. 16) was exhibited at the Chicago Architectural Club in March 1900, and apparently precedes Wright's designs.

FIG. 17 Robert C. Spencer, Jr. Gardener's Lodge, Charles A. Stevens estate, Lake Delavan, Wisconsin, 1901–2. Chicago Architectural Club *Catalogue* 1902

FIG. 18 Robert C. Spencer, Jr. Adams house, Indianapolis, Indiana, 1903. *Architectural Record* 1906

FIG. 19 Robert C. Spencer, Jr. Project: 'A Casement-Window House,' 1902. *House Beautiful* 1902

23 Photographs of the finished building, and a plan, were published in *House Beautiful, 21*, 1, 1906, 29.

24 Numerous other illustrations of the Adams house will be found in the *Architectural Record, 19*, 1906, 296–301.

25 George Robinson Dean (1864–1919) was born at Satara, India, graduated from Doane College, Crete, Nebraska, in 1885, worked for W.C. Whitney in Minneapolis (1886–9) and with Shepley, Rutan and Coolidge in Boston (1889–91) before going to Europe, where he studied in the atelier of Henri Duray in Paris from 1892 to 1893. He returned to the United States in 1893 and entered the Chicago office of Shepley, Rutan and Coolidge where he remained until entering private practice in 1895. In 1895 and 1896 he was president of the Chicago Architectural Sketch Club, and in 1903 went into partnership with his brother, Arthur Dean.

26 Illustrations of the Alpha Delta Phi chapter house will be found in the *Architectural Record, 18*, 1905, 211–16, and in the *Brickbuilder, 14*, 1905, plates 37, 38, and 40. My thanks are due to Stephen Jacobs for locating this material and obtaining photographs.

Other work by Spencer included a gardener's lodge (1901) on the Charles A. Stevens estate at Lake Delavan, Wisconsin (fig. 17). Here is discernible the influence of the English country cottage – combined with Spencer's predominantly horizontal farmhouses. The light stucco, dark trim, and rows of casement windows, indicate how English antecedents could be assimilated into the work of the prairie architects. This assimilation was even more apparent in the lodge as it was actually built.[23]

Spencer's affinity for English design was life-long, and among his work illustrated in the 1902 Chicago Architectural Club catalogue were two half-timber houses, one identified only as built in Evanston in 1894, while the other was the U.G. Orendorff house (1902) at Canton, Illinois. A stronger, more mature design than either of these was the Adams house in Indianapolis of 1903; although frankly Tudor, its clear, precise forms, basic simplicity, and pleasant proportions make it a most impressive design (fig. 18).[24]

'A Casement Window House' by Spencer was published (May 1902) by the *House Beautiful* (fig. 19). The three-storey project consisted of low-pitched hipped roofs grouped in pyramidal fashion with the entire design unified by strong horizontals – including bands of casement windows. The project was part of a promotional scheme, Spencer having founded the Casement Hardware Company to capitalize on the growing demand for casement windows.

Dwight Perkins, like Spencer, had a propensity for simplified medieval forms, as demonstrated by his Hitchcock Hall (1901), University of Chicago (where he constructed several buildings). It is a typical though not remarkable design (except perhaps for the sculpture by Richard Bock), and there is little in his work to attract our attention before 1908 when, as architect to the Chicago Board of Education, he made his greatest contribution. Educational architecture was his chief concern; residences interested him little.

George Dean,[25] like others among the Eighteen, occasionally flirted with unconventional ideas, as was demonstrated by the Alpha Delta Phi fraternity house at Cornell University, Ithaca, New York, a building long since destroyed by fire (figs. 20, 21, 22).[26] The ingenious T-shape plan extended down the hill with its stem terminating in a twelve-sided porch – with dining room below. The basement was of limestone, the high first storey of brick, and the second floor of smooth plaster. In appearance the design was rather heavy, and the windows were awkwardly placed. Yet the interior was striking, especially with its sensitively designed woodwork and unique furnishings (fig. 20).

Arthur Heun[27] was even less adventuresome than were Dean, Perkins, and Spencer, and his houses were aptly described by one reviewer as follows:

His work exhibits, as does that of a number of his associates, a respectful appreciation of the value of traditional forms mixed with a refreshing emancipation from the limitations of the mere copyist. It shows also, what is equally important, a desire for simplicity – an intention of reducing the elements of his design to the most fundamental and indispensable terms ... [28]

These values found Heun a ready clientele among Chicago's North Side society set and ultimately he received such coveted commissions as the

FIG. 20 George R. Dean. Alpha Delta Phi fraternity house, Cornell University, Ithaca, New York, 1902. Entrance hall. *Architectural Record* 1905

27 Arthur Heun (1864?–1946) was born in Saginaw, Michigan, although his exact year of birth is in question. Most of his life was spent in Chicago, where he began his training under Frank Waterhouse.

28 *Architectural Record, 19*, 1906, 59

FIG. 21 George R. Dean. Alpha Delta
Phi fraternity house. Plan. *Architectural Record* 1905

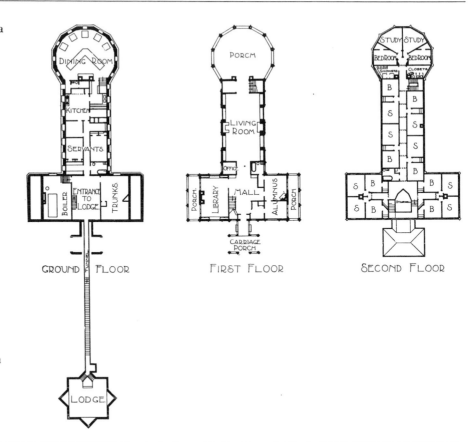

GROUND FLOOR

FIRST FLOOR

SECOND FLOOR

FIG. 22 George R. Dean. Alpha Delta
Phi fraternity house. South eleva-
tion, demolished. Courtesy Alpha
Delta Phi

J. Ogden Armour estate at Lake Forest, Illinois. About 1900, however, he had caught the enthusiasm that marked the Eighteen. His design for a 'Residence in Lake Forest' (fig. 23), exhibited in 1902, indicated his awareness of previously exhibited designs by Garden and Wright, but he made no attempt to accentuate their more novel features.[29] At approximately the same date Heun designed the Sedgwick S. Brinsmaid house on Grand Avenue in Des Moines, Iowa, a rendering of which was exhibited at the Chicago Architectural Club in 1902. The up-turned gable ends give this house an oriental flavor, while the detailing of the south porch recalls forms used by Sullivan and Wright; splendid Wright-inspired leaded glass adorns the interior.[30]

More skilled and successful as a society architect was Howard Van Doren Shaw (1869–1926). A graduate of Yale (1890) and student at MIT, he was in many respects the midwest counterpart of Sir Edwin Lutyens – his exact contemporary. Shaw's best architecture always had a tasteful dignity and repose, pleasant proportions, and a freedom – in spite of its lineage from the past – from excessive detail. His own house, 'Ragdale,' was a twin-gable, white stucco building that would have delighted C.F.A. Voysey, especially as the interiors were in the best tradition of William Morris.[31] With an eye

FIG. 23 Arthur Heun. Project: 'A Residence in Lake Forest,' 1902. Chicago Architectural Club *Catalogue* 1902

29 Heun's source was apparently Garden's project, 'A House at Highland Park,' illustrated in the Chicago Architectural Club catalogue of 1901, and its predecessor, 'A Home in a Prairie Town' by Wright. The Armour estate which Heun designed is now owned by the Lake Forest Academy; the house is profusely illustrated in Peter B. Wight's article, 'Melody Farm, the Country Home of J. Ogden Armour,' *Architectural Record*, *39*, 1916, 96–121.

30 The article by Wesley I. Shank, 'The Residence in Des Moines,' *Journal of the Society of Architectural Historians*, *29*, 1970, 56–9, contains documentation as well as numerous photographs, the plan, and the exhibited rendering of the Brinsmaid house.

31 Howard Shaw's home was illustrated with a photogravure plate in the *Inland Architect and News Record*, *33*, 6, 1899, while other views, including interiors, appear in the *Architectural Review* (Boston), *11*, 1904, 23–6.

to future clientele it was built in Lake Forest, but the more middle-class arts and crafts character of the design was hardly appropriate for great North Shore estates, for which Shaw ultimately found the English renaissance a more sympathetic point of departure. Thus the passage quoted above, about Heun, would aptly describe the simplified eclecticism embraced by Shaw.

FIG. 24 George W. Maher. James A. Patten house, Ridge Avenue, Evanston, Illinois, 1901. Demolished. *Architectural Record* 1904

FIG. 25 William E. Drummond. Project: An American Embassy, 1901. Plan. Chicago Architectural Club *Catalogue* 1902

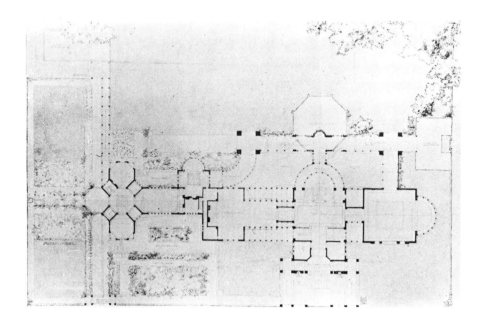

FIG. 26 William E. Drummond. Project: An American Embassy. Chicago Architectural Club *Catalogue* 1902

32 George G. Elmslie, 'Reflections on Rhythm,' *Illinois Society of Architects Monthly Bulletin*, 22, 1937, 6. The original typescript of this article is in the Burnham Library of Architecture, Art Institute of Chicago.

33 *House Beautiful*, 29, 1911, 159

34 George W. Maher, 'Art Democracy,' *Western Architect*, 15, 1910, 30

35 *Studio*, 30, 1903, 82. This was not Maher's first recognition in Europe. His J. MacMeans house was published in *Dekorative Kunst*, 4, 1899, 110.

36 Arthur C. David, 'The Architecture of Ideas,' *Architectural Record*, 15, 1904, 375. This article (pp. 361–84) contains numerous illustrations of the Patten and Rubens houses.

37 Illustrated in the *Architectural Record*, 15, 1904, 371, 380–2, and the *Western Architect*, 12, 6, 1908

Simplicity was a characteristic valued in design, and so was rhythm – rhythm existed in good design and architects thought that by the use of rhythm they could create better designs. Sullivan probably instigated this concern through his repeated mention of rhythm, and Maher, Irving Pond, Garden, Spencer, and Elmslie all wrote about it. Elmslie devoted an entire paper to the subject, saying, in part, that rhythm is 'the underlying influence that induces the vital and spiritual essence of organic design to disclose itself ... '[32] Garden noted that 'without these rhythms and accents, without the pattern, the [design] remains mere building. Style is the relation of these rhythms ... one to the other, to create a pattern.'[33] Maher developed a theory of design based on rhythm which he called the motive-rhythm theory. 'This theory,' he wrote, 'completely harmonizes all portions of the work until in the end it becomes a unit in composition ... since each detail is designed to harmonize with the guiding motif which in turn was inspired by the necessity of the situation and local color and conditions.'[34] But the theory was inherently a decorative concept and only superficially applicable to architectural design, though Maher spent years trying to apply it.

Maher's first attempt was with the James A. Patten house (1901), a rusticated granite mansion formerly on Ridge Avenue in Evanston (fig. 24). His theme, the thistle, was assiduously applied throughout the house, being painted on walls and ceilings, embroidered on draperies and table scarfs, carved in the woodwork, on fireplace mantels, and furniture, and on the exterior embellishing the broad decorative panel over the entrance. Yet it failed to govern the architectural design which, in effect, combined the asymmetrical massing of the Barrett house (fig. 3) with the more formal, austere, masonry-built Farson design (fig. 4).

Nevertheless the Patten house attracted international attention, and the *Studio* (and subsequently the *International Studio*) accorded it a four-page spread. They called it 'a gratifying example of art from the philosophical standpoint' and noted that 'this artist presents a system which is at once novel and enduring.'[35] Arthur C. David, in the *Architectural Record*, said enthusiastically of Maher's work, 'we are dealing with an architecture of ideas,' but then went on to observe that it 'is struggling not very successfully at formal expression.'[36] Certainly this was true of Maher's chief essay in motive-rhythm design – the house and stables for Harry Rubens (1902–3) at Glencoe, Illinois.[37] Here Maher substituted architectural motifs for floral ones. Two related motifs were used, a tall, inverted U-shape wall with colonnettes in antis, or a pair of these forms joined by a curved-edge gable roof. The motifs were repeated throughout the design, serving as everything from actual walls to lamp posts and rookeries. The result was appalling, and thereafter Maher restricted his application to more manageable limits, as seen at the F.N. Corbin house of 1904 (fig. 46).

The architects still to be mentioned shared one thing in common – all worked for Wright prior to executing their first designs. William Drummond was with Wright nearly two years when, in the spring of 1901, he submitted an American Embassy project in the competition for a traveling scholarship sponsored by the Chicago Architectural Club. The design was for a rambling structure punctuated by short towers, and featuring a great octagonal ballroom; public rooms formed a sequence of spaces along a main axis which was crossed by a secondary axis leading from the formal entrance to the ballroom (figs. 25–6). Some aspects of both Sullivan's and Wright's work seem implicit here, especially the latter's project for Cheltenham Beach – but the work remains a very personal design.

In 1901 and 1902 Drummond was listed at 172 Washington Street where he was apparently working for Schmidt – whose office was at that address. Probably the house project for L. Griffen in Buena Park (fig. 27), which Schmidt exhibited in 1902, was designed by Drummond, as well as the somewhat later and similar L. Wolff house, at 4234 N. Hazel Avenue in Chicago.[38] Thus Drummond, as well as Garden, was apparently assisting Schmidt with his work.

FIG. 27 William E. Drummond (for Richard E. Schmidt). Project: L. Griffen house, Buena Park, Chicago, 1902. Chicago Architectural Club *Catalogue* 1902

38 The correlation is significant because Drummond once told Barry Byrne that he, Drummond, designed the Wolff house for Schmidt (Byrne to the author, 22 February 1956). Photographs of the Wolff house are reproduced in the *Architectural Record, 15,* 1904, 365–7.

39 Barry Byrne recalls, as reported to the author, that the building committee asked Mahony for a design similar, but at smaller scale, to the Emmanuel Methodist Church (1892) in Evanston by Burnham and Root. The similarity is apparent. Plans, sections, and illustrations of Mahony's project and executed design are published in the *Prairie School Review*, 3, 2, 1966, 7–9.

While Marion Mahony was employed by Wright she designed a small Unitarian chapel in Evanston. The initial project, dated 1902, was for a low, domestically-scaled building with an octagonal front, but this design was rejected by the building committee, which insisted on Gothic forms.[39] These she provided in a steep-gabled building of random-cut limestone, with a central pointed arch for the entry (fig. 28). On the interior she had greater freedom and, while repeating the motif of the arch, she treated the broad surfaces in tinted stucco trimmed with wood.

FIG. 28 Marion Mahony. Church of All Souls, Evanston, Illinois, 1903. Demolished. Photo by Peter Weil, courtesy of Carl W. Condit

FIG. 29 Walter Burley Griffin. William H. Emery house, 218 Arlington, Elmhurst, Illinois, 1901–2. Courtesy *Prairie School Review*

Walter Burley Griffin (1876–1937)[40] – later Marion Mahony's husband – was raised in Oak Park and Elmhurst and studied architecture under Clifford Ricker at the University of Illinois.[41] After graduation he joined the group at 1107 Steinway Hall, and remained there about two years before entering Wright's employ. He also joined the Chicago Architectural Club, and attended the League convention of 1900, where he heard Sullivan's celebrated address. His first commissions were barns for various neighbors, and designing the Elmhurst Golf Club (1901, now demolished), a nearly square, one-storey hipped roof building with a wide veranda.

His earliest known design was for decoration, and here Sullivan's influence was apparent. After school hours Griffin worked at Christ Church in Elmhurst. His sister recalls that 'from church janitor he graduated to church interior decorator. He cut elaborate stencils which I now realize

---

40 Griffin was born in Maywood, Illinois, 24 November 1876, the son of an insurance salesman from Haverhill, Massachusetts. He was raised in Oak Park, where he attended elementary and high school before the family moved to Elmhurst, apparently in 1893. In September 1895, at age 18, Griffin began his studies at the University of Illinois under N. Clifford Ricker, the architectural educator who had headed the department since its founding some 22 years before. Illinois, like all architectural schools at the time, followed the Ecole des Beaux-Arts system in teaching, but Ricker introduced numerous German texts of his own translation into the course; among these was Otto Wagner's *Moderne Architektur*. Griffin's interest in landscape architecture, however, found little encouragement; the curriculum offered no courses in that field. Griffin was scholarly rather than athletic, and his high grades (except in certain math and engineering courses) resulted in his election to Tau Beta Pi, a national scholastic society. In June 1899 he was awarded the degree of Bachelor of Science in Architecture.

The most complete and accurate source of biographical data concerning Griffin appears in Frank W. Scott, ed., *The Semi-Centennial Alumni Record of the University of Illinois*, Chicago, 1918, p. 120, which is quoted here:

Architect; BS in Arch't.; b. Nov. 24, 1876, Maywood, Ill., s. George Walter (b. Mar. 20, 1851, Haverhill, Mass.) and Estelle Melvina (Burley) Griffin (b. Mar. 13, 1852, St. Charles, Ill.) Prepared in Oak Park HS Tau Beta Pi; Arch Club; Le Cercle Français. Arch. Draftsman, Chicago, 1899–1901; Arch. and landscape arch. with Frank Lloyd Wright, Oak Park, Ill., 1901–5; Practicing independently 1906–; Prize ($8500 for design of Australian Capital City, 1912; Working out plan for Capital City, Australia, 1914–. Mem., Chi Arch Club; Jefferson Club; Univ. Club; Ill. Chapter, AIA; City Club of Chicago. Married Marion Lucy Mahony Je 29, 1911, Michigan City, Indiana.

41 For an excellent account of Ricker and his school see Mark L. Peisch, *The Chicago School of Architecture*, London, 1964, Chapter I. Concerning Ricker's translations see Thomas E. O'Donnell (compiler), 'The Writings and Translations of Dr N. Clifford Ricker,' Urbana, 1926 (typed manuscript, Ricker Library of Architecture, University of Illinois). His translation of Wagner's classic work was published serially by the *Brickbuilder* (*10*, 1901, 124–8, 143–7, 165–71) and under the auspices of the Architectural League of America in a booklet which is so rare as to be all but unknown: Otto Wagner, *Modern Architecture, a Guide for His Pupils in This Domain of Art*, second edition, Vienna, 1898, translated by N. Clifford Ricker, Boston (Rogers and Manson), 1902. Part of Wagner's conclusion merits quotation because it expresses a sentiment so similar to that of the Prairie School: 'A direct question, "How should we build?" cannot be answered. *But our feeling must indeed say to us to-day that the antique horizontal line, the arrangement of surfaces in broad areas, the greatest simplicity, and an energetic prominence of construction and materials will thoroughly dominate ...*' [p. 171, italics original].

showed the influence of Louis Sullivan's designs – such as the elaborate metal work around the entrance of Carson Pirie Scott and Company. The stencils were painted in gold on a dull green background and were on the church walls for many years.'[42]

His first significant architectural commission, one which embodies the characteristics of all his later work, was received during the winter of 1901–2. The circumstances surrounding this commission are most revealing. The choice of architect, according to Mrs Emery's account,[43] was between Wright and Griffin, the house being a wedding gift from William H. Emery's father. Both architects were personal friends. Wright had just built some stables for T.E. Wilder,[44] Mrs Emery's father, and was then building the F.B. Henderson house only a block away from the Emery site in Elmhurst. Wright, however, was rejected because he was considered too uncompromising; William Emery wanted some of his own ideas incorporated into the design. Therefore the commission went to Griffin – a

42 Mrs Gertrude Griffin Sater, type-written biography of Walter Burley Griffin dated 7–8 November 1953, which (at the time of reading) was in the possession of H.A. Berens, Elmhurst. The stencil work mentioned was undoubtedly inspired by that at the Auditorium Building, where the color scheme was the same. The Griffin homestead, incidentally, still stands at 223 Kenilworth Avenue, Elmhurst.

43 As related to the author in 1956

44 Wilder helped found the Elmhurst Golf Club for which Griffin designed the club house.

FIG. 30 Walter Burley Griffin. William H. Emery house. Dining room. *Architectural Record* 1908

FIG. 31 Walter Burley Griffin.
William H. Emery house. Plan.
Brooks collection

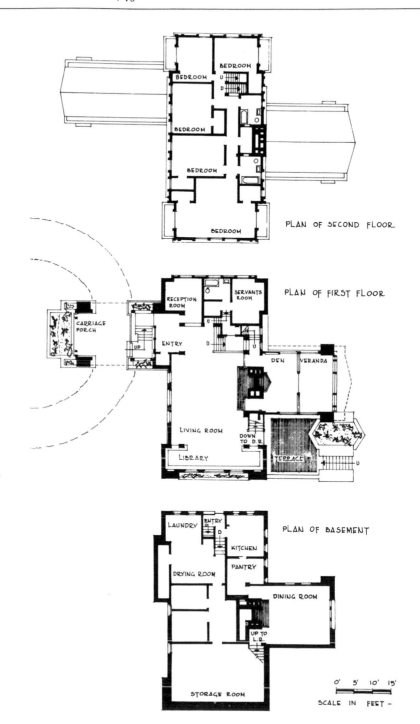

decision, as all others pertaining to the house, which Mrs Emery left strictly to her husband. The suggestions he made concerned the plan, and specifically that certain rooms should be placed at different levels. Construction began in the spring of 1902, and was completed during the autumn of 1903.

The design is amazing for its maturity. Griffin at that time thought in terms of mass, not volume. Containment of form ranked above free-flowing composition and emphasis on wall as surface took precedence over spatial penetration. His buildings rested securely upon the ground but did not nestle down. His hallmark was the corner pier which rose to the second floor, or beyond, and secured and confined the central mass. Appendages might protrude, but a static quality remained

Following are the characteristics of the Emery house (figs. 29, 30, 31, 32, 33). Great corner piers, topped by sleeping porches,[45] confine the two-storey mass, while a broad white plaster band accentuates the horizontal which

45 At the turn of the century sleeping porches were popular because outdoor sleeping was considered beneficial to one's health.

FIG. 32 Walter Burley Griffin. William H. Emery house. South elevation. Historic American Building Survey

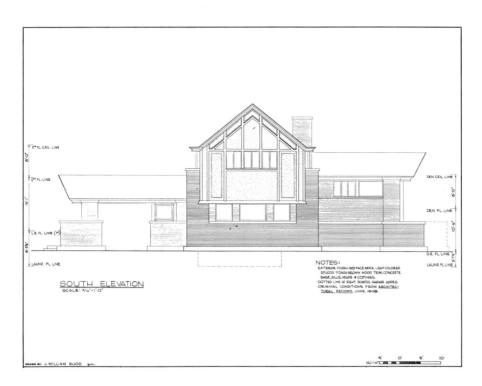

SOUTH ELEVATION
SCALE: 1/8"=1'-0"

NOTES:
EXTERIOR FINISH-RED FACE BRICK, LIGHT-COLORED
STUCCO, 7/DARK-BROWN WOOD TRIM, CONCRETE
BASE, SILLS, HEADS & COPINGS.
DOTTED LINE AT RIGHT DENOTES GARAGE ADDED.
ORIGINAL CONDITIONS FROM ARCHITEC-
TURAL RECORD, JUNE, 1908.

DRAWN BY: J. WILLIAM RUDD

is repeated in the steady rhythm of the windows. The end walls of the
second storey overlap the brickwork below and recall the thin, carefully
framed panels of Japanese design, an influence seen also in the extended
ridge of the roof. At right angles to the roof are two projections, a low
porte-cochère supported by brick piers and, at the rear, a storey-and-a-half
wing at split-levels with the house.[46]

The plan is ingenious and must be envisioned as a vertical rather than
horizontal space (figs. 31, 33). The wing at the rear is set a half-level below
the main house and contains the dining room, below, and a den above.
The vertical sequence of space, therefore, is from the dining room up
several steps to the living room, through which one must pass to reach the
stairs; these rise behind a head-height wall. Mounting the stairs to a height
above this wall gives one a sudden view across the living room; by walking
behind the huge chimney one enters the den which overlooks the living

FIG. 33 Walter Burley Griffin. William H. Emery house. Section. Historic American Building Survey

room, which is below. Other stairs continue to the bedrooms. The kitchen and related services are located in the basement a few steps below the dining wing. Just how much of this plan represents the owner's ideas is impossible to say, yet the split-level scheme was perpetuated in many of Griffin's later designs.

The interior color scheme was described as 'living room in light brown oak, pinkish tan brick, olive wainscot, tan frieze. Ceiling cream with old gold border. Dining room with golden terra cotta walls [and] old gold ceiling.'[47] The exterior combined off-white plaster, above, with common brick for the first storey and piers.

The date of the Emery house, when compared to Wright's chronology, is startling. It follows closely the Kankakee houses and the Henderson and Thomas designs, but apparently precedes those for Ward Willits and Arthur Heurtley, neither of which was exhibited by Wright in the spring of 1902. The roofs and trim of the Emery house recall the Kankakee houses, but little else; although Griffin was at the Studio, Wright has disclaimed giving him any help.[48] But the most telling comparison is not with Wright – it is with the popular English Tudor of the day. Compare, for example, Spencer's Adams house of 1903 (fig. 18). Here are the same basic massing, the banded casement windows, brick to the height of the first storey lintels, then, above a flaring sill of wood, stucco defined as rectangular panels by dark wood trim. Clear, sharp forms prevail. The distinction is not so much one of kind as of degree, and it plainly suggests that Griffin's source was not specifically Wright, but rather the same sources from which Wright drew so often – his own immediate architectural surroundings.

The exhibition of 1902 demonstrated the group's vitality as organizers and publicists, and more important, it showed them as designers with imagination and skill. The movement had gained momentum, and its character as a school was being defined. Yet many of the most significant designs of the period were not represented in the March exhibition, apparently being completed too late for inclusion in the show. Among these were Griffin's Emery house, Garden's Madlener house and Schoenhofen Brewing Company Building, Mahony's chapel, Nimmons and Fellows' Rosenwald house, and Wright's Willits and Heurtley houses. None of these was exhibited in 1903, and the reason is quite clear. A change had occurred in the executive of the club. The former officers and jurors were deposed, and a conservative slate was substituted in their stead – only occasionally thereafter, as in 1907, 1910, and 1914, did the former group reassert itself. The catalogue of 1903 reflected the change; classicism ruled

47 *House Beautiful*, 22, 2, 1907, 32
48 Wright told the author that he gave no assistance to Griffin; Mrs William Emery was of the same opinion.

49 In 1904 the composure of the jury of admissions confirmed this trend – only three jurors were from Chicago, while four represented the East.

50 *American Architect and Building News, 81*, 1903, 11

51 Robert Spencer's publication of 'The Work of Frank Lloyd Wright' (*Architectural Review*, 7 [New Series 2], 1900, 61–72 [and reissued by the Prairie School Press in 1964]) did much to enhance Wright's prestige among his colleagues at that time.

the day and eastern taste prevailed.[49] The consternation expressed by the *American Architect and Building News* in 1902 was supplanted by platitudes of contentment in 1903: 'The annual exhibition of the Chicago Architectural Club held in the Art Institute this spring was carried along legitimate lines more strictly than it was last year, and the result was a more dignified whole.'[50]

Six years had passed since Perkins, Spencer, Wright, and Hunt established their office in 1107 Steinway Hall. Years during which the group changed and expanded, formed the Eighteen, and actively participated in the local architectural club and the Architectural League of America. Initially they lacked a distinctive architecture of their own but, with the new century, this was forthcoming. Wright and Spencer experimented with low-lying horizontal forms while Garden worked toward simplification of the basic mass. Nimmons and Fellows endeavored to apply the ideas of commercial architecture to residential design. Sullivan, to whom all looked for guidance, offered continual encouragement but little practical help. It remained for Wright to present a strong, positive program of design, one which subsequently led to his becoming the dominant personality within the group.[51] While this was occurring, in the first years of the century, he attracted several of the more dedicated and adventuresome young architects to his Studio at Oak Park, there to receive their training. Included were Griffin, Drummond, and Mahony. Partly because of this, and partly because of the unwillingness of several of the more conservative members of the group to commit themselves fully, a lull began in 1903. Wright, Spencer, and Garden continued on their established course but not until about 1908–9 did the movement greatly expand. Griffin and Drummond were participating by 1908, as was Perkins with his school buildings for the Chicago Board of Education. Purcell and Elmslie commenced their fruitful partnership in 1909, and Tallmadge and Watson became active contributors by 1906. After 1910 many new names were added to an ever growing list. But during the interval from 1903 until after 1908, the focus of attention rested on Wright, his work, and his Oak Park Studio.

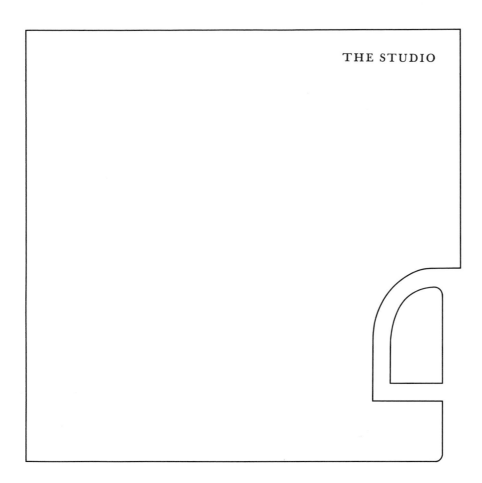

The Studio was the center of Frank Lloyd Wright's creative activity, and it was there that numerous architects received their training. As Wright wrote in 1908, it is 'our little university of fourteen years standing.'[1] Yet it was not a school, but rather an unconventional office where employees came in response to Wright's work, and assisted according to their skill. As employees, they were also pupils and apprentices, but there to learn by observation rather than by being taught.

The environment was congenial – it was an informal, pleasant place to work. There were four rooms: a reception hall, small octagonal library, Wright's office, and a two-storey drafting room accommodating a half-dozen desks. The furnishings were of Wright's design – Japanese prints and miniature casts of classical sculpture, numerous vases and bowls, and a profu-

1 Frank Lloyd Wright, 'In the Cause of Architecture,' *Architectural Record*, 23, 1908, 164

2 This chapter owes more to Barry Byrne than the footnotes can possibly divulge. In an earlier form, the text was read by Byrne, who made useful comments concerning both fact and interpretation. He was present at the Studio from 1902 to 1908 (except for a two- to three-month absence early in 1908 caused by an appendectomy) so his knowledge was extensive, though drawn from memory rather than written records. For the critical year 1909 the author has benefited from John S. Van Bergen's knowledge, supported by his detailed and extensive personal records and diaries (which, since supplying the information, have been [1964] destroyed by fire).

3 The Mahonys had no telephone, and as Byrne lived closer than the others, he was often sent to seek her out.

4 Notes taken in conversation with Barry Byrne (24 March 1965)

sion of foliage and wild flowers, either fresh or dried according to the season. In this home-like setting a close rapport existed among the members; much was shared in common – their work, their admiration of Wright (whose unusual attire some adopted), and even their political views – most supported La Follette and Henry George, and the Single Tax (especially Griffin, Drummond, and Wright). Herbert Spencer was read by all.[2]

Beside the Studio, and connected to it, was Wright's home. This was built in 1889, the Studio being added in 1895. Both were located on Forest Avenue, corner of Chicago, in Oak Park, a pious, self-righteous village nine miles west of the Chicago Loop. Wright, as announced on his stationery, was at the Studio from 8 to 11, at his Chicago office from 12 to 2, and at the Studio again evenings after 7. Thus it was his principal place of work, his drafting room at home.

Over the years employees came and went, no records being kept of their names or length of stay. Some contributed part-time assistance, as did Long, Corwin, Garden, and Elmslie, who have already been discussed. Others remained for varying lengths of time – a few weeks or many years. Most eventually found employment in other architectural offices; a few went into private practice. About six or seven ultimately made significant contributions on their own. Best known of these were Marion Mahony, Walter Burley Griffin, Barry Byrne, William Drummond, Francis C. Sullivan, and John Van Bergen; their role at the Studio, and their earlier training, is our immediate concern.

Marion Lucy Mahony (1871–1962) was born in Chicago on 14 February 1871, the year of the Chicago fire. She graduated in architecture from MIT (1894) – the second woman to do so – and briefly worked for her cousin, Dwight Perkins, preparing drawings for Steinway Hall. In 1895 she entered the Studio. Her attendance, however, was irregular – whether for reasons of health or merely inclination – yet her services were always in demand; Wright often asked her to return.[3] She was, said Barry Byrne, 'a thin, angular, shallow skinned person with a beak of a nose; she was so homely that she looked almost distinguished. She had a fragile frame and walked as though she were falling forward. She was a good actress, talkative, and when around Wright there was a real sparkle.'[4] Elsewhere Byrne wrote, 'Her mordant humor always attracted me as a fellow Celt, and I can well remember welcoming her advent (she came irregularly) because it promised an amusing day. Her dialogues with Frank Lloyd Wright, who, as we all know, is no indifferent opponent in repartee, made such days particularly notable.'[5]

Mahony was a gifted designer, but perhaps more an artist than an architect. She was renowned for her renderings, many of which were exhibited and published by Wright. She designed, under Wright's direction, many of the furnishings and decorations for his houses – tables, chairs, murals, and mosaics – but the task of preparing architectural drawings was usually left to others.

Another addition to the Studio staff was William E. Drummond.[6] He came about 1899 and stayed until 1909 except for the period between 1901 and 1903 or 1904 when he worked downtown for such people as Richard E. Schmidt and D.H. Burnham.[7] Both departures, in 1901 and again in 1909, were apparently prompted by financial need; payment of salary at the Studio was seldom a regular thing.

Drummond was tall, dark, and romantically good looking, as remembered by Byrne, and respected by Wright for his skill. Their personalities were not complementary though, and the lively interchange so characteristic of Wright's relation with Griffin and Mahony did not exist between Wright and Drummond. Due to lack of prior training, Drummond initially undertook only routine tasks, but later assumed responsibility for the working drawings of several well-known commissions. These, Byrne notes, included the Larkin Company Administration Building, the Cheney house, and also the Isabel Roberts house for which he prepared the scale design from Wright's preliminary sketches.

When Griffin entered the Studio in 1901 he was reasonably well trained, having a degree in architecture and nearly two years of experience at Steinway Hall (see pp. 30 and 71 above). He increasingly took charge of running the office, and eventually became the office manager – and a job superintendent as well. Less time, therefore, was spent at the drafting boards; he seldom prepared drawings from rough sketches, as did Drummond. Temperamentally he was a good-natured, intensely likeable person, open and interested in exchanging views. Wright found him most stimulating, and discussed with him, at length, work that he was designing.[8] This was characteristic of Wright; he would discuss his work with others, accepting or rejecting their views as he saw fit. Griffin, therefore, served as a useful critic, a lens through which Wright could re-examine his own ideas. What, if any, influence he had on Wright was largely intangible, being more completely assimilated and less profound than that from more extraneous sources.[9]

5 Barry Byrne, 'The Chicago Movement,' paper delivered before the Illinois Society of Architects, 28 November 1939, typed manuscript in the Ricker Architectural Library, University of Illinois, p. 4

6 William Eugene Drummond (1876–1946) was born in Newark, New Jersey, 28 March 1876, the son of a carpenter contractor. When about eight his family moved to Austin (now incorporated with Chicago), where Drummond attended public school. He spent a year (1896–7) at the University of Illinois Academy (a preparatory school) before entering the Department of Architecture at the university, where he stayed one year (1897–8). He then worked 'several months' for Louis Sullivan, and perhaps others, before entering Wright's Studio.

The only reference to Drummond in Sullivan's office is in a paper, now in the author's collection (apparently written for the *Monthly Bulletin* of the Illinois Society of Architects), dated 4 January 1940. Drummond, while discussing Sullivan, stated (p. 2): 'Of me, who spent several months in his employ, I have heard that he said: "Drummond is alright but he can hardly get thru the door" – which was a great surprise in that I did not suppose that he even knew that I was around.'

7 Dates calculated from directory listings and the above manuscript

8 Information concerning Griffin from Barry Byrne

9 The great corner piers of the Larkin

Building are sometimes cited as Griffin's contribution, but it is difficult to confirm this proposition (embryonic corner piers appear in Wright's work in 1902, thus the possible precedence of the Emery house). More germane, perhaps, is Wright's planning solution for the projected H.J. Ullman house (1904–5), where Griffin's executed work (the Emery house), rather than his presence in the Studio, may have been a contributing factor. The proposed Ullman plan is by no means a copy of the Griffin scheme, yet the theme is sufficiently similar to suggest that Wright may have been conscious of the Emery interior (unless Griffin himself prepared the Ullman design for Wright). Common to both is the split-level arrangement with the dining room set at right angles to, and a half-level below, the living room; the use of a mezzanine level containing a study overlooking a storey-and-a-half living room (separated from it by a chimney); stairs which rise beside the living room but separated from it by a low partition wall; and, finally, a covered veranda above the dining room. (Plans and a perspective drawing of the Ullman house will be found in *Ausgeführte Bauten und Entwürfe von Frank Lloyd Wright*, Berlin, 1910, pl. 16, and *The Buildings, Plans and Designs of Frank Lloyd Wright*, New York, 1963, pls. 45 and 46.)

When Wright departed on his three-month trip to Japan in mid-February 1905,[10] Griffin was left in charge of the Studio; this event helped precipitate their break. Griffin apparently failed to expedite the Ullman commission to Wright's satisfaction (due, it seems, to a family feud), and Wright was further annoyed on learning that Griffin, while pressed to complete a personal project for the Chicago Architectural Club design competition, had elicited aid from the Studio staff.[11] Griffin for his part was annoyed at not being paid. Eventually he was discharged, receiving Japanese prints in lieu of overdue salary. The rupture was complete; the two men apparently never spoke to each other again.

The Studio match-makers paired off Griffin with Isabel Roberts, but this came to naught. She was Wright's secretary and bookkeeper, and occasionally she assisted with the drafting. She remained at the Studio for many years, and in 1908 Wright designed her well-known River Forest home.

Barry Byrne (1883–1967),[12] without prior experience or training –

10 The exact date of Wright's first trip to Japan has long been uncertain, yet Robert C. Twombly, to whom the author is indebted, found the following in the Oak Park *Oak Leaves* of 25 February 1905: 'Mr and Mrs Frank Lloyd Wright left last week for Japan, where they expect to remain three months.'

11 Information from Barry Byrne. The Griffin project, although listed in the catalogue, was not illustrated and apparently is no longer extant.

12 The story of Byrne's early life is well told in his own correspondence:
I was born in Chicago, December 19, 1883, and my parents were Charles Emmett Byrne, a native of Prince Edward Island and my mother, a native of Chicago, was Mary (Barry) Delaney, whose mother was a Barry out of Wexford, Ireland. My father was a blacksmith and miscast in the role, for he was an avid reader of Shakespeare and also wrote verse. He died when I was fourteen ...

I was the eldest of six children with a reed-like mother, as far as this world's misfortunes affected her, for they engulfed her and her brood, receded and there she remained, with God's help, upright, steadfast, and believing. If I may say, as I believe, that my tendency toward the life and work of an artist, is a heritage from my thwarted father, it is from my mother that whatever I have of stability and steadfastness came as her bequest.

At fourteen I left St Columkille Parochial School and went to work at the then downtown mail order house of Montgomery Ward. As I had known since the age of nine years that architecture was my chosen life work, there is no need to emphasize the fact that my career in mercantile though long determined to be an architect – was so impressed by Wright's Chicago Architectural Club exhibit of 1902 that he sought an interview. This was granted (apparently in May or June 1902) and within a week Frank – as Wright preferred to call Francis Barry Byrne – was working at the Studio. He was a short, quiet-spoken person with a dry sense of humor who, although entering as a novice, learned quickly and was soon entrusted with ever greater responsibility. 'Drummond initially, and later [Harry] Robinson and myself,' Byrne writes, 'were handed rough preliminary designs of buildings to develop into working drawings. ... During the last few years of my stay I executed the working drawing of the Beachy house, the complete remodeling for N.G. Moore of an old house adjoining his own, the Boynton house in Rochester, NY, the Tomak house in Riverside, Unity Temple and the Coonley house. For most of these I wrote specifications, supervised construction, and dealt directly with the clients during construction.'[13] The last mentioned, Unity Temple and the Coonley house, were nearly complete at the time of Byrne's leaving the Studio in August 1908.

The Studio staff numbered five when Byrne entered in 1902: George Willis – a Texan who later returned home – was head draftsman (apparently leaving late in 1902 after some four years of service); Cecil Barnes (?), another Texan who soon departed; Griffin; Isabel Roberts; and Andrew Willatzen. Mahony, as so often, was absent and Drummond was away. Willatzen (later changed to Willatsen; b. 1876) later became Byrne's partner. He came to America from Denmark in 1901 and briefly worked at construction before joining the Studio staff. He remained three or four years, then worked for Spencer and Powers, and Pond and Pond, before departing for Spokane, Washington, in 1907.[14] There he worked for others until entering partnership with Barry Byrne in Seattle during the winter of 1908–9.

Drafting was the major Studio activity, and this allowed little latitude for personal expression. One area existed, however, where individuality emerged, particularly during the middle years of the decade. This was in preparing renderings – the magnificent perspective drawings made for clients or, more often, created expressly for exhibition and publication. Wright had long been interested in visual representation; he was an avid amateur photographer and had always concerned himself with creating a setting for his perspectives. Oriental painting, the Japanese print, photography, and the prevailing mode of architectural rendering (cf. Harvey Ellis and H.H. Richardson) were combined in these splendid, soft-toned representations, renderings where the setting appeared as flat planes stepped

work was far from happy.

My escape from it was to the symphony concerts in the incomparable Auditorium. The Art Institute and the Public Library were also refuges, and my memories of the last named recalls the difficulties I had in persuading the attendants that I really wanted the bulky volumes of architectural history I requested and not the works of Horatio Alger which they suggested were my real desire.

In many ways it seems that my life actually started when, in an answer to my letter to him, the great architect gave me a date for an interview. In his autobiography, written of course from a not too perfect memory, Wright tells the story of that interview with, what he termed, the 'Little Boy.' [Letter from Barry Byrne to Sister Mary Guala, OP, dated 28 March 1963. Quoted with the writer's permission.]

13 Letter to the author (10 October 1962)

14 Biographical information concerning Andrew Willatzen furnished through the kindness of James F. O'Gorman

15 For a detailed discussion of the drawings and a check list of attributions see my 'Frank Lloyd Wright and the Wasmuth Drawings,' *Art Bulletin, 48*, 1966, 193–202. Therein is illustrated the comparison between drawings and their photographic sources.

back in space in contrast to the thin, dematerialized, three-dimensional perspectives of the house. Flowers and shrubs, cascading over walls or nestling close to the building, were usually rendered with greater naturalness and more plasticity than other parts of the foliate setting. Ink, either brown or black, pencil, and colored pencil (in various combinations), were the usual mediums – occasionally there was an ink wash or white highlight. The material used was ordinary tracing paper, the size varying greatly but often approximating 12 to 30 inches. Frequently renderings were made only after the house was built, and these eye-level perspectives were often based upon – indeed actually traced or copied from – a photograph of the building. For this and other reasons it is impossible to isolate various hands involved in preparing the building perspectives, despite the individuality which appears in the rendering technique of the foliate setting.[15]

Wright was magnanimous in acknowledging the rendering skill of others. While with Silsbee and Sullivan he himself made renderings, which he signed; those for Silsbee had a foliate setting, those for Sullivan did not. After entering private practice, however, he often sought the aid of others. Five of the six water colors he displayed at the 1894 Chicago Architectural Club exhibition were credited to Ernest Albert, and Wright's single entry the following year was drawn by Corwin and Garden. Thereafter, however, the catalogues ceased to list delineators, and as neither Wright nor his staff signed the later drawings, the problem of attribution is most difficult.

Several drawings published by Spencer in 1900 ('The Work of Frank Lloyd Wright') are probably the architect's own, notably the renderings of the Studio, the Winslow house, and (most characteristic of all) the Husser house – the light, feathery branches, often delineated with the merest suggestion of leaves, being quite distinctive. But most drawings from about 1900 are more difficult to ascribe, although the renderings of Long (who left Chicago about 1903) and Mahony seem discernible as well as Wright's. At this time visual reality, almost photographic likeness, characterized the renderings, but this was soon modified to a simplicity particularly reminiscent of the Japanese print (recalling Wright's 1905 trip to Japan). During mid-decade, especially between 1905 and 1907, Mahony was the prime producer, and it was then that she did her finest and most characteristic work. Her renderings of the Hardy house are outstanding, but the Cheney, Shaw, and de Rhodes (on which Wright later wrote 'Drawn by Mahony – After FLlW and Hiroshige') house drawings, and the side view of Unity Church, all record her brilliant draftsmanship and unusual artistic skill. Her drawing of 'A Fireproof House for $5000,' the Wright project (1906) for the *Ladies' Home Journal*, is unusual because it displays her monogram – MLM.[16] Griffin, in spite of his interest in landscape, had no talent for rendering; Drummond occasionally helped with the drawings but the degree of his contribution is uncertain; Byrne assisted but so completely adopted Mahony's style that late in life, when questioned by the author, he could no longer isolate his work. Many of these fine renderings were exhibited at the Chicago Architectural Club in 1907, Wright's first showing since the eventful year of 1902.

The culminating event concerning these drawings, however, was their publication by Ernst Wasmuth in *Ausgeführte Bauten und Entwürfe von Frank Lloyd Wright* (Berlin, 1910) – a magnificent 100-plate folio in which drawings, plans, and ornamental details were printed (direct lithography) on different types of paper in ink of several colors, including gold. Most of the requisite drawings had been prepared by 1907; those for the intervening years before 1910 are less distinctive, making it more difficult to distinguish individual artists. Most, if not all, were retraced prior to publication, much of which work was done at Fiesole, Italy, by Wright, his eldest son Lloyd (Frank Lloyd Wright, Jr), and Taylor Wooley. Some Italian tracers were also employed. Apparently it was Wright who reworked several of the previously completed renderings, at Fiesole, in a style approaching geometric abstraction – a flat style based largely on squares and triangles; the Bock studio and Westcott house drawings are a notable case in point. This technique was of immense significance for the future. First it served as the basis for his decorative designs and furnishings (cf. especially Midway Gardens and the Imperial Hotel), and later it was reflected in his architectural designs and plans.

Wright had left Oak Park in late September 1909, proceeded to Berlin where he met his publisher, and then settled at Villino Belvedere in Fiesole where he completed work on the drawings. To assist with this undertaking he sent for his son Lloyd, who stayed two and one-half or three months, and Taylor Wooley, who remained about four months.[17] Neither can be isolated in terms of the renderings. Wooley was a gentle-natured Mormon from Salt Lake City who had joined the Studio staff in 1908.[18]

The only Studio apprentice to return to Wright's employ after the latter's European sojourn was Harry F. Robinson (1883–1959),[19] an enigmatic figure insofar as the renderings are concerned. Robinson had entered the Studio after graduating from the University of Illinois in 1906. He departed before 1909, worked for Griffin, and then returned to Wright's Orchestra Hall office where he remained until about 1918–19. He was

16 One of the most perplexing problems in attributing work to Marion Mahony is that her signed work is of two distinctly different styles, both of which seem to co-exist, although the lighter, more delicate style becomes dominant in later years. Her signed drawing of 'A Fireproof House for $5000' (fig. 62) – like the side view of Unity Church – is rendered in a more solid, heavy style, yet among the drawings she did for Wright this was often combined with delicately rendered parts. The same is true, but to a lesser extent, of drawings she later did for Griffin (see especially the Griffin house project, fig. 168, but also 'Solid Rock,' fig. 104). On other occasions only the more delicate style was used, as for the Melson house (fig. 170), which bears her monogram.

17 Information obtained from Lloyd Wright, in conversation, 8 February 1965.

For an account by Lloyd Wright of his, and his father's, trip to Europe, and the preparation of the drawings for Wasmuth, see Edgar Kaufmann, Jr, 'Crisis and Creativity: Frank Lloyd Wright, 1904–14,' *Journal of the Society of Architectural Historians*, 25, 1966, 292–6.

18 Taylor Wooley is not mentioned in Wright's list, published in March 1908, yet he arrived sometime prior to Byrne's departure in August of that year.

19 The University of Illinois Alumni Record of 1918 lists Robinson's birth

date as 1881 and his occupation as manager, Frank L. Wright architectural office. Robinson's son (Joe R.) informs the author that the family Bible gives 1883 as the birth date.

20 Letter to the author of 22 April 1970

21 *Architectural Record*, 23, 1908, 164

22 Sullivan's work is discussed in chapter 8, pp. 272-9

23 John S. Van Bergen was born in Oak Park 2 October 1885, where he graduated from high school in 1905, then briefly visited California before working for his uncle, a speculative builder. In January 1907, without previous architectural training, he entered Griffin's office (the Griffins were close family friends). Griffin took pains to carefully instruct him in the fundamentals of drafting, but with insufficient work in the office to keep him busy, Van Bergen left in October 1908. He then took special training at the Chicago Technical College (21 October 1908-25 January 1909) in preparation for the architectural licensing exams. At the end of January he began working for Wright. (All dates are from Van Bergen's own records, now destroyed.)

actively engaged in such commissions as the William B. Greene house (1912), Aurora, Illinois. Indeed so great was his involvement that when additions were later made to the house, the Greenes asked Robinson to be their architect.

Since the rendering style identified with the Studio continued until about 1914, it is not illogical to attribute Robinson with its continuum. Such, however, was apparently not the case. According to John Lloyd Wright (who was then working with his father) it was Emil Brodelle who prepared the beautiful bird's-eye renderings such as those of Taliesin and the Imperial Hotel.[20] Brodelle, tragically, was among those murdered at Taliesin in 1914.

In 1908 Wright published a list of Studio employees in his article 'In the Cause of Architecture.' He said: 'the members, so far, all told here and elsewhere ... are: Marion Mahony, a capable assistant for eleven years; William Drummond, for seven years; Francis Byrne, five years; Walter Griffin, four years; Andrew Willatzen, three years; Harry Robinson, two years; Charles E. White, Jr, one year; Erwin Barglebaugh and Robert Hardin, each one year; Albert McArthur, entering.'[21] For lack of other documentation, this list has often been misinterpreted; total years are referred to here, not (as has been assumed) the time since first employment. Those briefly employed some years before are omitted, whereas still active short-timers, including Barglebaugh, Hardin, and McArthur, are mentioned. Of the latter only Albert McArthur is well remembered, and he primarily for the Arizona Biltmore Hotel (1928) for which he sought Wright's assistance with the design.

Not mentioned in Wright's list was Francis C. Sullivan, a Canadian who was probably at the Studio briefly during 1907. He subsequently became a devoted promoter of Wright's work in Canada, where he practised for several years.[22]

The last addition to the Studio staff was John S. Van Bergen (1885-1969).[23] He came in January 1909 with some technical education and nearly twenty months of experience in Griffin's office at Steinway Hall. Present on his arrival were Drummond, as chief draftsman, Mahony, McArthur, Wooley, and Roberts, but before the year was out Wright had left for Europe and only Isabel Roberts and Van Bergen remained – to close the Studio and end this phase of Wright's career. 'When Wright finally went off with Mrs Cheney,' Van Bergen writes, 'I was the only one, except Miss Roberts, on the payroll. I doubt if I ever received my last few weeks pay (quite the custom with FLW). I completed the work then in the office, with much help from Miss Roberts. There were many problems to be settled with various contractors (and) as a youngster I had my troubles.'[24] One trouble was that Wright had collected final fees on various jobs and left Van Bergen and Roberts to get the work completed.[25] Other commissions, not nearing completion, were turned over to Hermann von Holst, a move that has long puzzled historians. Von Holst had neither sympathy nor understanding for Wright's work; he was a well-educated and well-trained architect working in a simplified classical style.[26] His office was in Steinway Hall, however, and probably this coincidence prompted Wright, in desperation, to approach him.

Wright's trip, contrary to the generally held impression, was premeditated, and before asking von Holst for assistance, the more logical alternatives were explored. Wright wrote Barry Byrne (then in Seattle, Washington) but Byrne, though tempted, refused, believing another financial arrangement with Wright to be unwise. Mahony, although hardly suited for the task, was asked, but she declined.[27] Wright and Griffin were not on speaking terms, and Drummond had just departed with harsh words while trying to collect his overdue pay.[28] Thus fifteen years after the Studio opened Wright found himself with no well-trained former assistant willing to share his work – an almost unbelievable situation: the alternative was to seek a relative stranger from Steinway Hall.

With mistrust and ill-will the life of the Studio came to an end. In 1908 Wright had written fondly of the 'New School of the Middle West' and his 'little university of fourteen years standing,' but by 1914 ('In the Cause of Architecture: Second Paper'), he lashed out against his former assistants and the entire movement which he, and they, had helped to set in motion. But his work remained, and that, ultimately, was the important thing.

The Studio years had witnessed Wright's maturity, and the designing of many of his greatest works. With the Ward Willits house (1902) his revolutionary concept of interior space was first fully expressed – an axial, interpenetrating, merging, and often overlapping concept of space, one which defined, rather than always enclosed, a given area. An appropriate external form was also achieved, one which was dynamic, yet at rest, being locked together by a massive chimney at the center. Wright had re-thought the problem of the single-family private house, and the result was the destruc-

24 Letter to the author (16 May 1961), quoted with the writer's permission

25 Ibid. Van Bergen specifically mentions completing supervision of the Mrs Thomas Gale house and the Peter Stohr arcade.

26 Hermann V. von Holst (1874–1955) was a graduate of the University of Chicago (1893), where his father had taught since emigrating from Germany in 1891. He took his BS in architecture at MIT in 1896, and worked for Shepley, Rutan and Coolidge in their Chicago office. In 1901 he traveled extensively in Europe, taught architectural design at Armour Institute from 1904 to 1906 (IIT), and subsequently wrote several books on the subject.

27 In 'The Magic of America,' an unpublished manuscript at the New York Historical Society (p. 170), Marion Mahony Griffin wrote: 'Later this architect went abroad. He asked me to take over the office for him. I refused.' The unnamed architect, of course, was Wright, whom she ultimately disliked so much that she refused to use his name. A carbon copy of this manuscript is at the Burnham Library in Chicago; illustrations for the two sets are not identical. The jumbled text, which abounds in vindictive comments concerning Wright, discusses the careers of Walter and Marion Griffin. Although the text is undated, internal evidence suggests that it was written during the 1940s.

28 Van Bergen says (letter of 16 May 1961) that Drummond left Wright with harsh words while endeavoring to collect his back salary.

29 *Architectural Record, 23*, 1908, 164

tion of the box; he opened the house within itself and opened it out to nature.

He did not abandon, however, the more traditional rectangular form of a house. The solid monumentality of the William Winslow house (1893), with its dominating roof and more static, classical order, was restated in the new century at the Arthur Heurtley house (1902) and in its successors. The massive, cubic form of Unity Church, especially its suggestion of a slab-like roof, had an immediate impact upon Wright's domestic designs. And his 1906 project for the *Ladies' Home Journal* ('A Fireproof House for $5000,' fig. 62) revitalized the typical vernacular home of the period – in terms of Unity Church. This closed cubic form, however, was soon modified by Wright's concern (as at the earlier Willits house) for broad, space-defining planes, as ultimately best expressed in the little house for Mrs Thomas Gale (1909), where the traditional wall is eliminated and the slab-like roof is echoed by the cantilevered balconies. Meanwhile this more abstract play of horizontal forms, punctuated by short, sharp vertical accents (piers, mullions, etc.), altered Wright's vision of the prairie house, leading to a synthesis so brilliantly achieved in the Robie house (1908). The closing of the Studio marked no break in Wright's gradual evolution of form, as the project (1911) and executed design (1912) for the Avery Coonley playhouse make clear. The basic massing (though more rigidly symmetrical) here hearkens back to the earliest prairie houses, but the low-pitched hipped roof has completely given way to the slab, and the lively interplay between horizontals and verticals is intensified. This trend culminated at Midway Gardens in 1914.

Wright was mindful that his pupils would 'inevitably repeat for years the methods, the forms and habits of thought, even the mannerisms of [my] present work,' but he noted that 'for me one real proof of the virtue inherent in this work will lie in the fact that some of the young men and women who have given themselves up to me so faithfully these past years will some day contribute rounded individualities of their own, and forms of their own devising to the new school.'[29] This prophecy of 1908 proved true, and the consequences of the training will be discussed below – from the earliest, patently Wrightian early phase through that of personal maturity when former assistants did make a contribution of their own. But first we must review other developments occurring during the years prior to 1909, since many of the most dynamic Prairie School architects were never employed at the Oak Park Studio.

The unity and drive which produced the Annual Exhibition of 1902 was not sustained and the group from Steinway Hall started to disperse. The less adventuresome architects went their independent ways. Hunt, Dean, Heun, indeed most of the Eighteen, forsook the unfamiliar course which momentarily had captured their youthful imaginations. The initial Sullivan-dominated phase of the movement was drawing to a close; his message of elimination and simplification did not result in a uniform expression. There followed a gradual reorganization of the group, as increasingly Wright and his work became a source of inspiration. This reorganization produced, toward the close of the period, a greater consistency of expression, which was to be expected among Wright's previous employees, but it was also seen in the work of others, particularly among newcomers to the field. Because the peak of Wright's influence followed so soon

1 Arthur C. David, 'The Architecture of Ideas,' *Architectural Record*, *15*, 1904, 361–2

after men like Spencer, Garden, Schmidt, Perkins, and Maher abandoned their search for a more original expression, the trend toward consistency seemed especially marked. The last of these men's more inventive work, as well as the earliest designs of Wright's former apprentices, is the subject of this chapter; the years concerned are those from 1903 to 1909.

This period covers the time span between the Chicago Architectural Club exhibition of 1902 (with the subsequent waning importance of the Steinway Hall group), and the closing of the Studio after Wright's departure for Europe in the autumn of 1909. The latter date also coincides with the founding by Purcell and Elmslie of the most active and productive partnership within the Prairie School. During these intervening years, even while the Studio was most active, the school was recognized and its early characteristics defined. It is therefore appropriate to recall the remarks, cited in the introduction (see p. 9), of Arthur C. David, who so aptly summarized the situation typical of the period prior to 1909.

It is true, nevertheless, that there is a group of western architects, resident chiefly in Chicago, who are ... departing from the allegiance to the strict European tradition which prevails in the East. The number of the protestants is not as yet very great; several of the architects whose work shows the influence of the different ideal are by no means consistent in their devotion thereto; and the different members of the group differ considerably in the extent to which they push their search for an original vehicle of expression. In the cases of some of them the desire to free themselves from tradition does not go much further than a search for irregularity in exterior design and for certain novel details in the interiors. Others have become absolutely revolutionary in their ideals and in their technical machinery. They are seeking to make one big jump from a condition of stylistic servitude to that of irreverent and self-assured independence. They do not seek originality, however, as the "great American architect" once did by combining a number of traditional types into one incongruous architectural hodge-podge. The radicals among the group are seeking for a rational and consistent basis for American design and ornament. The more conservative are merely seeking to reduce their debt to the European tradition to a few fundamental forms and to work out on the basis of those forms some new type of design.[1]

These remarks were written in 1904, the year of the Louisiana Purchase Exposition in St Louis. This potentially significant architectural event was patently intended to challenge Chicago's triumph of eleven years before. It was the last round in St Louis' keen but unsuccessful bid for supremacy

FIG. 34 Robert C. Spencer, Jr.
August Magnus house, 655 Sheridan
Road, Winnetka, Illinois, 1905.
Staircase. *Western Architect* 1914

2 Irving K. Pond, 'German Arts and Crafts at St Louis,' *Architectural Record*, 17, 1905, 118–25; Gustav Stickley, 'The German Exhibit at the Louisiana Purchase Exposition,' *Craftsman*, 6, 1904, 489–506, which is also an excellent source for illustrations of the installations

3 Information from Barry Byrne in conversation, 12 November 1956

in the Midwest, and as commercial gateway to the West. Yet the vast neo-baroque exhibition lacked the magic of its Chicago predecessor and even the architectural profession showed little enthusiasm. Only the German pavilion, with its furnished rooms by Joseph Olbrich, Bruno Paul, and others, roused much interest among visiting architects. Irving Pond wrote an enthusiastic review of these interiors for the *Architectural Record*, while Stickley was ecstatic in the *Craftsman*.[2] Spencer, Maher, and Griffin visited the exhibition and Wright was so impressed by the German installation that he gave train fare to Byrne so that he too could see it. Byrne was particularly moved by the slickness and nicety of finish in these German interiors.[3] Yet the fair had surprisingly little impact on the midwestern scene. The heavy baroque character typified in most of the pavilions was out of step with the times.

During the years immediately following the St Louis fair Spencer was producing some of his finest work. Certain of his projects from about 1900 had taken a course parallel to that of Wright, although he never became a true follower of his close friend. Rather he sought inspiration from English sources and especially from such contemporaries as Voysey and Baillie Scott, who likewise were reinterpreting and simplifying architecture from the medieval past. Spencer's largest commission at this time, actually 1905, was the August Magnus house and gatehouse, which were built on a splen-

FIG. 35 Robert C. Spencer, Jr. August Magnus house. Lake front. *Architectural Record* 1906

FIG. 36 Robert C. Spencer, Jr. August Magnus house. Stair tower. *Western Architect* 1914

4 A special number of the *Studio*, edited by Charles Holme and entitled *Modern British Domestic Architecture*, was published during the summer of 1901. It was readily available in the United States, and many designs by Voysey, Mackintosh, Baillie Scott, and others were illustrated therein. Plate 64, the hall at Dixcot, Streathan Park, by Walter C. Cave, is strikingly similar to the front hall of the Magnus house and was probably Spencer's source. His design, however, has greater breadth and sensitivity.

Numerous illustrations of the Magnus house were published in the *Western Architect*, 20, April 1914 (the entire issue was devoted to Spencer's work and included Jens Jensen's landscape layout for the Magnus grounds), in the *Architectural Record*, 20, October 1906, and in the *American Architect and Building News*, 91, June 1907.

did site overlooking Lake Michigan at 655 Sheridan Road, Winnetka, Illinois (figs. 34, 35, 36; old photographs are used because the house is now painted entirely white, thereby impairing its visual unity). A strong cornice line, low hipped roof, and horizontal massing give the house a characteristically midwestern air, but the curved bow window on the lake front is reminiscent of Voysey's work or that of Parker and Unwin in England. The dark trim, establishing a rigid, abstract pattern of verticals and horizontals, relates to English half-timbering, although here it functions as a device to unify the fenestration and accentuate the major elements in the design.

On approaching the Magnus house the most stunning feature is the octagonal tower, its window lengths being determined by the inside stairs (fig. 36). The paneling of the interior, laid horizontally, corresponds to the stair risers, while a simple, graceful handrail curves upward from the newel post (fig. 34). The adjoining rooms, however, are less striking in their finish.[4]

Jens Jensen (1859–1951) landscaped the Magnus estate by creating a

FIG. 37 Robert C. Spencer, Jr. Robert C. Spencer, Jr house, 926 Park Avenue, River Forest, Illinois, 1905. Photo by H.A. Brooks

naturalistic midwest setting; into this setting he introduced the native hawthorn, from which Spencer drew inspiration for his decorative glass designs. He stylized the thorny shrub in its leafless winter guise for the first floor windows and represented it in full leaf on the floor above. These splendid windows, possibly Spencer's finest, have unfortunately been destroyed, their loss altering entirely the character of the house.[5]

In the same year Spencer built his own modest home on Park Avenue in River Forest. It was closed, solid, and had an almost Palladian sense of

FIG. 38 Spencer and Powers. Edward W. McCready house, 231 N. Euclid Avenue, Oak Park, Illinois, 1907. Historic American Building Survey photo by Richard Nickel

5 Drawings of these windows will be found in the *Western Architect*, 20, April 1914. A small window is still in place at the base of the stair tower, in which the original color scheme can be seen. Concerning Jensen see: Leonard K. Eaton, *Landscape Artist in America: The Life and Work of Jens Jensen*, Chicago, 1964.

order – yet was decidedly more contemporary in appearance because it lacked the half-timber effect of the Magnus house (fig. 37). A broad hipped roof covered the rectangular building, while an off-center entrance pavilion

FIG. 39 Spencer and Powers. Edward W. McCready house. Detail of entrance. *Brickbuilder* 1914

introduced a mild vertical thrust. The exterior stucco was rough textured and tinted buff, the roof was a deep red tile, and the window casements were painted white. The trim was dark, and decorative glass filled the windows.[6]

Late in 1905 Spencer formed a partnership with Horace S. Powers (1872–1928), a native Chicagoan and graduate (1899) of Armour Institute of Technology. Powers had worked previously for Nimmons and Fellows, Howard Shaw, D.H. Burnham and Company, and as chief draftsman for the United States Commission at the Paris exposition of 1900.[7] He managed the office while Spencer continued as designer, so no outward change was apparent in their work.

Spencer's journalistic activities, however, did change in 1905. Previously

6 The house, as illustrated, is now painted white, thus destroying the original harmonious color scheme. Some idea of the intended effect can be gained from the poor photographs published in the *Western Architect*, 20, 1914, 35 and 37.

7 Biographical information from the *Western Architect*, 20, 1914, 33

FIG. 40 Spencer and Powers. John W. Broughton house, 530 Keystone Avenue, River Forest, Illinois, 1908. *Brickbuilder* 1908

he had written primarily for professional magazines (the *Architectural Review* and the *Brickbuilder*), but in 1905 he began writing for the *House Beautiful*, producing more than 20 articles by 1909. These were chatty and informal, and directed to the layman. The opening titles typify the series: 'Planning the Home,' 'Plaster Houses and their Construction,' and 'Kitchens and Pantries.' Although the contents were inconsequential, the illustrations usually represented Prairie School work, thereby implying that these designs were the most appropriate for the American home. This publicity was invaluable in attracting clients. It was during these same years (1905–9) that Sullivan was writing for the *Craftsman*, an undertaking which brought to him the Owatonna bank commission.

Two of Spencer's best designs date from 1907–8. The earlier, its building permit dated 6 September 1907 (with the estimated cost given as $17,000), was for Edward W. McCready at 231 N. Euclid Avenue in Oak Park (figs. 38–9). A dignified simplicity characterizes this design, its Palladian formality recalling Spencer's own house of 1905 except that brick, rather than

FIG. 41 Spencer and Powers. John W. Broughton house. Plan for first floor. *Brickbuilder* 1908

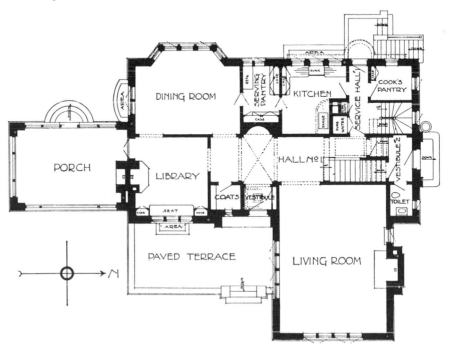

less expensive stucco, was the main material. Balance, not symmetry, prevails. The varied internal requirements are reflected in the fenestration, which is carefully ordered and scaled to produce a harmonious effect on the exterior. The high string course adds monumentality to the design, and the closed, solid building form is precisely defined by long Roman bricks – golden-tan in color and fired to a hard glaze. The horizontal joints are raked. The soffit of the low hipped roof is broad, and painted a deep cream to reflect the tonality of the brick.

The central pavilion is striking (fig. 39). The doorway, with its handsomely carved stone casement and lintel, is placed off-center and balanced by the decorative glass windows of the staircase landing. Behind this pavilion the plan of the house seems clear. To the left are the living and dining rooms and the porch; the right is primarily for services, with a one-storey wing extending along Erie Street and terminating in a three-car garage – an arrangement reminiscent of H.H. Richardson's imposing Glessner house in Chicago.

Splendidly proportioned, yet less remarkable as a design, is the John W. Broughton house at 530 Keystone Avenue in River Forest of 1908 (figs. 40–1). The L-shaped plan terminates in a low porch (with its own fireplace) at the left, thus adding breadth and balance to the massing. Casement windows are grouped in strong horizontal bands and a high string course adds both unity and monumentality to the design. A curt description of colors and materials was furnished by the architects: 'Chicago common brick faced with Danville, Illinois, kiln-run pavers laid in pale red mortar [for the walls, with the] base, sills, and coping buff Bedford stone. Roof light red Kentucky Shingle Tile. All windows of ornamental glass in zinc bar with rose motif in dull amber and iridescent glass.'[8]

The plan of the Broughton house presents a pleasant disposition of rooms in which the spatial experience derives from one's movement between the different areas rather than from interpenetrating interior spaces (fig. 41).

After this date the most inventive phase of Spencer's career was nearly over. He had never entirely abandoned English medievalism (see the Adams house, fig. 18), and by 1910 the revival of these forms became increasingly pronounced in his work, as it was among his English contemporaries.

In 1905 Garden was still – unofficially – assisting Schmidt with his designs. Garden's precise role, however, was now less distinct; perhaps he was becoming less adventuresome (there was a slight falling off in the quality of

8 *Brickbuilder*, 20, 1911, 231. The architects' specifications for this house are dated 3 November 1908.

his work), and perhaps both men occasionally worked on the same design. This collaboration took place at the Chapin and Gore Building (1904), 63 E. Adams Street, Chicago, where Garden assisted, but Schmidt retained

FIG. 42 Richard E. Schmidt (assisted by Hugh M.G. Garden). Chapin and Gore Building, 63 E. Adams Street, Chicago, 1904. Historic American Building Survey

control (fig. 42).[9] The resulting mannerist tensions are not characteristic of Garden's work. The narrow mezzanine windows, with their wide frames, are disquieting (contrast Norman Shaw's New Zealand Chambers), as are the stout mezzanine piers. Frank A. Randall notes that the first three floors were designed for a heavier load than the floors above, a fact often cited to justify these mezzanine piers.[10] However, doorways exist under two of the piers, while under the third only a window mullion apparently supports the eight-storey building – a complete denial of the adage that form follows function!

The last major work executed solely under Schmidt's name was the Michael Reese Hospital (1905–6), where the proportions of the whole are more refined than the details, suggesting, perhaps, that Garden assisted only at the early, conceptual, stage. In 1906 the two men entered into a partnership, thus formalizing what had long existed in fact. The corporate

9 Garden took the author on a tour of his Chicago buildings in 1955, and at the Chapin and Gore Building he remarked that he had 'helped' Schmidt with it, intimating that he did not have full control over the design and was not particularly happy with the result. Stylistic evidence suggests both men worked on the design, with the upper floors and cornice (now, unfortunately, removed) probably by Garden and the ground floor and mezzanine apparently by Schmidt – perhaps after Garden had presented an initial design.

10 *The History of the Development of Building Construction in Chicago*, Urbana, 1949, p. 224

FIG. 43 Richard E. Schmidt, Garden and Martin. Montgomery Ward Warehouse, W. Chicago Avenue at Chicago River, Chicago, Illinois, 1906. Photo by H.A. Brooks

11 The working drawings are dated in November 1906 with the architects listed as Richard E. Schmidt, Garden and Martin. The building is illustrated in Carl W. Condit, *The Chicago School of Architecture*, Chicago & London, 1964, plate 153, with numerous illustrations in W.R. Hasbrouck, ed., *Architectural Essays from the Chicago School*, Park Forest, 1967, p. 14.

12 *Brickbuilder*, *14*, 1905, 77. Also illustrated in the *Prairie School Review*, *3*, 1, 1966, 16

13 Stated in conversation with the author

name was Richard E. Schmidt, Garden and Martin; Edgar D. Martin (1871–1951) was a structural engineer. The division of labor was henceforth more distinct: Schmidt was the front-office man, Garden the designer, and Martin the engineer.

Two buildings from 1906 indicate that ambiguities were now resolved – the Pavilion and Boat House at Humboldt Park and the Montgomery Ward Warehouse in Chicago. The warehouse is unique in Chicago for its early reinforced concrete frame, prodigious size, and splendid design (fig. 43). The brickfaced spandrels create a dynamic and unbroken horizontality along the lengthy, eight-storey façade, an effect weakened now that the brickwork is painted a concrete gray. The piers of the first two storeys (as seen from the street – on the river façade, as illustrated here, the basement windows spoil the effect) rise uninterrupted by spandreds, a design innovation that visually lifts the structure off the ground in the manner of Le Corbusier. The exposed concrete, in fact, is the structural frame; one actually sees the load-bearing structure itself. Never had the Chicago School achieved so direct an expression of structure (largely, of course, because a metal frame building must be overlaid with fireproofing).

The Humboldt Park Pavilion and Boathouse, unlike the buildings already discussed, has always been credited to Garden, an ironic fact since it is among the smaller and less significant of his works.[11] Yet there is a dignity and simplicity in the three-arch motif that forms the pavilion, with the rectangular service rooms at either end being sheltered under the same hipped roof. This arch theme was used earlier by Garden in his Village Block project, published by the *Brickbuilder* in 1905.[12]

In 1906 Garden was only 33 years old, but so far as the Prairie School was concerned his contribution was all but complete, perhaps because of his responsibilities in a large and prosperous firm, but more likely because of the nature of the man himself. Garden was a brilliant designer, but his buildings did not result from deep-seated convictions or from a strong personal architectural philosophy. Late in life (and this may have been true earlier) he liked to enumerate the most appropriate styles for different uses – English renaissance for city dwellings and apartments, Tudor for country estates, and Chicago School for commercial buildings.[13] He had the capability and *savoir faire* to bring it off; for a less talented designer such views would have been disastrous.

Only occasionally after 1907 did Garden avoid the historical styles, as when designing the ten-storey Dwight Building in Chicago of 1911. This was an excellent reminder of days gone by. It indicated that the architect understood no other 'style' quite so well.

Tallmadge and Watson met while working for D.H. Burnham and founded their own firm in 1905. Thomas E. Tallmadge (1876–1940) had joined Burnham's staff after graduating from MIT in 1898 and remained until he won the Chicago Architectural Club Traveling Scholarship in 1904. Upon his return from Europe he joined Vernon S. Watson (1879?–1950), a graduate of Armour Institute, in a partnership that lasted many years. Watson was probably the chief designer, yet Tallmadge is the better known because of his activities as teacher and historian. He coined the name 'Chicago School' in 1908, and in 1927 published an excellent historical study, *The Story of Architecture in America*. His firm was renowned for ecclesiastical architecture (First Methodist Episcopal Church, Evanston; First Presbyterian Church, Woodlawn Avenue, Chicago), although initially it specialized in residences, many being built in Evanston, where Tallmadge lived, or in Oak Park, where Watson constructed his home at 643 Fair Oaks Avenue in 1906.[14]

Among their earliest commissions was the Gustavus Babson house (1906) at 412 Iowa Street in Oak Park, a neat and self-consciously precise little

14 Many illustrations of their work will be found in the article 'The Work of Tallmadge and Watson, Architects,' *Western Architect*, 22, 1915, 47–50.

FIG. 44 Tallmadge and Watson. T.S. Estabrook house, 200 N. Scoville Avenue, Oak Park, Illinois, 1908. Photo by H.A. Brooks

15 For plans and photo of the Gustavus Babson house see the above-mentioned source.

design which is L-shaped with a porch, a massing derived either from Wright or the vernacular.15

Judging by its publicity, the T.S. Estabrook house (1908), 200 N. Scoville

FIG. 45 Tallmadge and Watson. T.S. Estabrook house. Plan. Saylor *Bungalows* 1911

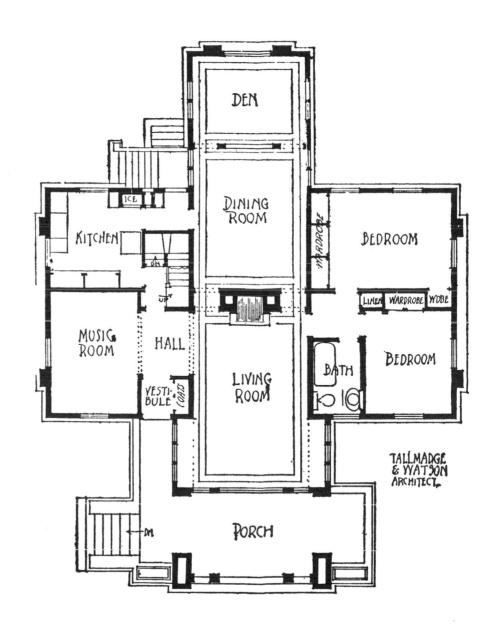

Avenue, Oak Park, was the most popular of Tallmadge and Watson's designs (figs. 44–5). It was illustrated repeatedly in books and magazines, and was described by Henry H. Saylor (the bungalow authority) as 'A midwestern type of one story house that typifies the "Chicago School" [but] it would be difficult to trace any connection between this and the bungalow of India.'[16] The association with the bungalow had a strong public appeal; so did the thin and delicate proportions that contrasted sharply with Wright's more robust, masculine designs. Price was also a factor; the building permit, dated 25 January 1909, estimated that this shingle and stucco house would cost $4000. The cruciform plan was bisected by a strong axis running through the den, dining, and living rooms with only a free-standing fireplace to break spatial flow (fig. 45). The disadvantage of this arrangement, however, was the darkness of the inner rooms.

The earlier Tallmadge and Watson house for C.C. Linthicum (1907) at 1315 Forest Avenue, Evanston, was more substantial.[17] Its heavy, sym-

16 Henry H. Saylor, *Bungalows*, Toronto, 1911, p. 66

17 An elevation drawing of the Linthicum house was published in the Chicago Architectural Club catalogue in April 1907. A photograph of the house appears in Condit, *The Chicago School*, plate 171.

FIG. 46 George W. Maher. F.N. Corbin house, 533 Roslyn Road, Kenilworth, Illinois, 1904. Photo by H.A. Brooks

18 The Lake house is well illustrated (exterior and interior photographs and plan) in the *Inland Architect and News Record, 46, 3,* October 1905.

metrical massing, tripartite division of the façade, long open porch, and other features seem to owe much to Maher.

By 1904 Maher was consciously turning to Europe for inspiration, and in this search the St Louis exposition provided encouragement. His variations on the Farson house type virtually ended in 1904 with the W.H. Lake house at 826 Hutchinson Street (4250 N.) in Chicago – a rather dry, precise design where the interior is open, yet totally lacking in subtilty and refinement.[18]

Earlier, Maher had sought originality through application of his motif-rhythm theory of design, as at the Harry Rubins house in Glencoe of 1902. But the bizarre result dissuaded further pursuit of this particular course, and in search of forms more appropriate to his theory Maher looked seriously at contemporary European design, particularly in Germany, Austria, and England.

FIG. 47 George W. Maher. F.N. Corbin house. Dining room. *Inland Architect* 1905

The F.N. Corbin house (1904), 533 Roslyn Road, Kenilworth, Illinois, opened this new phase in his career (figs. 46–7).[19] The segmental arches with short lateral flanges probably derive from English sources, and perhaps specifically from C.F.A. Voysey, whose work Maher knew from the *Studio* magazine where patterns for Maher's decorative glass may also be found. The large, swelling house-shape is Germanic in character, while the pergola and sharp, clean interior details – such as seen in Olbrich's work at St Louis – were typical of Austrian Secession design. Thus by eclecticism Maher endeavored to combine the best that contemporary European architecture had to offer, hoping to produce something personal and substantially new.

The C.R. Erwin house at 530 N. Euclid Avenue in Oak Park of 1905 retained the long rectangular shape and broad hipped roof so typical of the midwest scene (fig. 48). Some motifs were European, however, such as the curved pediment over the entryway which perhaps derived from Vien-

19 The original exterior color scheme, unlike that of my photograph, had dark trim for the cornice, casements, pergola, and balcony railing. This contrasted with the off-white plaster walls. An early, tree-shrouded photograph of the Corbin house will be found in the *Inland Architect and News Record, 46, 4,* November 1905.

FIG. 48 George W. Maher. C.R. Erwin house, 530 N. Euclid Avenue, Oak Park, Illinois, 1905. Photo by H.A. Brooks

20 A photograph showing the original fence, posts, and a splendid Art Nouveau wrought-iron gate is in the *Inland Architect and News Record, 51,* 2, February 1908; the original decorative glass windows have also been destroyed. The building permit was issued 5 July 1905, with the cost estimated at $18,000.

Related to the design of the Erwin house was that of the E.B. Blimm house in Pasadena, California, both of which were exhibited by Maher at the Chicago Architectural Club in 1906.

21 A house of almost identical design was built by Maher at 2360 Sheridan Road in Highland Park, Illinois.

nese sources, a motif repeated in the now destroyed wrought iron fence and gate-posts – a design unity that Maher always sought to achieve.[20] The interior was organized around a spacious living hall off which opened a study, dining room, and living room; over the entrance was an impressive triple-flight staircase. Comfort and gracious living characterized the interior, the openness being a trait of Maher's work at the time. The exterior betrayed Maher's habitual concern for wall as an enclosing surface, a quality long associated with his work, but not until 1902–4 did thickness give way to thinness, as is also evident in the trim and decorative details.

Maher enjoyed considerable social success, and most of his houses were built in the wealthiest of Chicago's suburbs. Kenilworth, where Maher lived at 424 Warwick Road, had the largest concentration, with Oak Park and Evanston vying for second place. The designs were usually low and rectangular with broad hipped roofs and, often, a central projecting entryway.

The increasing symmetry and clarity of his work are exemplified in the Henry W. Schultz house (1907) at 19 Warwick Road, Winnetka (fig. 49).[21] The slanting corner piers, repeated at the entrance, and the thin segmental

FIG. 49 George W. Maher. Henry W. Schultz house, 19 Warwick Road, Winnetka, Illinois, 1907. *Western Architect* 1909

FIG. 50 George W. Maher. Kenilworth Club, Kenilworth Avenue at Richmond Road, Kenilworth, Illinois, 1906. *Inland Architect* 1907

FIG. 51 George W. Maher. Kenilworth Club. Detail of entrance (now remodeled). *Inland Architect* 1907

arch over the door are motifs found in Voysey's work, and the cottage-like character of the house also reflects English inspiration. Simplicity has been achieved by reducing the building to a basic rectangular shape and by a symmetrical arrangement of the fenestration. The paired casement windows of the second storey create a strong yet disciplined rhythm; they are confined between the flush underside of the broad hipped roof (above) and the long planter box (below) – which doubles as a sill. Larger windows flank the entrance and add balance to the scheme. Rough gray-white plaster is the exterior finish and although some remodeling has been done (an addition on the left, a dormer window, and a new roof which lacks the striated bands of the original) the house remains, inside and out, in splendid condition with all of its magnificent ornamental glass still in place.

Less imposing, in spite of its semi-public nature, is the Kenilworth Club, which harmoniously combines certain midwestern and European sources. Completed in 1906, this is the closest of Maher's designs to the work of the Prairie School (figs. 50–1). It is a timber frame and stucco building, and sited on a slight rise of ground, its long hipped roof (originally striated) creating a restful silhouette. Paired vertical timbers, interspersed with slender diamond-headed decorative motifs, mark off the bays and are contrasted against the plaster walls. A spacious assembly hall is on the left, a

FIG. 52 George W. Maher. Northwestern University Gymnasium (demolished), Evanston, Illinois, 1908–9. Chicago Architectural Club *Catalogue* 1911

smaller room and service area on the right, the two sections originally being joined by an open pergola-covered entrance which has since been enclosed. The window glazing is among Maher's finest, as indeed is the entire design.

More typical of Maher's non-residential work were his designs for Northwestern University. The Northwestern University Gymnasium, now demolished, was built in 1908–9 with funds donated by Maher's former patron James A. Patten (fig. 52).[22] The formal, imposing façade was dominated by a monumental arch which, being vigorously modeled, contrasted with the smooth masonry surface of the walls. Except for the university crests above the doors, the decoration was restricted to two pairs of slender shafts topped by diamond-shaped tablets bearing the letter N. This motif was much favored by Maher, who used it with variations at the Kenilworth Club (fig. 50), Swift Hall of Engineering, Joseph Sears School, and Watkins Medical Buildings (fig. 133).

A podium in front of the gymnasium was formal in layout and spatially defined by handsome lamp standards consisting of rectangular bars grouped around a rectangular core. The terrace, raised several steps above the street, led to the entrance and was dominated by the arched silhouette of the façade. This shape echoed the long vaulted space of the interior, with its triple-hinged, single-span steel arches.[23]

Swift Hall of Engineering at Northwestern is the stylistic counterpart of the gymnasium except that the façade is rectangular, three stories in height, and divided into thirds by decorative shafts. It is bounded by a continuous moulding which adds monumentality to the design.[24] Maher was consciously endeavoring to create a new collegiate architecture but the Northwestern buildings were merely a continuation of his post-Farson house commercial designs. These included his store and office block, called University Building (1905–6), at Chicago Avenue and Davis Street in Evanston, and the Watkins Medical Company Building (1911) in Winona (fig. 133). All have the same emphatic cornice, the same emphasis upon wall as surface (with precise apertures for doors and windows) and the same sky-gray stone veneer.

George Maher also prepared a campus plan for Northwestern University that brilliantly recognized the aesthetic potential of the university's lakeside setting. But unfortunately the plan was not adopted, even in modified form, and for another 60 years Northwestern turned its back on Lake Michigan, as though embarrassed by the natural beauty of the site.

Thus throughout the opening decade of the new century, Maher con-

22 The complete collection of Maher's original architectural drawings has been needlessly destroyed, but the author had access to them before this destruction occurred. Before 1908 Maher did not date his drawings. Those for the Northwestern University Gymnasium were dated 1908 with corrections from October 1908 until 1909.

23 For a description of the structural system see Condit, *The Chicago School*, p. 196.

24 An illustration will be found in Condit, *The Chicago School*, plate 160.

tinued his search for an appropriate architectural expression, a search which led him to seek ideas from the European avant-garde, assimilating these ideas into something which was substantially his own creation. Maher houses inevitably had a personality of their own; they were spacious and livable. Yet as the years passed his borrowings became more literal,

FIG. 53 Dwight H. Perkins. Carl Schurz High School, Addison Street at Milwaukee Avenue, Chicago, Illinois, 1908. *Brickbuilder* 1911

and the personal, if not always sophisticated, character of his designs became less distinct.

Another architect concerned with educational work was Dwight H. Perkins, whose Hitchcock Hall, field house, and settlement house for the University of Chicago gave him some claim as a specialist. His appointment in 1905 to a five-year term as architect to the Chicago Board of Education, therefore, was not undeserved, and in this role he performed a distinguished service. His earliest public schools were not outstanding, but those constructed between 1908 and 1910 have long been recognized for their planning innovations as well as for their design. The Jesse Spalding (Crippled Children) School of 1907 was a rather uninspired Queen Anne

FIG. 54 Dwight H. Perkins. Grover Cleveland Public School, 3850 N. Albany Street, Chicago, Illinois, 1909. *Brickbuilder* 1911

25 The unexecuted project for the Bowen School was illustrated in the *Inland Architect and News Record, 48,* November 1906, while that for the Trumbull School appeared in volume *49,* January 1907. Both drawings were initialled E.P.P. A photograph of the completed Trumbull School is in Condit, *The Chicago School,* plate 164.

design that continued a trend established by Perkins in several commissions during the late 1890s. However, in 1906 and 1907 the *Inland Architect and News Record* published several projects signed by Perkins for schools of a markedly different character. These projects were not subsequently built, although two of the named schools were constructed according to different designs. The Lyman Trumbull School (Ashland Boulevard and Foster Avenue) was a heavy, almost fortress-like structure of brick laid in polychromatic bands – emphasizing the megalithic quality of the design. The other published project was for the James H. Bowen High School which, as built in 1910, was similar in concept to the Carl Schurz School of 1908.[25]

The project for the Carl Schurz Public High School at Addison Street and Milwaukee Avenue was displayed at the Chicago Architectural Club annual exhibition in March and April 1908, and the final working drawings were signed by Perkins on 21 October 1908. The school was opened in 1910. This strong, almost expressionistic design, executed in a rich, warm-toned brick with stone and terra cotta trim, owes something not only to Sullivan in its closely spaced piers and recessed spandrels, but possibly to German architecture as well (fig. 53). The spirit of Alfred Messel's 1904 Warenhaus Wertheim, Berlin, seems manifest here. The building, now much enlarged, is capped by a steep gable roof with symmetrical wings at either side. The massiveness of the design is enhanced by a robust ground floor, topped by a strong belt course that serves as a plinth for the vigorous and assertive piers above. The inverted U motif embracing two columns (cf. Maher's Harry Rubins house of 1902–3), is a tour de force of questionable validity.

The finest design prepared under Perkins' stewardship was for the Grover Cleveland Public School at 3850 N. Albany Ave (fig. 54; the 1909 Joseph Gray School, 30th and Lawndale Ave, is similar). The approved drawings are dated 25 May 1909; construction was largely completed in 1910. The plan is a truncated T shape, four storeys high, and the principal materials are brick with stone trim. The vigorous plasticity of earlier designs is not characteristic here. Wall plane predominates but is vitalized in two ways – first by the rich tapestry brickwork establishing a broad, continuous border along the sides and across the top (the cornice hardly projects at all); and, second, by the superimposed grill of piers which rests on a plinth that, in turn, caps the projecting posts and lintels of the ground floor. There is dignity and repose in the design; it is monumental without being formidable.

The year of his appointment to the Board of Education (1905), Dwight Perkins entered into partnership with John L. Hamilton; in 1911 the firm was expanded to include William K. Fellows who, prior to 1910, had been with George C. Nimmons. Hamilton served primarily as engineer and Fellows as designer. Known as Perkins, Fellows and Hamilton, the firm continued until 1927. When writing of Perkins in 1915, Tallmadge said, 'we think of him as a citizen and a patriot almost before we think of him as an architect.'[26] And for Perkins public service was always a matter of priority. His particular concern for more and better parks and playgrounds led him to service on numerous commissions. Along with Jensen and others he was instrumental in establishing the famed Cook County Forest Preserves, one of which, in tribute, bears his name. His efforts to improve school facilities led to a conflict with the Board of Education, which, in effect, accused him of malpractice. At public hearings conducted in 1910 he cleared his name, but subsequently declined the proffered reappointment.

Perkins' reputation as an architect of the avant-garde is based upon his schools of c. 1908–10, and one naturally assumes that he created other designs of a similar nature. Such, however, is not the case; there are few highly inventive designs among his works. It is possible, therefore, that these schools were produced by some anonymous designer temporarily assigned to his office staff.

Although Perkins was not of the avant-garde he often lent support to the cause. He did so at Steinway Hall, at the Chicago Architectural Club, and also during his mandate as architect for the Chicago Board of Education. But as a designer he perhaps lacked the capacity, and probably the will, to stray very far from the conventional course. His choice of medieval revival – whether the modified Queen Anne of his early career or the Tudor Gothic later on – typified the vast majority of his schools. His mentor in the latter respect was certainly William B. Ittner of St Louis, his senior by three years. Ittner, who, like Perkins, had studied architecture at Cornell, was selected Commissioner of School Buildings for his native city in 1897.[27] By 1903 his work was nationally publicized,[28] and in design quality it perhaps surpassed that of the Perkins firm.

Charles E. White, Jr (1876–1936) was another whose work only occasionally showed an affinity with that of the Prairie School, although his final year of training had been with Wright. He entered private practice in 1907 or early 1908 in Oak Park, and almost immediately enjoyed considerable success. In 1908 he listed seven commissions in the Chicago Architectural

26 *Brickbuilder*, *24*, 1915, 146

27 For a short biography of Ittner see the *Brickbuilder*, *24*, 1915, 101.

28 S.L. Sherer, 'Recent School Building in St Louis, William B. Ittner, Architect,' *Brickbuilder*, *12*, 1903, 206–12, 229–31. This well illustrated, two-part article discusses the innovations and architectural designs of Ittner; more illustrations of his work appeared in the *Architectural Record, 23*, 1908, 136–54.

Club catalogue, with fifteen the following year. His artistic disposition was decidedly English, and half-timbering often appeared in his work. The large J.F. Skinner house (estimated in its building permit of 27 March 1909 to cost $20,000) typifies his early work (fig. 55). The massing is emphatic, yet the various parts seem awkwardly related to the whole. The interior is spacious and versatile; the rooms are arranged around a generous hall that forms the most notable aspect of this house, located at 605 Linden Avenue in Oak Park.

Between 1910 and 1914 White published over 20 articles in *House Beautiful*, a continuation of the series begun by Spencer in 1905. Initially he illustrated his own work, but later presented a rich variety of designs, including some by the Prairie School. Editorially he showed no preferences, implying thereby that all were appropriate for the home. His *Successful Homes and How to Build Them*, first published in New York in 1912 and running through five editions by 1918, illustrated numerous prairie houses. But in the text, although one chapter was devoted to 'How to Know the Architectural Styles,' he avoided mention of the characteristically mid-

FIG. 55 Charles E. White, Jr. J.F. Skinner house, 605 Linden Avenue, Oak Park, Illinois, 1909. Photo by H.A. Brooks

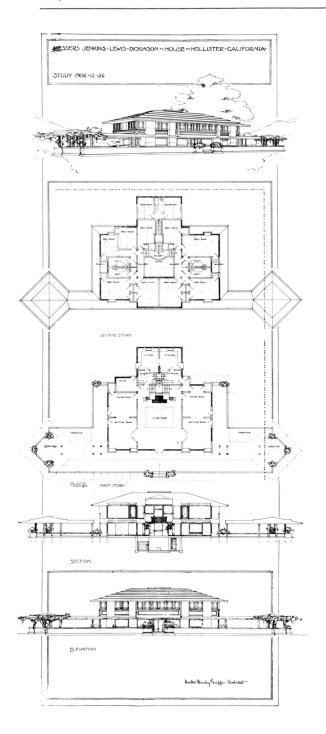

FIG. 56 Walter Burley Griffin. Project: Messrs Jenkins, Lewis, Dickinson house, Hollister, California, 1906. Courtesy Northwestern University

western house. Nevertheless, such publicity, while not actually champion-
ing the cause of the prairie architects, played a useful role.

The work just discussed bears little relation to that of Wright; indeed
it is closer to certain contemporary European developments than anything
occurring in Chicago. Not so, however, with Griffin, Drummond, and others
who spent long years under Wright's tutelage. Such is to be expected. After
leaving Wright each had to seek his own course and develop his own personal expression. This development often took several years. For Griffin,
who left the Studio in the winter of 1905–6, the process took until 1911. No
intermediate design was nearly so much his own as the William Emery
house of 1901–2, executed in the first year of his apprenticeship.

The project for 'A City Residence,' exhibited by Griffin at the Chicago
Architectural Club in 1905, has not survived, so the earliest extant post-
Emery design is a project for the Messrs Jenkins, Lewis, Dickinson house;
this was proposed for a site near Hollister, California, and dated 26 December 1906 (fig. 56). The elevations are bold and incisive, plastically conceived, and harmoniously unified. The massive piers counterbalance the
emphatic horizontality of the second-storey windows, the broad hipped
roof, and the continuous shelf roof that projects between the storeys. This
roof, and the foundation wall, help to integrate the detached pergolas with
the house. The interior reflects the unusual demands of the clients: two
parallel apartments are connected by a common two-storey living room,
and eleven bedrooms and five baths are located on the upper floor. The
plan is laid out on a four-foot module, a device much favored by Griffin
which, however, tended to restrict his freer development of the plan. The
design source was probably Wright's Francis Little house at Peoria, Illinois,
while the pergola recalls Sullivan's project at the Chicago Architectural
Club exhibition in 1902 (fig. 14).

The twin houses built by Griffin in 1908 for Dr W.S. Orth at 38 and 42
Abbottsford Road in Kenilworth look almost like scale models; they are
small and appear cramped, as indeed they are, especially in the interior
(fig. 57). This quality was characteristic of Griffin's early houses where he
rarely achieved a real sense of spaciousness, except in designs where he
manipulated the vertical rather than the horizontal dimensions. Although
the living and dining rooms at the Orth houses are divided by only a free-
standing fireplace, the sense of confinement remains.

By contrast, the two houses built by Griffin for F.W. and Philip Itte on
Morse Avenue, Chicago, now demolished, were dissimilar in plan but
carefully integrated in design; happily they lack the doll-house quality of

the Orth houses (fig. 58). The single family dwelling for F.W. Itte was based on a cruciform plan with a central fireplace separating the major rooms, as at the Orth houses, yet here a comparison with the Estabrook plan by Tallmadge and Watson (fig. 45) shows Griffin to be the greater master of the theme. The Philip Itte house was rectangular, two storeys in height, and intended for two families with one complete apartment on either floor.

Common to each house were their hipped roofs set on flat slabs, rows of windows held tight against the soffit (with central bays projecting), and shelf roofs along the sides – all reminiscent of the project for Hollister, California. By these means unity was achieved in the designs. The working drawings are dated in October and November 1908;[29] the houses were exhibited at the Chicago Architectural Club in 1910 and were published in England the same year by Alexander Koch in *Academy Architecture*.[30]

Other work from the 1908–10 period included a two-family house for Mrs Mary H. Bovee at 1710 Asbury Street in Evanston (with tiered balconies and overhanging roofs), a one-storey bungalow for R.L. Blount in Tracy, Illinois, a two-storey store and apartment building for William H.

29 Microfilms of the original drawings are in the Burnham Library and the Ricker Library.

30 Vol. 37, 1910[1], 132, from which our illustration was made. Koch had earlier published a house by Tallmadge and Watson in vol. 35, 1909[1], 118.

FIG. 57 Walter Burley Griffin. Dr W.S. Orth houses, 38 and 42 Abbottsford Road, Kenilworth, Illinois, 1908. Chicago Architectural Club *Catalogue* 1909

Fox and Company in Chicago, the Niles Club at Niles, Michigan, with its cross gables and elaborately trellised porches (now much remodeled), and the William B. Sloan house at 248 Arlington Avenue in Elmhurst, Illinois (fig. 59). The last may have been under study as early as 1907, for Griffin exhibited three studies of 'a house at Elmhurst' that year at the Chicago Architectural Club; the finished design was exhibited in 1910. The cubic mass of the central portion is given breadth by low flanking wings and this

FIG. 58 Walter Burley Griffin. F.W. and Philip Itte houses (demolished), Morse Avenue, Chicago, Illinois, 1908. *Academy Architecture* 1910

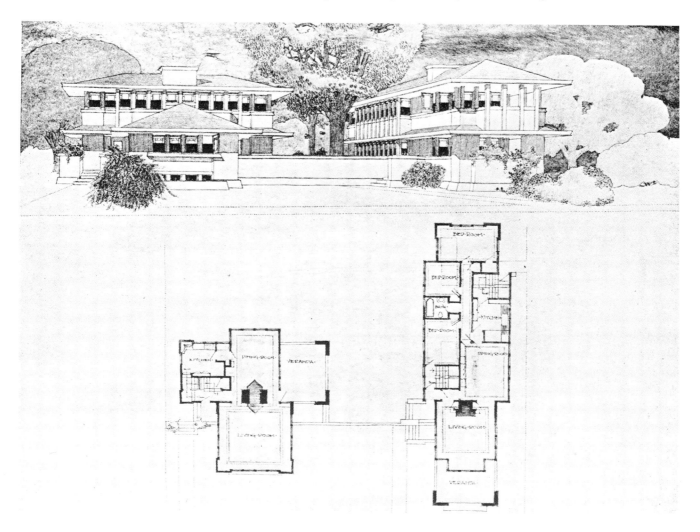

characteristic along with the thin, crisp character of the design, recalls the
Stevens gatehouse and lodge by Spencer (fig. 17) more than the robust and
plastic conceptions of Wright. Strong horizontals unite the wings with the
central mass while grouped windows – patterned with inexpensive wood
mullions rather than elaborate lead and colored glass – create strong accents on the façade. At the right was an open carport (later enclosed as a
garage) which must be one of the earliest examples of this now prevalent

FIG. 59 Walter Burley Griffin. William B. Sloan house, 248 Arlington Avenue, Elmhurst, Illinois, c. 1909. Photo by H.A. Brooks

FIG. 60 Walter Burley Griffin. Ralph Griffin house, 705 St Louis Street, Edwardsville, Illinois, 1909–10. Perspective and plans. Courtesy Northwestern University

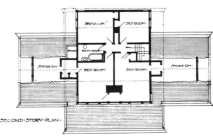

31 The attached garage and the carport apparently derive from the covered unloading area called a porte-cochère, which did not, because of the complex housing requirements of horse and carriage, serve as a terminal resting place for horse-drawn vehicles. The relatively clean, compact automobile, however, could be stored within the house and, following the porte-cochère tradition, many of the earliest attached garages had doors both front and back. The garage at Griffin's Melson house, Mason City, Iowa (fig. 170) still exemplifies this development with the driveway circling through the garage.

The carport, unlike the porte-cochère, is usually a dead end, as at the Sloan house where it is intended as the terminal station for the vehicle. For an early photograph and plan showing the carport at the Sloan house before it was enclosed as a garage, see the *Western Architect, 19,* August 1913, 98, or the *Architectural Record, 32,* 1912, 381, where the house is incorrectly identified as that of Ralph D. Griffin.
32 The exterior design was probably derived from Wright's Walter Gerts house at Glencoe, a drawing of which is in the Wasmuth portfolio of 1910. The rendering of the Ralph Griffin house used for our illustration is unquestionably by Marion Mahony, who may also have prepared the Gerts house drawing published by Wasmuth.

type of vehicle shelter. The size of this budget-built house was not great, yet some feeling of interior openness was achieved by uniting the dining and living areas in a single axial space from front to rear. Four corner bedrooms with cross ventilation are grouped on the second floor.[31]

For his brother, Ralph Griffin, the architect designed a small yet spatially intricate home in Edwardsville, Illinois, in 1909–10 (figs. 60–1). The interpenetrating arrangement of exterior masses and broad sheltering roofs is more compact than it appears; it also gives some indication of the multi-level space within. Griffin here re-employs the vertical spatial planning first developed at the Emery house (figs. 29–33) combining it, however, with a totally different exterior design.[32] Four levels exist in which only the bedroom storey has a uniform floor height. The storey-and-a-half living room (fig. 61) is at ground level near the entry; from it one descends to a billiard room (under the dining room) or goes up several steps to the so-called first storey overlooking the living room and containing the den, dining room,

FIG. 61 Walter Burley Griffin. Ralph Griffin house. Perspective of living room. *Western Architect* 1913

kitchen, and veranda, as well as a separate stairway system leading to the upper floor (fig. 60). Movement – procession – is an important feature of this interior, and although the rooms are not large the house is full of variety and interest. Both the stair hall and the den overlook the living room, which has indirect electric lighting and a cove ceiling – a space-enhancing device often used by Griffin, especially for bedrooms. The interior is sand-finished plaster and wood trim with a color scheme worked out in greens, buffs, tans, and yellow. Similar materials were used on the exterior, the wood being stained and the plaster tinted off-white. The landscaping was also planned by the architect.

Throughout these years Griffin often signed his architectural drawings 'Walter Burley Griffin, Landscape Architect and Architect,' thus indicating his preference for landscape design. Yet he rarely received such commissions and few were actually carried out. In later years (after 1912) these were usually for residential subdivisions, but he also landscaped individual residences, laid out campus plans, and undertook city planning, as in his prize-winning concept (1912) for the federal capital at Canberra, Australia. All had certain points in common: they included formal and informal elements in the design and utilized local flora for the planting. Although an informal setting always predominated, with meandering spaces and varied clusters of shrubs and trees, Griffin inevitably introduced axial roads and paths, or at least a geometric flower bed, in his scheme. In this he differed from the Danish-born midwest landscape architect Jens Jensen, who restricted himself exclusively to native plants and trees and rarely included formal elements in the design.

When Griffin left Wright's Studio in 1905 he returned to Steinway Hall, where he shared the loft with Spencer and Powers, Tomlinson, Pond and Pond, and Heun having offices on the floors below. Wright also maintained an office in room 1106, using it for meeting clients rather than for work. The old comradery was thus partially revived and before long Jensen, von Holst, and Drummond also moved in, with Drummond joining Griffin, Spencer, and Powers in the upper loft.

The reconstitution of this group helped infuse new vigor into the Chicago Architectural Club, judging, that is, by the annual exhibitions beginning in 1907. That year Irving Pond, Alfred Granger, and Howard Shaw comprised the local jury with Griffin entering four house and two landscape designs, Jensen showing photographs of his landscaping for the Harry Rubins and August Magnus estates and Humboldt Park, and Tallmadge and Watson exhibiting two houses. Von Holst's single entry was a sketch

FIG. 62 Frank Lloyd Wright. Project: 'A Fireproof House for $5000,' published by the *Ladies' Home Journal*, April 1907. Marion Mahony, delineator.

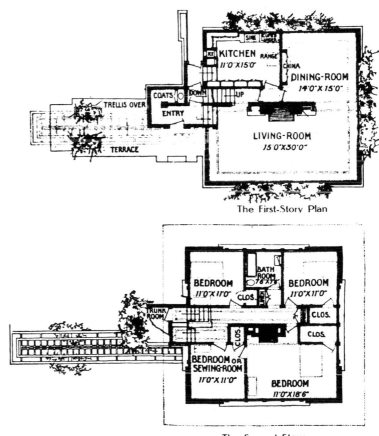

The First-Story Plan

The Second Story

of the Porta della Carta in Venice. Wright exhibited a staggering 34 build-ings and projects, his first entry since the memorable year of 1902. Many of these were illustrated by Mahony's splendid renderings.

For Wright these years were highly productive; they saw fruition of such masterpieces as the Isabel Roberts, Avery Coonley, Frederick Robie, and Mrs. Thomas Gale houses with their increasing emphasis on space-defining cantilevered planes and abstractly juxtaposed geometric masses. These houses had less appeal, though, among Wright's students than did his compact reinterpretation of the cube-shaped vernacular house, a form he revised in accordance with such non-residential designs as his Larkin Building and Unity Church. The resultant design he published in the *Ladies' Home Journal* in 1907 as 'A Fireproof House for $5000' (fig. 62; for actual construction detail see fig. 63).[33]

FIG. 63 Frank Lloyd Wright. Construction detail. Plaster or stucco as used on the exterior of a house. Sheathing boards are laid flush over studs and covered with felt paper and metal lath. Over this a tinted cement plaster is then troweled. The wood coping offers some protection at the top. Pictured is a damaged portion of Wright's Dr G.C. Stockman house, Mason City, Iowa, 1908, the design of which is based on the project: 'A Fireproof House for $5000.' Photo by H.A. Brooks

33 Fireproof because it was to be con-structed of concrete, yet as executed by Wright (cf. Stephen Hunt house, La Grange, or Dr G.C. Stockman house, Mason City, fig. 63, etc.) it was built of wood and plaster.

FIG. 64 William E. Drummond. First Congregational Church, 5701 Midway Park, Austin (Chicago), Illinois, 1908. *Western Architect* 1915

FIG. 65 William E. Drummond. First Congregational Church. Interior. *Western Architect* 1915

To the crude, ungainly box Wright had imparted style. He flattened the roof, strengthened the cornice, ordered the window openings, and married the building to the ground. He vanquished the compartmentalized interior by opening the living and dining rooms as a single L-shaped space which pivoted around a central fireplace. To gain apparent breadth and horizontality he extended the entrance as a low, trellised terrace at the side. The design – in its traditional form or as revised by Wright – had many virtues. It was compact and economical to maintain and build. It required little land and its orientation was readily changed. And its appeal was broadened by identity with prevailing forms. For Drummond, Bentley, Purcell, Elmslie, and others it served as inspiration; blended into the vernacular, it served the speculative builder.

Drummond undertook his first private commission while still in Wright's employ for the First Congregational Church in his home town of Austin (now part of Chicago) Illinois (figs. 64, 65, 66).[34] This was in 1908 when Wright's Unity Church was nearing completion in neighboring Oak Park.

34 It will be recalled that Griffin designed the Emery house while working for Wright and, although the reasons are not actually known, Drummond may have received the church commission for similar reasons; i.e., he was a local boy and perhaps could furnish a Wright-type design without the difficulties and delays often encountered when dealing with Wright (the moderate-sized Unity Church in Oak Park was still not completed in the summer of 1908, although Wright had begun designing it in mid-1904).

FIG. 66 William E. Drummond. First Congregational Church. Plan. *Western Architect* 1915

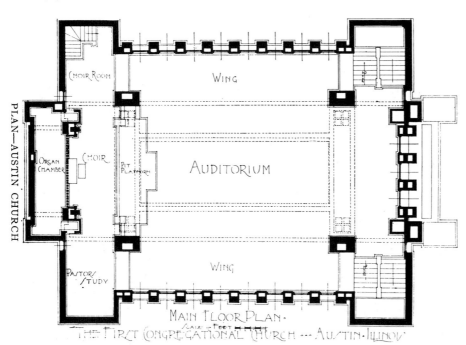

FIG. 67 William E. Drummond. William E. Drummond house, 559 Edgewood Place, River Forest, Illinois, 1910. To the right, at #555 Edgewood Place, is the Badenoch house by Drummond of 1925. Photo by H.A. Brooks

FIG. 68 William E. Drummond. William E. Drummond house. Interior. *Western Architect* 1915

For inspiration, however, Drummond turned to Wright's non-ecclesiastical work, specifically the Larkin Company Administration Building with its galleried, nave-like interior, a building for which Drummond had prepared many of the drawings.[35] His transformation, nevertheless, was almost complete and little was retained but the great towers, the stout window-dividing

35 Information concerning Drummond's role in preparing the Larkin working drawings from Barry Byrne (who was then at the Studio) in conversation, 22 February 1956

FIG. 69 William E. Drummond. William E. Drummond house. Plan. *Architectural Record* 1916

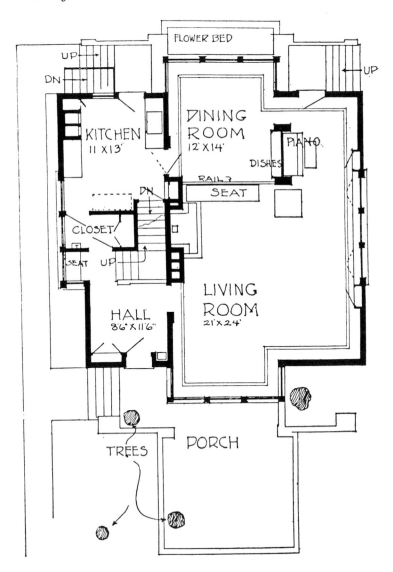

36 These fixtures have been removed but otherwise the interior is well preserved, in spite of the fact that it has served several denominations over the years (most recently as Our Lady of Lebanon Roman Catholic Church).

37 The building permit, dated 19 March 1910, describes the house as 'a two storey concrete residence costing $6000' yet the *Historical American Building Survey: Chicago and Nearby Illinois Areas* (Park Forest, 1966, p. 39) confirms it as being of 'stuccoed frame with wooden trim.'

piers, and the stone-trimmed brickwork. The bold, forceful façade admirably expresses the high nave and lower, symmetrical 'aisles.' Large, vertical windows with ornamental glass dominate the façade, and around the cavernous entrance is a framework of posts and lintels which clearly state the vertical-horizontal theme repeated throughout the design. Massiveness and rugged plasticity characterize the design, and the raked-joint brickwork is used with expressionistic vigor. The structural system is of masonry bearing walls with heavy timber framing.

Through the low entrance and ornamental glass doors one enters a small narthex with lateral stairs leading up to the sanctuary (or down to the social and Sunday-school rooms a half level below). The church has two aisles with pews along the side. The nave is lit by an ornamental glass skylight rather than clerestorey windows and spherical and cube-shaped light fixtures originally hung from the ceiling.[36] The materials are warm sand-tinted plaster, tan brick, and a stained wood trim. The treatment is heavy and severe, the latter being in character with the Congregational tradition of simplicity and lack of symbolic decoration.

The maturity of this design is extraordinary when judged as the architect's first independent commission. Certain details are perhaps unnecessarily heavy and robust, but the general massing, highly original façade, and novel spatial organization of the entrance indicate a designer of considerable ability.

Two years after his marriage in 1907, Drummond designed his River Forest home, having purchased a lot beside that of Isabel Roberts on Edgewood Avenue. The building was completed in 1910. Its inspiration owed much to Wright's Stephen Hunt house in La Grange, the first executed variant of 'A Fireproof House for $5000' (cf. figs. 62 and 67, 68, 69). The Drummond design – like Wright's – envisioned the use of concrete, but was constructed in wood and plaster with a decorative wood trim, the area enclosed being tinted slightly darker than the surrounding walls.[37] A crisp angularity prevails throughout, suggesting a tension between the various parts. The walls read as thin, enclosing planes and, unlike those in Wright's example, the upper rooms are cantilevered to the edge of the broad, overhanging roof (except in front). The terrace was originally open but was later enclosed as a sun porch by the architect.

The interior of Drummond's house breaks entirely with Wright's prototype (cf. figs. 62 and 69). Instead of a square plan with living and dining rooms juxtaposed in an L-shape divided by the fireplace, Drummond's plan is a stunted Greek cross with the left-hand third (hall, stairs, and kitchen) closed off by a lateral extension of the huge fireplace as a wall. The remaining two-thirds of the plan is open except for double supporting piers which serve as a wall for the display of a single Japanese print and which help define the immediate spatial limits of the living room. An alcove at the side affords access to the dining room, which is separated from the living room by a low wood-slat screen against which is placed the fireplace seat – an arrangement ingeniously increasing the apparent size of the interior space. A low-tempo interplay exists between broad horizontals and short staccato-like verticals. Exterior materials find repetition on the interior with rubbed or stained wood trim defining surface areas of ceiling and wall, and with the sand-finished plaster tinted different shades. The furniture is also of the architect's design.

In final analysis, therefore, both the house and the church demonstrate Drummond's capacity to devise fresh concepts from Wright-inspired ideas, a capacity that became more apparent in his designs of 1910.

Passing all but unnoticed in 1907 was Purcell's entry into private practice.[38] William Gray Purcell (1880–1965) was raised in Oak Park and early became interested in the work of Wright, a close and well-known neighbor. In 1899 he graduated from the Oak Park High School and four years later from Cornell University, where he studied architecture. Through the

38 The author is much indebted to David Gebhard, who over the years has generously offered help and information concerning Purcell and Elmslie and whose dissertation 'William Gray Purcell and George Grant Elmslie and the Early Progressive Movement in American Architecture from 1900 to 1920' (University of Minnesota, 1957) contains a fund of information. Much of the biographical material used herein was initially collected by Dr Gebhard.

FIG. 70 Purcell and Feick. Charles A. Purcell house, 628 Bonnie Brae Avenue, River Forest, Illinois, 1909. Photo by H.A. Brooks

39 In the competition sponsored by the *Brickbuilder* the project by Purcell received 'Mention' and was published in elevation and plan in vol. 13, 1904, pp. 18–19.

40 From the time of his graduation Purcell was an active participant in the Chicago Architectural Club. In 1904, with address given as 319 N. Kenilworth Avenue, Oak Park, he entered his library project and 'A Suburban House'; in 1905, with address as 2312 Durant Avenue, Berkeley, California, he submitted a 'Dwelling for Mr Oliver Esmond, Seattle, Washington' and 'A City Bank' (the Bank of Reno), the latter being illustrated in the catalogue. In 1906 his home address in Oak Park was again listed and there were three entries: a college dormitory, a metropolitan riding club, and a bank and office building in a small midwestern city. There was no listing in 1907 when he was apparently still in Europe and by 1908 the firm of Purcell and Feick was listed with offices at 1007 New York Life Building, Minneapolis.

41 Concerning their eight-month tour of Europe and meeting with Berlage, see Purcell's account in the *Northwest Architect*, 17, August 1953, pp. 40–2. Late in life Purcell was on the editorial board of this magazine, for which he wrote numerous articles, including reminiscences.

42 David Gebhard, dissertation, pp. 109–10

43 David Gebhard, ibid., p. 109, notes

kindness of George Elmslie he obtained work with Sullivan and although this lasted only five months (1903), it established a lasting friendship between Purcell and Elmslie that six years later resulted in their partnership. Even while with Sullivan these men began informal collaboration, with Elmslie assisting the young apprentice with a library project that was submitted to and published by the *Brickbuilder*.[39] But Sullivan had insufficient work to keep Purcell and after Christmas the midwesterner departed for California, where he visited Myron Hunt and Elmer Grey in Los Angeles and then, for a year and a half, worked for John Galen Howard in San Francisco. In August 1905 he left for Seattle and found employment there until returning to Oak Park about March 1906. After a brief stay at home, during which he entered three exhibits in the annual exhibition of the Chicago Architectural Club,[40] he departed with his former college classmate George Feick, Jr (1881–1945), an engineer, for an extended trip in Europe. They traveled from Scandinavia to Asia Minor and visited many architects, including P.H. Berlage in Holland for whom Purcell in 1911 arranged an American lecture tour.[41] Upon their return, Purcell and Feick established the partnership which Elmslie joined in 1909.

With Purcell's proclivity for public relations the firm soon had a larger and more diversified practice than Wright, a fact not apt to please the master of Taliesin. They built more banks than Wright and Sullivan combined, and what with residences, churches, town halls, courthouses, fire stations, and other types of buildings, they executed over 70 commissions in a decade and prepared innumerable other unrealized designs.

Nevertheless, the first years were relatively lean, with most commissions deriving from relatives or family connections. In 1907 a house was built for Catherine Gray, Purcell's grandmother, at 2409 E. Lake of the Isles Boulevard, Minneapolis, the design of which (now much remodeled) is indebted to Wright's 'A Fireproof House for $5000.' David Gebbard records that Purcell sought guidance from Elmslie in preparing the design, and then took the completed drawings to Wright for a critique.[42]

Two years later, and without Elmslie's assistance, Purcell designed the Charles A. Purcell house at 628 Bonnie Brae Avenue in River Forest (fig. 70). This is closer to contemporary English work than the Gray house.[43] The broad wall surfaces appear as thin coverings over the structural frame

that Purcell at this time was studying the published works of certain English architects, especially buildings by Baillie Scott.

with the gable roofs reiterating this feeling of lightness, a personal characteristic often found in Purcell's designs. Windows, carefully grouped, add strong accents to these walls. The lower storey is orange-brown brick; above is tinted plaster with wood trim. The decorative sawed woodwork and leaded glass windows were added in 1914.

For J.D.R. Steven, Purcell and Feick designed a house at 216 Hudson Avenue, Eau Claire, Wisconsin, which was of seminal importance for its plan (fig. 71). The cruciform shape, dominated by a free-standing fireplace around which internal circulation was arranged, was the basis of such later designs as the Bradley bungalow and Decker house where, however, the exact placement of the fireplace was somewhat modified.

The largest commission undertaken before Elmslie joined the firm was the Stewart Memorial Church at 32nd and Stevens Avenue S. in Minneapolis. Although constructed of brick, the walls and slab roof seem thin and

FIG. 71 Purcell and Feick. J.D.R. Steven house, 216 Hudson Avenue, Eau Claire, Wisconsin, 1909. Plan. *Western Architect* 1915

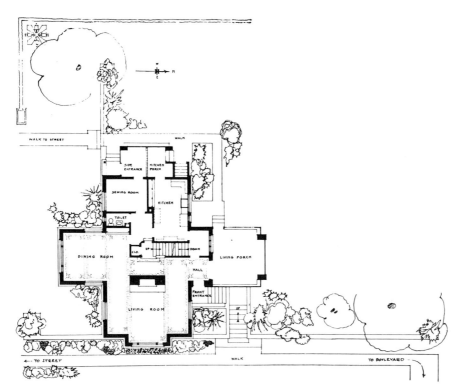

almost fragile, a characteristic already noted in the house for Charles A. Purcell. The plan is dominated by a cube-shaped auditorium to which, like a stem, is added an entrance with a balcony overhead. At one side is a larger multi-purpose room which can serve for social functions or be

FIG. 72 Harvey Ellis (for Leroy Buffington). Project: Security Bank, Minneapolis, Minnesota, 1891. *Western Architect* 1912

FIG. 73 Frank Lloyd Wright. Project: 'A Village Bank,' published by the *Brick-builder* 1901

opened through folding doors into the auditorium, the capacity of which is thereby vastly increased. On the opposite side a great glass window floods the interior with light. Although not a brilliant design, the Stewart Memorial Church does indicate strong personal characteristics and a willingness to experiment with problems of internal planning.

The design of banks had always interested Purcell; the problem was central to those men, like Purcell, who were dedicated to creating a fresh and original architectural expression in the Midwest. No other buildings, excluding houses, were so characteristic or so prevalent among their work, and in no type of building, including houses, was there a freer interchange of ideas among the various men.

The bank was a prominent architectural feature of every midwestern town. It was the 'Temple to the God of Money, as modern Temples go,'[44] according to Wright, and its location was more conspicuous than the church, the latter being relegated to the side streets and placed among the homes (a situation quite different from that typical of New England). The bank, by contrast, was on Main Street – not usually at mid-block but at some prominent crossing or, if the town had a park, on the adjacent corner. Only civic buildings, those associated with democracy, took precedence over banks, and if the town was a county seat an entire block might be devoted to the courthouse which, if space permitted, was placed in a landscaped park.

Visually, Main Street was exceedingly dull. It was but a segment in the unbending prairie road – widened to suggest a grandeur that was never present. Characteristically it was without trees or a central mall to relieve the harsh confrontation of low façades of one or two storeys, which seemed insignificant in relation to the breadth of the street itself. On either side lay the numbered residential streets, projecting their grid into the very farmland from which the community drew its strength. These streets were tree-lined, usually by arched elms, and each house was centered on a relatively large, comfortable looking plot of level ground. The church, often Methodist, set the character of the coffee-drinking, teetotalling home life over which it effectively stood guard. The bank, on the other hand, represented the material life and economic well-being of the region.

The outstanding era for Prairie School banks was between 1906 and 1917, dates established by Sullivan's most brilliant essays in bank design – that at Owatonna, his first, and that at Sidney, Ohio, his penultimate such design. Many splendid banks by various architects were created during the intervening years, but their basic character was largely determined before

44 *Brickbuilder, 10,* 1901, 160

45 Although first published in 1901 this project is sometimes dated 1894. The reason for the earlier date is two-fold – that the design is avowedly related to the loggia of Wright's Studio of 1895, and that an early rendering of the project carries the notation 'Early Study Concrete Monolith Bank 1894.' This caption, however, is not part of the original drawing, nor is it probable that Wright was aware of concrete as early as 1894. When the drawing was published in 1901 Wright described the building as being 'constructed entirely of brick ... the ornamental members throughout are of terra-cotta, except the window sills and caps which are cast in bronze' (*Brickbuilder, 10*, 1901, 161). Brick, of course, would have been the material stipulated by the publisher.

46 *Brickbuilder, 10*, 1901, 161

1906 as seen in the three specific projects described below; the prevailing mode of bank design also played an influential role. Past were the days of high, complex gable massings which reigned during the Victorian era, and in their stead one finds ordered compositions with low, quiet silhouettes expressing a simple yet monumental dignity: permanence and security. The vocabulary was often classical; a free-standing portico might adorn the façade but the solidity of the box-like form was always retained. These designs inevitably affected the form of Prairie School banks which, in turn, eventually exerted an influence back upon the prevailing mode.

The first midwest bank to break with tradition was Harvey Ellis' project for the Security Bank in Minneapolis. Dated 1891 and prepared for the architect Leroy Buffington, the long, severely rectangular shape suggests a safety deposit box; its heavy, solid walls are pierced only by an entrance under the powerful Richardsonian arch (fig. 72). Niches and a tile or terra cotta decorative pattern, near the door, offer some enrichment to offset the rigorous form; this relation between richness and severity recalls the Spanish colonial. A low saucer-like dome, too low to be seen easily from the street, and with bull's eye windows around its circumference, is primarily for interior effect. The basic shape, but not the ornament, sets the theme for many later banks.

In 1901 Frank Lloyd Wright published 'A Village Bank' in the *Brickbuilder* which was emphatically rectangular but not as long as the Ellis project (fig. 73).[45] An enframed area in front contained clerestorey windows, ornamental terra cotta panels, and the bronze doors of the entrance; each bay was divided by piers which merged, near the bottom, into the battered walls. The interior, lit by the high windows, was divided longitudinally by the counter and, according to Wright, 'the screen is to be constructed of terra-cotta and antique bronze, the terra-cotta being worked out in a soft Pompeian red, and the bronze finished in verdigris.'[46]

These projects by Ellis and Wright established the severe, rectangular shape assumed by many later banks. In stressing mass and large areas of smooth, unadorned surfaces of wall, however, they lacked the lively interplay of horizontals and verticals so often associated with prairie banks. This interplay also was proposed by Wright, about 1904, in a hitherto unpublished project for the Frank L. Smith Bank in Dwight, Illinois (fig. 74). Basic to the design was the classical theme of columns in antis, here combined with a high attic storey rather than a pediment. The articulation of the columns cum piers, with their capitals, as well as the recessed spandrels and broad attic, have their antecedents in the Larkin Building and ultimately in Sullivan's skyscrapers such as the Wainwright Building. The combination is undeniably Wright's own, although the design must have been known to Elmslie, who occasionally assisted Wright at the Studio; it served

FIG. 74 Frank Lloyd Wright. Project: First National Bank and Offices of Frank L. Smith, Dwight, Illinois, 1904. By permission of The Frank Lloyd Wright Foundation. Copyright © 1970 by The Frank Lloyd Wright Foundation

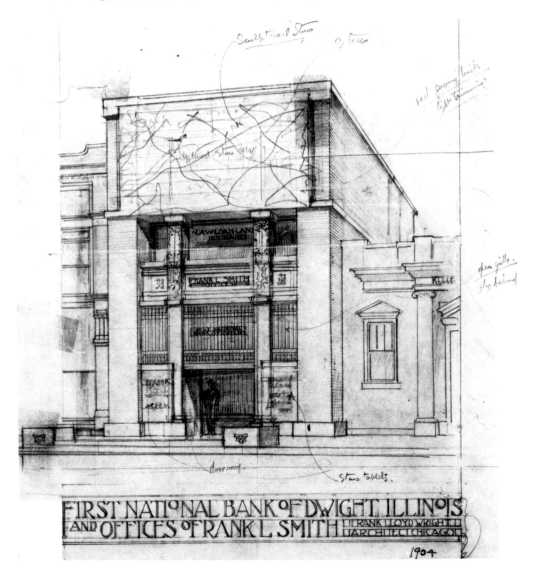

FIG. 75 Louis H. Sullivan. National Farmers' Bank, Owatonna, Minnesota, 1906–8. Photo by Richard Nickel

FIG. 76 Louis H. Sullivan. National Farmers' Bank. Interior, as remodeled. Photo by Richard Nickel

as the source for Purcell and Elmslie's Merchants Bank of Winona in 1911 and the Edison Shop the following year.

In contrast to this fascinating project, the building built by Wright for Frank L. Smith in 1906 was rather uninspired, and produced no progeny in spite of its early date. It is commendable for its clear, straightforward solution to the problem, but lacks the verve of the initial project. Probably it derives from the first-storey, side elevation of Wright's All Souls project – with an intensified interplay between the vertical and horizontal members.[47]

The most famous midwest bank, and the first to receive national publicity, was Sullivan's masterpiece at Owatonna – the National Farmers' Bank (figs. 75–6). Monumental in concept and richly colored, its gigantic voussoired arches and nearly square shape recall the splendid Golden Door of the Transportation Building. Yet the bank, befittingly, has greater dignity and reserve. The sweeping arches, executed in a deep-toned tapestry brick, suggest the enclosure of space as they spring from the red sandstone base which, with its small windows, is scaled to the height of a man. Richly colored terra cotta enlivens the enclosing shell of brick. A band of blue frames the arches, and paired cartouches, brilliant in rich greens and warm browns, accentuate the walls. Corbeled bricks create a powerful cornice. A lower, two-storey block of rentable offices is at the side, its scale clearly distinguishing it from the bank.

The exterior shell creates a single great volume of interior space which is lit by a skylight and the two arched windows of varicolored glass; four heavy and richly ornamented chandeliers hang from the ceiling. Pastoral murals by Oscar Gross adorn the walls opposite the windows and establish the green-brown tonality prevailing throughout. Elaborate cast and stenciled ornament abounds but the total effect is never overbearing because there is an overall harmony and because the richest ornament is kept far from the eye. Nearby objects, such as desks, counters, and partition walls, are simple – almost severe – except for certain highlights of ornament (such as the tellers' wickets).

Sullivan's commission for the National Farmers' Bank of Owatonna resulted from his article 'What is Architecture?', which appeared in the 1906 *Craftsman* and was read by Carl K. Bennett, vice-president of the bank. The officers, it seems, had rejected the prevailing classical style as inappropriate for their building and had sought an architect who could create a more uniquely expressive form. This search, according to Bennett,

47 The Frank L. Smith bank was not published in its own time. An illustration, however, will be found in Hitchcock, *In the Nature of Materials*, pl. 115, and All Souls is illustrated by Manson, *Frank Lloyd Wright to 1910*, fig. 103.

48   Carl K. Bennett, 'A Bank Built for Farmers,' *Craftsman*, *15*, 1908, 183

49   Hugh Morrison, *Louis Sullivan, Prophet of Modern Architecture*, New York, 1935, p. 210

'was made largely through the means of the art and architectural magazines,'[48] thus indicating the importance of non-professional journals in apprising clients of an architect's work. The design, the first sketches of which date from the autumn of 1906, was prepared with Elmslie's assistance. Hugh Morrison writes that 'Elmslie, who was never formally a partner of Sullivan, was at this time a truer collaborator in design than Adler had ever been,' and that Elmslie designed most of the interior details as well as suggesting the single exterior arches instead of triple arches as shown in Sullivan's earliest sketch.[49] More recent authors have emphasized Elmslie's participation, and largely credited him with the design. This judgment seems unwarranted; Morrison's assessment seems correct, that is, Elmslie offered judicious critiques and designed – in the manner of Sullivan – much of the ornament. This is a far cry from being the designer, a matter which will shortly be discussed in greater detail.

While Elmslie was still with Sullivan, Purcell was also gaining experience in bank design. In 1905 he submitted 'A City Bank' project, called the Bank of Reno, to the annual exhibition in Chicago (he was then resident in Berkeley, California), and this was illustrated in the catalogue. The theme, apparently arrived at independently, was similar to Wright's Smith project except that the two columns in antis, with attic overhead, were somewhat more classical in derivation. The following year another bank project was

FIG. 77   Purcell and Feick. Project: First National Bank, Winona, Minnesota, 1907. P&E Archives, courtesy David Gebhard

exhibited, but not published, while in 1907 the newly-founded firm of Purcell and Feick received its first bank commission. This was for the First National Bank at Winona, Minnesota, a design undoubtedly derived from Wright's Unity Church, yet imaginatively reinterpreted by carrying the piers that support the raised slabs of the roof down to the level of the foundations (fig. 77). H.C. Garvin, bank president and close friend of Purcell's father, was delighted with the model, but neither he nor the architects could sell the directors on the scheme. A trip to Owatonna to see Sullivan's bank only confirmed the directors' desire for an oyster white, rather than brick and glazed terra cotta, building, and preferably one of classical design.[50] Such a building they eventually built, designed by different architects, only to see their new edifice eclipsed by the rival Merchants National Bank, which built a design by Purcell's firm in 1911.

The Owatonna bank of 1906–8 marked the start of a modest increase in Sullivan's activity, resulting in 13 buildings, eight of them banks, over the next 16 years. Earlier, since the turn-of-the-century building of the Carson Pirie Scott Store, only three relatively insignificant works had been completed, two for the Crane Company and a small store for Eli B. Felsenthal. Residences now re-entered his repertory for the first time in nearly 20

50 William Gray Purcell, 'Parabiography, 1907' (unpublished manuscript), 1940, p. 15

FIG. 78 Louis H. Sullivan. Henry Babson house (demolished), Riverside, Illinois, 1907. *Brickbuilder* 1910

years, and for Henry Babson he built a large home in Riverside, Illinois, in 1907 (figs. 78–9). This house, now demolished, had great dignity and repose. It rested in the landscape like a huge ship at berth, its appendages, like tenders, gathered at its side. The delicate wooden balcony might well recall the sidewheel housing on a Mississippi River boat.

FIG. 79 Louis H. Sullivan. Henry Babson house. Plan. *Brickbuilder* 1910

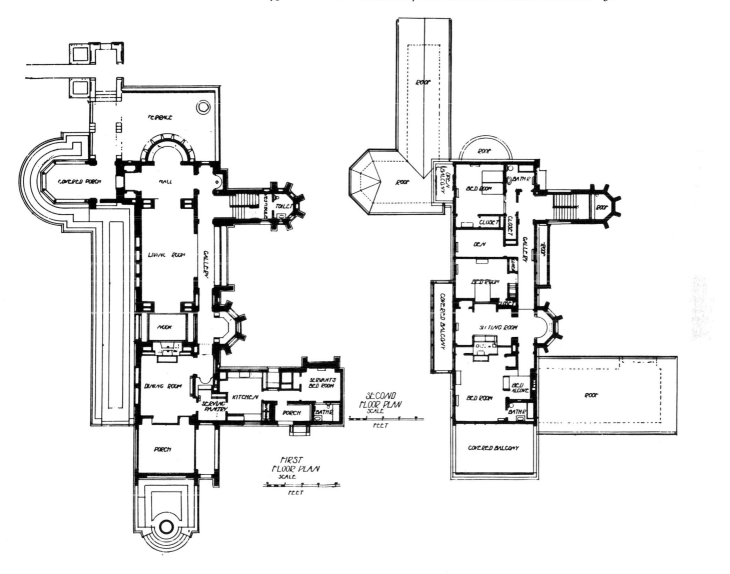

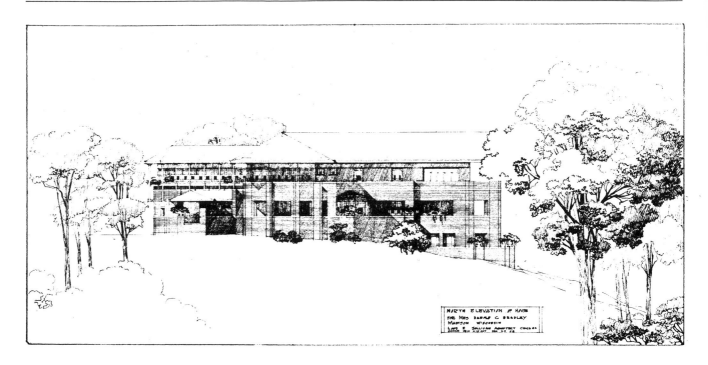

NORTH ELEVATION OF HOUSE
FOR MRS HAROLD C. BRADLEY
MADISON WISCONSIN
LOUIS R SULLIVAN ARCHITECT CHICAGO

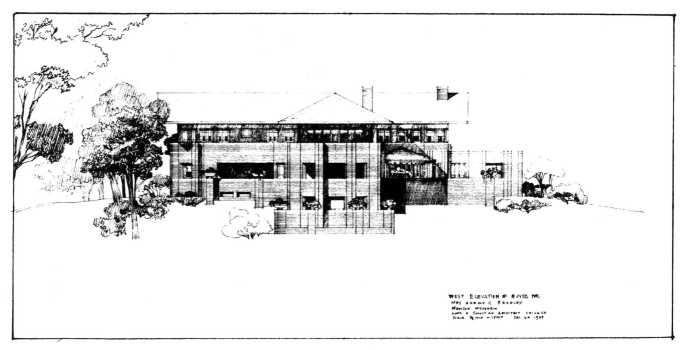

WEST ELEVATION OF HOUSE FOR
MRS HAROLD C. BRADLEY
MADISON WISCONSIN
LOUIS H SULLIVAN ARCHITECT CHICAGO
SCALE 1/8 INCH = 1 FOOT   DEC 24 1908

FIG. 80 Louis H. Sullivan. Project: Harold C. Bradley house, Madison, Wisconsin, dated 24 December, 1908. North and west elevations. P&E Archives, courtesy David Gebhard

In the materials, both color and variety were introduced. A deep red tapestry brick formed the walls to the height of the second-storey sills; above was stained cypress siding laid horizontally with battens. The openings for the grouped windows were clean-cut and precise; the glass was ornamented with leading and bits of color; and the casements were painted white. Enrichment was introduced in the sawed and carved woodwork of the balcony, and in the bright terra cotta bas relief set underneath. The setting was landscaped by Jensen.

The rectangular shape of the exterior, with its appendages, clearly reflected the interior plan. The house was open throughout its length, with an unobstructed view along the single axis; each of the rooms opened generously into the next (fig. 79). Subsidiary functions were located outside the basic rectangle – covered entrances, porches, and staircases as well as servants' quarters and the kitchen. The scheme was entirely un-Wrightian in its concept of interior space.

The extent of Elmslie's contribution to the Babson house design has long been subject to debate. That Sullivan was averse to residential work

FIG. 81 Louis H. Sullivan. Project: Harold C. Bradley house. Plan for ground floor. P&E Arichives, courtesy David Gebhard

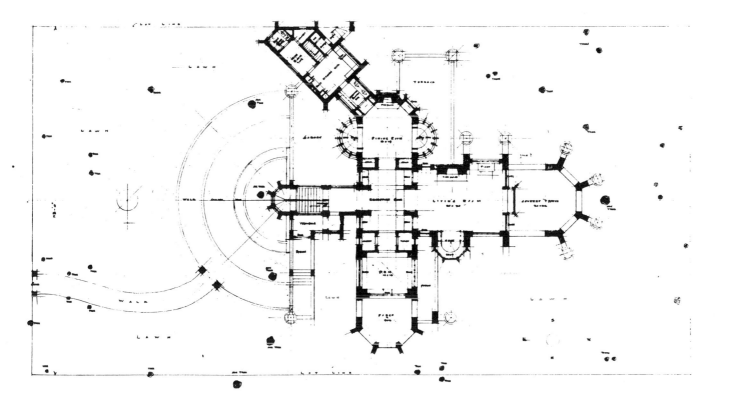

(Wright had, in his time, relieved Sullivan of the task) favors Elmslie's participation, as does the fact that both Babson and the Bradleys, Sullivan's two residential clients, later patronized only Elmslie. This question was broached in connection with the Owatonna bank, and is of special interest since it also concerns the relation between Purcell and Elmslie.

That Elmslie was a brilliant designer there is no doubt. But temperamentally he did not work well alone. He needed a thoughtful, intellectual co-partner-in-design; without a spark there was no flame. He required assistance to formulate, and then keep sight of, the basic idea. This situation contrasts sharply with Wright's; he discussed his work with others but used their notions only as a lens through which to re-examine his own ideas.

Purcell's evaluation of Elmslie seems entirely sound, and although the following quotation concerns a specific collaboration (the Merchants National Bank of Winona) the conclusions are of wider application:

I find it contrasting our different approaches to basic design. The one begins in analysis, the other in synthesis. Mine must pass through the word laboratory, his passes through the graphic meadows, on the way to the building forms.

Behind the "logic," which he very properly rejects as inadequate, are the subconscious pressures from his having fully experienced the mental conditioning of logic while recognizing its limitations and dangers. On my part, I am not fooled by the sophistries, and my thinking goal is also preservation of "feeling," and disclosure of a life in the building, which defies the very analysis I am at pains to set forth.

So at very base, we operate as architects, rejecting the over-pressures of both graphics and dialectics.[51]

This appraisal goes far toward explaining the successful partnership between Purcell and Elmslie – each man so perfectly complementing the talents of the other. It also implies much concerning Elmslie's relation with Sullivan who, like Purcell, possessed an analytical, inquiring mind. The Babson design, for example, is indicative of Sullivan's thought process at almost every stage, yet apparently it was Elmslie who translated many of the ideas into specific forms – forms which in themselves owe much to Sullivan, or to Wright. Elmslie alone could not have created this design, nor could Sullivan. Yet judging by each man's residential work over the years it seems that the more significant responsibility here rests with Sullivan. A collaboration between Purcell and Elmslie, by contrast, owed less to Sullivan and more to other external sources, including Frank Lloyd Wright.

51 William Gray Purcell, 'Parabiography, 1912' (unpublished manuscript), 1951, p. 51

The residential commission received by Sullivan from the Harold C. Bradleys (Mrs Josephine Crane Bradley was the daughter of Charles Crane, the Chicago industrialist for whom Sullivan had built two buildings) had a complex history. The initial design was made in 1908 for a house in Madison, Wisconsin. By Christmas the blueprints were ready (figs. 80–1), but these were rejected as too grandiose for the needs of a college professor. Another set was prepared, accepted in 1909, and the house built (fig. 82). However, when completed, the owners found it too large, so they commissioned Purcell and Elmslie (Elmslie had left Sullivan by that time) to build them another house in nearby Shorewood Hills. This was constructed in 1914–15, and their first house was sold to the Sigma Phi fraternity, the present owners. Meanwhile, in 1911–12, the Bradleys also built a summer home on the Crane estate at Woods Hole, Massachusetts, with Purcell and Elmslie as architects (figs. 135–7). Thus within seven years the Bradleys built three houses, two by Purcell and Elmslie and one by Sullivan.

FIG. 82 Louis H. Sullivan. Harold C. Bradley house, 106 N. Prospect Street, Madison, Wisconsin, 1909. Photo by Richard Nickel

The unexecuted Bradley project of 1908 was cruciform in plan with rooms laid out on axis; the entire main floor was therefore visible from the crossing while the service wing was appendaged at the side (fig. 81). This axial arrangement of interior space recalls the Babson house, as do the long horizontals of the exterior, the heavy proportions, the great gable roofs, and the octagonal projections for staircases and porches. Brick, trimmed with stone, was the intended material.

The Bradley house as actually built in 1909 at 106 N. Prospect Street in Madison retains many features from the earlier design (fig. 82). But the plan, while open, is more compact, being T-shaped and based on Wright's project for 'A House in a Prairie Town.' The exterior materials are brick with shingles above the string course, which is a continuation of the first-storey window sills. Piers establish a broken rhythm along the sides, giving a 'lift' to the massive building and serving as the spring-point for the boldly cantilevered sleeping porches projecting at either end. These porches, now winterized, are constructed of wood (with steel core for the cantilevered beams) and ornamented with sawed patterns in the wood. The effect is striking. The splendid ornamental glass windows, as well as the original furnishings – lamps, tables, and chairs, many of which are still in use – were undoubtedly designed by Elmslie. As for the design of the house itself, Sullivan probably took a more active interest in the unexecuted project than in the final scheme,[52] although even the latter bears the unmistakable character of his control.

The Bradley house was the last commission completed before Elmslie left Sullivan to join Purcell and Feick in partnership in the autumn of 1909, a date which coincides with Wright's departure for Europe. By then the character of the movement was well formulated, having changed from one marked by variety of expression and a conscious endeavor to achieve a uniquely expressive form, to one – after mid-decade – dominated largely by Wright-trained architects who, though still under his influence, were seeking their own identity. These men were often slightly younger, and inevitably more unswerving in their dedication to an ideal, than those who had first congregated at Steinway Hall, although of the men discussed in this chapter – Spencer, Garden, Schmidt, Tallmadge and Watson, Maher, Perkins, White, Griffin, Drummond, Purcell, Sullivan, and Elmslie – the majority had no direct training under Wright. This situation, however, was soon to change, especially as those still in training and/or traveling – Byrne, Willitzen, Van Bergen and others – established their own practices. California and Washington had attracted several of the architects, yet the

52 The revised plan, which closely follows Wright's project for 'A House in a Prairie Town,' was probably Elmslie's recommendation as a means of reducing the size of the house while retaining the openness Sullivan apparently desired.

53 It should be noted that support for the midwest movement came only from periodicals founded in the 1890s, i.e., the *Architectural Record* (1891), *Brickbuilder* (1892), *Architectural Review* (1891), and the *House Beautiful* (1896). The older *American Architect and Building News* (1876) and *Inland Architect and News Record* (1883) largely ignored the movement, as did publications founded after 1900 such as the *Craftsman* (1901) and the *Western Architect* (1902), prior to its conversion late in 1911.

west coast work of Irving Gill and Greene and Greene reached maturity (1907–8) too late to influence the earlier development of the Prairie School; only in Byrne's work after 1914 is the influence of Gill to be seen.

Formal recognition of the school was accorded in the architectural journals by 1904, followed in 1908 by the coining of names by both Tallmadge and by Wright. Significantly, it was eastern rather than midwestern journals which recognized and publicized the movement, specifically the *Architectural Record*, the *Brickbuilder*, and the *Architectural Review*, in that order. The *Inland Architect and News Record* (Chicago) and, prior to 1911, the *Western Architect* (Minneapolis) paid no heed; the *House Beautiful*, founded in 1896, was the only midwestern periodical to distinguish itself in terms of support for the Prairie School.[53] Thus it is no coincidence that Wright's series 'In the Cause of Architecture' appeared in the *Architectural Record* or that the *Architectural Review* (Boston) published Spencer's famous article of 1900 on 'The Work of Frank Lloyd Wright,' and Thomas Tallmadge's 1908 article on 'The "Chicago School." '

Professional Chicago, like the journals, was loath to support the new movement. Only when the members themselves dominated an organization such as the Chicago Architectural Club were their interests accorded recognition; the local chapter of the A.I.A., controlled by more senior practitioners, offered little or no encouragement. And the once lively Architectural League of America had long since been dominated by the establishment.

Yet these were the years when Charles R. Ashbee made his second pilgrimage to Chicago, and Kuno Francke, a visiting German professor at Harvard, was so impressed by Wright's work as to recommend its publication by Ernst Wasmuth of Berlin.

The culminating event, however, was Wright's departure from the scene, and the release of the last of his trainees from the Studio; all, now, had to learn to stand alone. The result was not a restraint; on the contrary, the school soon flourished as it never had before.

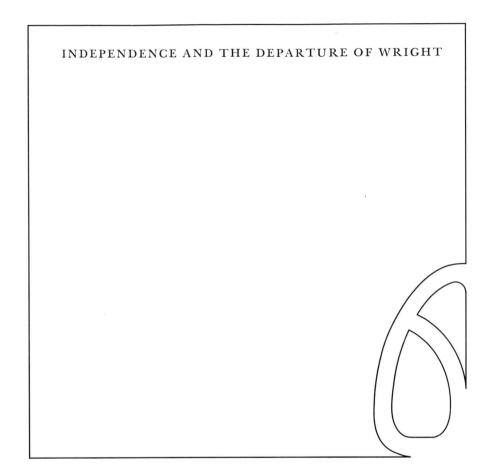

Wright's departure from Oak Park inevitably had its repercussions. Yet contrary to popular opinion the movement did not falter and collapse; it gained vigor and momentum instead. The last of the Studio employees were free to practice on their own as the focus of attention shifted from the Studio to the school itself. Those left behind developed greater independence, and work previously available to Wright was distributed by his clients among his former pupils.

On the detrimental side, however, the group lost, and never fully regained, its strongest and most dynamic member. Soon after returning from Europe Wright moved to rural Wisconsin, and increasingly spent time in California and Japan. Honored abroad, he had become a social maverick at home. Few of the clients he abandoned were to return (except for Mrs Avery Coonley). The classic example occurred at Mason City where Wright

1 *Western Architect, 19*, 1913, 38–9

had built a house, a bank, and a hotel before 1910, yet in 1912 when he desperately needed work James Blythe, his former client, commissioned Griffin as architect for his Mason City subdivision. The implication is that client dissatisfaction was with Wright himself, and not with his architecture; the stigma of unorthodox behavior was personal and not associated with his work. One result was that his contemporaries became more active and prosperous than he; inevitably this caused Wright to become increasingly bitter and antagonistic toward his erstwhile friends.

After Wright had gone, Van Bergen supervised the work already under construction – such as the splendid little house for Mrs Thomas Gale and the arcade building for Peter Stohr. Commissions still to be designed, or requiring working drawings, were turned over to von Holst at Steinway Hall. The clients involved included Henry Ford and C.H. Wills of Detroit, the Ambergs of Grand Rapids, and the E.P. Irvings and Adolph and Robert Muellers of Decatur. Attribution of these designs must depend largely on stylistic evidence, and of the six only one is easy to assign – the Irving house at Decatur, Illinois.

When the E.P. Irving house was published by the *Western Architect* in 1913 the text stated that it was 'designed by Mr Frank Lloyd Wright ... with whom was associated in the work Mr H.V. von Holst. ... The original sketch, which is the only drawing made by Mr Wright's office, contemplated a house entirely of plaster, but Mr Irving concluded, after Mr Wright left, to change it to a brick house, which necessitated considerable changes, and out of which developed the combination of brick and plaster. ... The designs of the decoration and furnishings ... are the co-operative work of the architects and the firm of Neidecken and Walbridge.'[1] This information was undoubtedly supplied by von Holst; it seems equally certain that Wright's participation extended well beyond the 'original sketch' if only because of the pleasing proportions and total harmony of the parts. Even such details as the leaded glass seem subject to his control, although that would have been one of the last things designed. Mahony probably assisted with the furnishings, but this was normal Studio procedure at that time. In point of fact, therefore, von Holst probably had little to do with the design except to modify the materials and change a few insignificant details. The design, including its remarkably open interior planning, deserves to rank among Wright's more brilliant achievements, yet because of its uncertain attribution, and in spite of its intrinsic quality as a design, it has not been published since 1913.

Design responsibility for the other houses is much more difficult to ascribe due to their complex histories. In every case the initial commission went to Wright, he handed it over to von Holst, and von Holst subsequently went into partnership with James Fyfe. They, in turn, confided authority in Mahony, who produced the final design. Dates vary from 1909 to 1912, which is well beyond the time of Wright's return.

Of her role, Marion Mahony has said:

after [Wright] had gone Mr von Holz [*sic*], who had taken over, asked me to join him so I did on a definite arrangement that I should have control of the designing. That suited him. When the absent architect didn't bother to answer anything that was sent over to him, the relations were broken and I entered into partnership with von Holz [*sic*] and Fyfe. For that period I had great fun designing.[2]

Three things in this statement are of particular importance: first, that the writer says she did the designing for von Holst, second, that this was done by prearrangement and is not a draftsman's subsequent claim to active participation in the design work of a firm and, third, that attempts were made to remain in touch with Wright but that he failed to reply. The latter point emphasizes how completely Wright broke with his past, a factor which has generally been overlooked. Rationally it is difficult to explain; one can imagine his lack of interest in mundane affairs, but the Henry Ford commission was perhaps a once-in-a-lifetime opportunity. He could have prepared designs in Europe, and remained in contact with Ford by mail until his return in October 1910. Yet he did not. Moreover, no attempt was apparently made after his return to pick up where he had left off, which is indeed curious. The assumption has always been that these commissions were dealt with while he was away but, in point of fact, this was not true. The Ford project was designed by Mahony in 1912 – why, at that late date, had Wright not re-established contact with Henry Ford? It seems that Wright had closed the door on his past; in Europe he had prepared a post-mortem retrospective exhibition and monograph on his life work, and then he had returned to America to begin life anew.

In all five house designs for which attributions are required common characteristics exist. Each has an axial interior extending the length of the living quarters and coinciding with the center line of the terminal spaces (except at the Robert Mueller house) but this axis does not coincide with the center line of certain intermediate rooms. These off-center rooms are set at 90° to the prevailing direction with their own axis terminating in a

2 Marion Mahony Griffin, 'The Magic of America,' unpublished manuscript, New York Historical Society, p. 170.

FIG. 83 Marion Mahony. Project: C.H. Wills house, Detroit, Michigan, 1909. Chicago Architectural Club *Catalogue* 1911

FIG. 84 Marion Mahony. C.H. Wills house. Interior of second project. Courtesy New York Historical Society

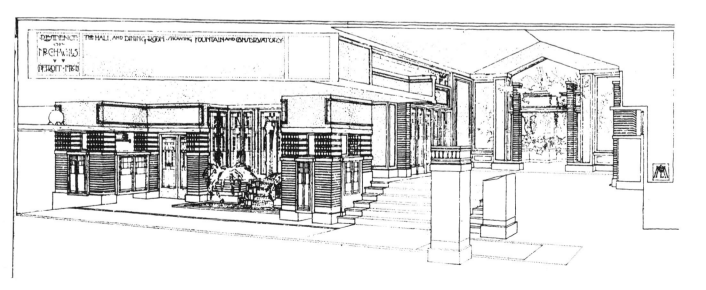

fireplace, a major window, or both. The simplest exposition of this is seen in the Amberg plan (fig. 87); the most complex in the Wills and Ford plans (figs. 85 and 96). In all five houses there is a change in floor level (but apparently not ceiling level) somewhere along this axis (see interior views, cross sections, and plans). These characteristics of plan are not found among the work of other prairie architects and probably result from Mahony's Beaux-Arts training at MIT combined with her subsequent experience under Wright. Among the latter's work the closest comparison is

FIG. 85 Marion Mahony. C.H. Wills house. Plan. Courtesy New York Historical Society

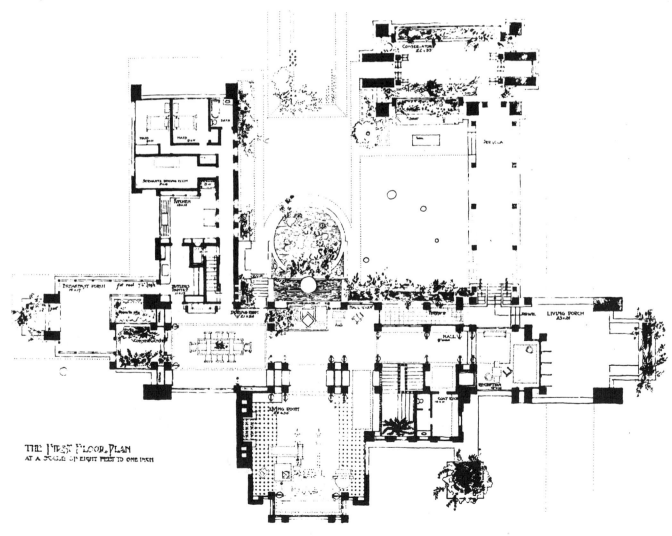

3 The plan of Walter Burley Griffin's Emery house was pinwheel in shape and there was also a slight change in floor level between the dining room and living room (but they were not on axis). This raises the question as to whether Marion Mahony was consciously drawing on Griffin's earlier work. If so, did this encourage Griffin to do the same, as for the Carter and Ricker houses?

4 Significantly, this is the one Wright building that Mahony implied was largely her own design ('The Magic of America,' p. 170).

with the J.W. Husser house of 1899. The individuality of Mahony's plans can best be appreciated in relation to such counterparts as Sullivan's less complex axial space at the Babson house (fig. 79), or Wright's more rigidly symmetrical Edwin Cheney house and Coonley playhouse, all quite different from Mahony's more casual arrangement of rooms along a skewer-like axis.

With an axial layout one expects the outline of the plan, and the massing, to be rectangular or cruciform, yet in each case it is pinwheel in shape.[3] Related to this is the consistent full height, off-center projection in front, as at the Amberg house (fig. 86), a characteristic also found in Wright's work dating back to the 1901 Thomas house.[4]

Keeping this family resemblance between the designs in mind, the individual buildings or projects can more easily be discussed. Other evidence, primarily stylistic, will be presented to confirm Mahony's contribution.

For instance, the rendering of the Childe Harold Wills house, dated December 1909, was unquestionably drawn by Mahony. All of her stylisms are present – the striated bark of trees, the feathery silhouette of foreground plants, and the inimitable spiral vines (fig. 83); her monogram also appears on one of the interior sketches (fig. 84). Similarly, the architectural

FIG 86 Marion Mahony and Frank Lloyd Wright. David M. Amberg house, 505 College Avenue S.E., Grand Rapids, Michigan, 1909–10. *Western Architect* 1913

FIG. 87 Marion Mahony and Frank Lloyd Wright. David M. Amberg house. Plan.
Western Architect 1913

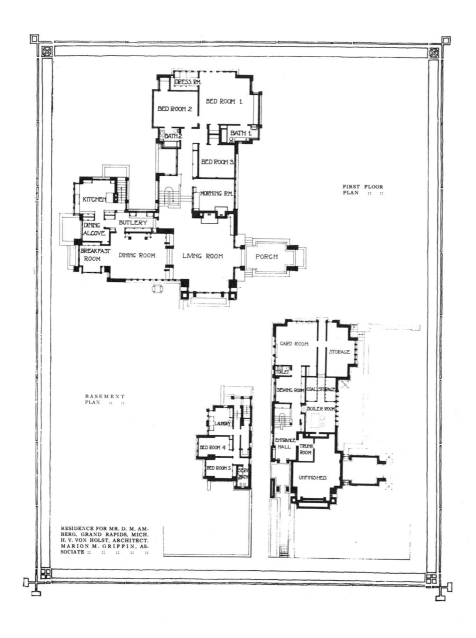

FIG. 88 Marion Mahony. David M. Amberg house. Dining room (above), living room (below). *Western Architect* 1913

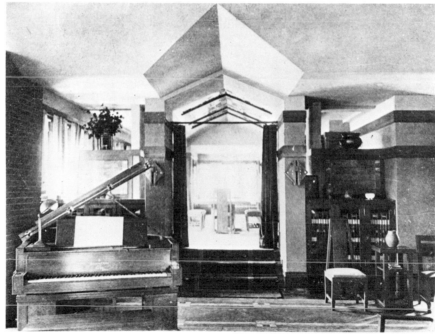

design should be assigned to her. The plan is typical of her work with its central axis symmetrical at the lateral ends (fig. 85). Typical too are the exterior vertical elements, which are rather tight and narrow; these proportions are entirely unlike those of Wright. The caption credits the design to von Holst, yet it is certainly not his work, although Wright handed him the commission. This project was exhibited at the Chicago Architectural Club in 1911 but because of the client's domestic difficulties it was never built.[5]

A final assessment of the D.M. Amberg house at 505 College Avenue S.E. at Logan in Grand Rapids would require knowledge of presently inaccessible drawings which Hitchcock reports to be at Taliesin, as well as confirmation that these drawings do not pertain to an earlier project.[6] Yet the plan, and the detailing of the exterior, tend to confirm this as Mahony's work (figs. 86, 87, 88).[7] That the plan is not obviously pinwheel in shape is perhaps because bedrooms were incorporated on the main floor which, incidentally, is elevated with a driveway passing underneath, as was also

5 David T. Van Zanten's study of 'The Early Work of Marion Mahony Griffin,' *Prairie School Review*, 3, 2, 1966, 5–23, deals at length with this and Mahony's other work of the period. For my information about Wills as client I am indebted to this source (p. 18).

6 Henry-Russell Hitchcock, *In the Nature of Materials*, New York, 1942, pp. 118–19, says Wright 'made preliminary sketches for the Amberg house' but identifies the owner as J.H. rather than D.M. Amberg.

7 When extensively published by the *Western Architect*, 19, October 1913, the Amberg house was credited to 'H.V. von Holst, Architect, Chicago, Marion M. Griffin, Associate.'

FIG. 89 Frank Lloyd Wright and Marion Mahony. Robert Mueller house, 1 Millikin Place, Decatur, Illinois, 1909–11. Photo by H.A. Brooks

intended for the Wills project. Tight, angular forms predominate on the interior, where the living room is three steps lower than the dining room. The latter has a tent-like ceiling and leaded glass skylight.

The two Mueller houses on Millikin Place, Decatur, present a challenging problem in attribution, the Robert Mueller house being the more difficult because of several inconsistencies. First, its proportions seem too broad and relaxed to be designed by Mahony, and even the four tall, narrow piers in front suggest no tension or tautness (fig. 89). The plan, although pin-

FIG. 90 Frank Lloyd Wright and Marion Mahony. Robert Mueller house. Plan. *Architectural Record* 1916

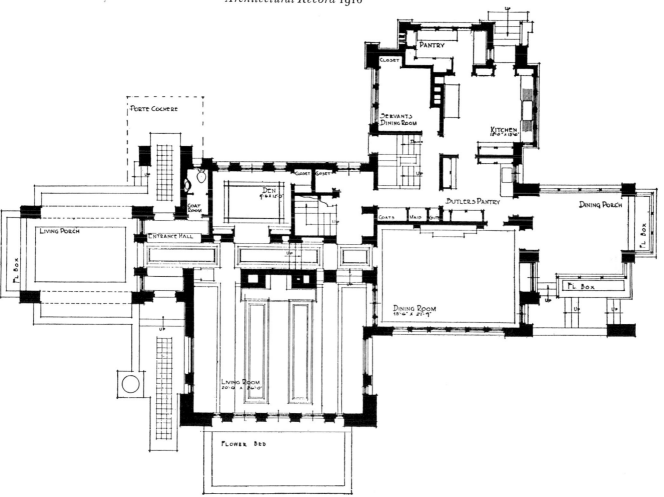

FIG. 91 Marion Mahony. Adolph Mueller house, 4 Millikin Place, Decatur, Illinois, 1910. Photo by H.A. Brooks

FIG. 92 Marion Mahony. Adolph Mueller house. Side view. Photo by H.A. Brooks

wheel, is modified in its axial scheme with the right terminal not on axis, and the central axis passing behind the chimney rather than through the living room (fig. 90). This results in a more intricate and interesting spatial experience, but it is inconsistent with the other four plans. Perhaps the reason for this is that Wright left behind some elevation drawings which Mahony utilized, and in so doing was forced to accept certain pre-conditions regarding the plan. A change in level does occur, this in the corridor behind the chimney so that the entrance hall, den, and living room are three steps lower than the dining room, breakfast porch, and service wing. The way the various rooms open off the changing level corridor is very

FIG. 93 Marion Mahony. Adolph Mueller house. Interior: living room with view through hall and dining room to porch. *Architectural Record* 1916

pleasant, as a maximum amount of spatial variety and interest is thus achieved.

Common brick, a cool gray color, and stained casements with leaded glass, are combined with a red tile roof. Small balcony-like projections at the sides are surfaced with plaster, as are the soffits of the roof. Colored tile set in plaster panels decorates the area between the front piers, the design being a stylized flower pattern which recalls the tulip motif at the Coonley house. But here it is placed as at the Ford project (fig. 95) or as at Griffin's Ricker or Blythe houses (figs. 102 and 179). Roman brick, plaster, wood,

FIG. 94 Marion Mahony. Adolph Mueller house. Plan. *Architectural Record* 1916

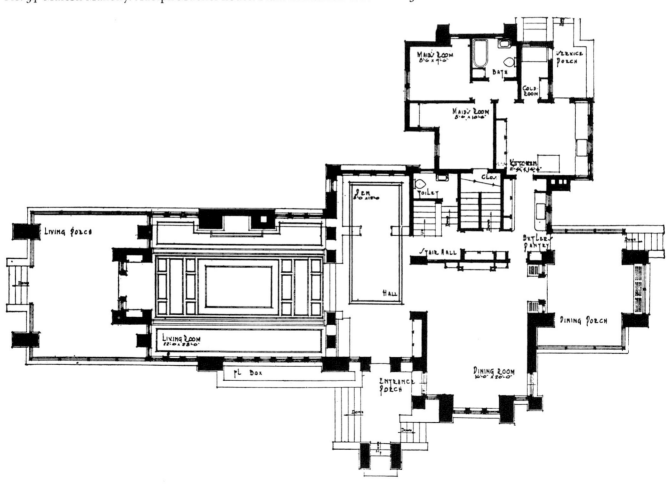

and tile are the materials of the interior, the bright, verging on gaudy, tile of the breakfast porch recalling the not always subtle colors at the Amberg house. The blueprints for the Robert Mueller house are dated 21 September 1911, and the architect is given as von Holst. Apparently the formal recognition of Mahony as 'associate' began only after von Holst and Fyfe entered partnership – an event post-dating her marriage to Griffin in June 1911.

The Adolph Mueller house exemplifies all the characteristics thus far associated with Mahony: exterior massing like that of the Thomas house, long, restful horizontals combined with rather tight, narrow verticals, foundations that are high and heavy, and crisp, sharp (gable) roofs (figs. 91–2). The interior has the same sharp, angular quality in the details, and the inevitable low tent-like ceiling (fig. 93). The plan has a central axis passing through the major rooms with the two terminal spaces (porches) centered on this axis (fig. 94). Certain intermediary rooms are set at 90° to this axis; the plan is not bilaterally symmetrical and in outline suggests a pinwheel shape. Plaster rather than masonry was the exterior material. The blueprints are dated 30 November 1910, with all revisions in April and May 1911. Although Mahony was not given credit for the Adolph Mueller drawings, it may safely be considered the most complete, authentic house ever built to her designs.

FIG. 95 Marion Mahony Griffin. Project: Henry Ford house, Dearborn, Michigan, 1912. Courtesy Northwestern University

FIG. 96 Marion Mahony Griffin. Henry Ford house. Plan. Courtesy Northwestern University

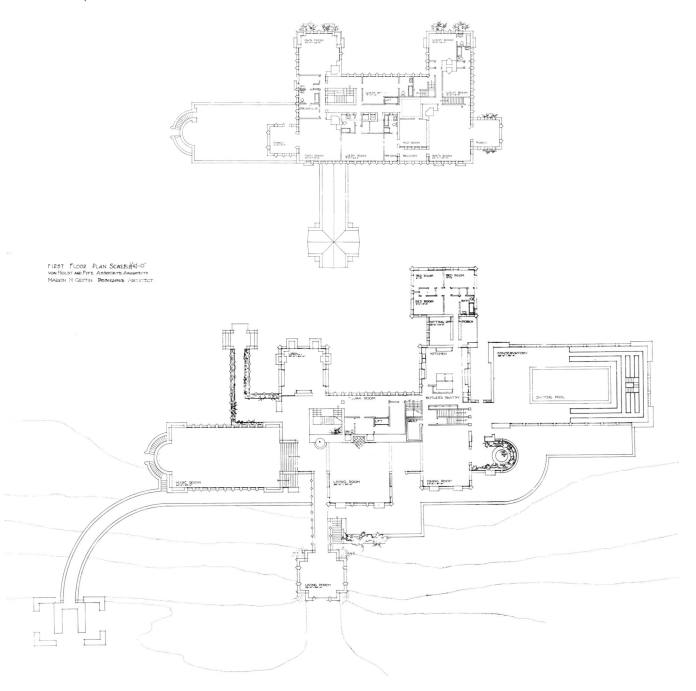

8 Marion Mahony Griffin often obliterated (usually with black India ink), and occasionally altered, the captions of drawings, this probably at the time she was preparing the manuscript of 'The Magic of America.' Her motive in most instances is unclear.

9 Van Zanten, 'The Early Work of Marion Mahony Griffin,' p. 21

The last among the so-called von Holst designs was that for Henry Ford. It is known only through several sepia drawings on linen given to the Art Department at Northwestern University by Marion Mahony Griffin. One has a caption reading 'von Holst and Fyfe Architects Marion M. Griffin Associate,' yet this was subsequently altered to read 'von Holst and Fyfe Associate Architects Marion M. Griffin Designing Architect.'[8] The latter version more correctly represents the truth. The only date was neatly added in pencil to the lower right corner of the perspective drawing – 1912. This is probably correct since the von Holst and Fyfe firm was not founded until 1912 and the Griffin name must post-date Mahony's June 1911 marriage; her MMG monogram appears on the section drawing. Stylistic evidence also indicates a date of 1912 (cf. Griffin's own house project and the Melson house both of 1912, figs. 168 and 170).

Size and materials distinguish the Ford project from its predecessors, as does the sloping hillside site (figs. 95, 96, 97). Quarry-face limestone, such as Mahony used at All Souls' Unitarian Church, Evanston (fig. 28), forms the foundations and merges into the walls. These continue to the height of the first-storey windows, above which there is a band of diaper patterned stucco and colored tile. Heavy mullions, splayed and one or more storeys in height, divide the windows and support the low hipped roof. The water level viewpoint of the perspective obscures the windows of the main floor (but not those of the bedrooms) behind a terrace wall – except at the left where the music room can be seen. At the right, raised on great arches, is the indoor swimming pool. Porches project forward to the water's edge, and at the rear the service wing extends to complete the pinwheel effect.

But the plan of the Ford project is rather dull (fig. 96). Rooms are laid out monotonously along a main axis – music room, hall, living room, hall, dining room, conservatory – in a spatially uninteresting manner. Each opens generously into the next permitting little in the way of privacy or subtlety of interrelation; the plan is far less imaginative than the Wills project, where the axial scheme had some validity in terms of human habitation. Size, unfortunately, has resulted in looseness, not sophistication.

Construction was actually undertaken and, according to David Van Zanten, the foundations were laid in 1913 before a dispute arose between Ford and the architects. A law suit resulted and ultimately Ford hired the Pittsburgh architect W.H. Van Tine to prepare a new design to be built on the old foundations.[9] The services of Jens Jensen, however, were retained, and it was he who designed the grounds for Fairlane at Dearborn, Michigan.

In sum, therefore, the attribution of these designs nominally credited to von Holst should probably be as follows: the E.P. Irving house was designed by Wright in 1909 but slightly modified in execution. The Robert Mueller house was designed by both Wright and Mahony with Wright primarily responsible for the exterior, Mahony for the interior. Its design date must have extended over a two-year period from 1909 to 1911. The Adolph Mueller house was designed by Mahony in 1910. The David M. Amberg house was also designed by Mahony, perhaps with the aid of some preliminary sketches by Wright; thus the date would have been 1909 and onward. The project for C.H. Wills, dated 1909, was entirely by Mahony, as was that for Henry Ford of 1912.

Superficially at least, the appearance of these works suggests a highly personal, well-developed design maturity, yet the family resemblance is so strong among them as to imply that a basic formula underlies each design. Was Mahony sufficiently imaginative as a designer to devise a continuing series of rich variations on the theme or might she have proven relatively inflexible – as Maher was with his repetitions of the Farson house theme? This we shall never know. After her marriage she so completely sublimated herself to her husband's career that – although she participated in developing certain of his designs – she did no designing entirely on her own. But to hypothesize, it is probably true that she lacked the imaginative mind to create a wide and rich variety of outstanding designs.

Millikin Place, where the Mueller and Irving houses were built, is a short, dead-end extension of Prairie Avenue in Decatur. It is set apart by an entrance gateway (now remodeled) and given distinction by handsome

FIG. 97 Marion Mahony Griffin. Henry Ford house. Section along main axis from music room to dining room. Courtesy Northwestern University

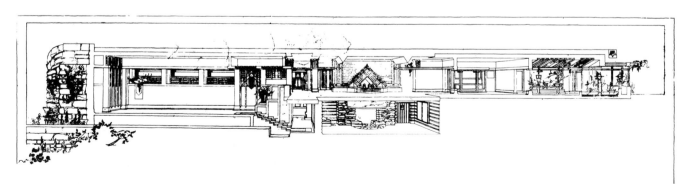

10 *Architectural Record*, 28, 1910, 307–10

brick and wrought-iron lamps and a unified landscaping scheme. The landscaping was planned by Griffin; the driveway lamps were most likely by Mahony. At least the original project showing a combination fountain and light post was unquestionably Mahony's rendering and the heavy scaled, neo-baroque sphere and podium atop the brick and iron pier seem more in context with her work than with Griffin's. This ambitious scheme, however, was modified prior to construction when only narrow brick piers, flanked by iron bars and cross pieces, were built.

The collaborative work at Millikin Place, and Mahony's move into von Holst's office at Steinway Hall – where Griffin had his office – reunited these former Studio apprentices with the result that (as vividly recorded in 'The Magic of America') Marion fell inextricably in love with Walter, offered her rendering services to him as bait and on 29 June 1911, married him. That same month the international competition for the design of Canberra was announced. Griffin entered and, aided by his wife's superb renderings, was acclaimed winner on 23 May 1912. These events completely altered the course of their careers.

In the first five years (1906–10) after Griffin left the Studio, his work was largely Wrightian in character, but gradually he developed a strong, personal style of his own. His 15 designs exhibited at the Chicago Architectural Club in 1910 summed up his early career, as did the article concerning his work in the *Architectural Record* of 1910. Illustrated were the two Orth houses (fig. 57), the F.W. and Philip Itte houses (fig. 58), the Bovee house, and the Moulton house, complete with interior and exterior photographs or drawings. All were indebted to Wright, as the critic justly noted, and although he praised Griffin's 'bold and discreet ... handling of his adopted forms,' he concluded by saying that Griffin must now 'make a genuine personal contribution' of his own.[10]

And this is exactly what Griffin did. He shed the Wrightian mantle he had been trained to wear and subconsciously seemed to revert ten years to his own William Emery house of 1901–2. This became his new point of departure, and with the B.J. Ricker house at Grinnell of 1911 he seemed, almost literally, to wipe his Wright indoctrination off his slate. His inborn preferences once more were manifest – hard, masonry materials and solid, massive forms; simple square or rectangular shapes bounded by large corner piers; interiors confined rather than spreading; spatial variety and interest achieved through manipulation of multi-level space.

While still typifying his early work, the first hint of impending change

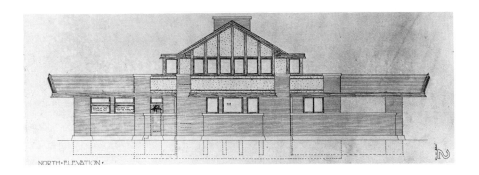

FIG. 98 Walter Burley Griffin. Project: Frederick B. Carter, Jr house, Glencoe, Illinois, 1909. North elevation. Original drawing, brown ink and ink wash on linen, Brooks collection

FIG. 99 Walter Burley Griffin. Frederick B. Carter, Jr house, 1024 Judson Avenue, Evanston, Illinois, 1910. Photo by H.A. Brooks

FIG. 100 Walter Burley Griffin. Frederick B. Carter, Jr house. Plan and section. Courtesy Northwestern University

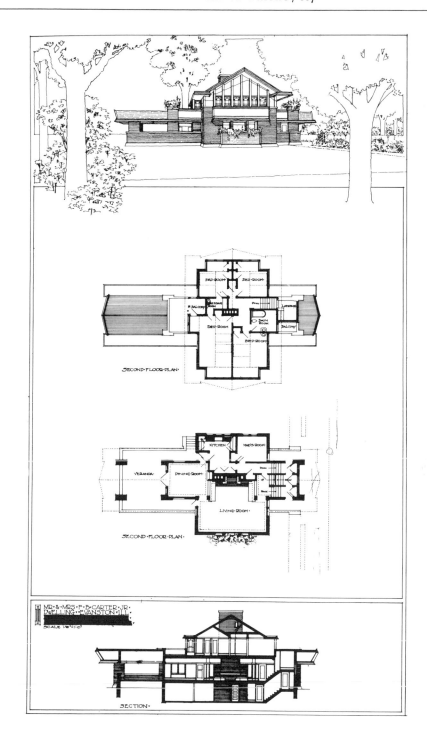

appears at the Frederick B. Carter, Jr house which Griffin designed in 1909 for a site in Glencoe, Illinois (fig. 98). This lot was exchanged, however, for a smaller one at 1024 Judson Avenue in Evanston; the house was accordingly reversed and reduced in size. New drawings were prepared, dated between January and April 1910 (figs. 99–101).[11]

11 The Carter house was known in Germany through photographs published in *Architectur des* xx *Jahrhunderts*, *14*, 1914, plate 86.

FIG. 101 Walter Burley Griffin. Frederick B. Carter, Jr house. Living room. Historic American Building Survey photo by Richard Nickel

In the Carter design Griffin tried to reconcile his Wright training with the ideas expressed earlier at the Emery house (fig. 29). The combination of materials (brick below, stucco and wood above), corner piers, cantilevered second storey, and roof shape recall his first house, but the lateral extension of porches and most of the formal vocabulary derives from Wright. The compact plan contradicts the apparent breadth of the design. The crisp, angular quality is Griffin's own, as is the height of the central mass.

Griffin seldom used leaded or colored glass for his windows (except for interior cupboards and cabinets), preferring clear glass ornamented with mullions of wood. These were more robust than the delicate leading cherished by Wright. The designs were abstract in pattern and bilaterally symmetrical. Usually they were composed of verticals and horizontals (although at the Carter house the 45° angle was also used) with only a limited number of the wooden bars actually touching the window frame.

With the B.J. Ricker house (1911) at 1510 Broad Street at 10th in Grinnell, Iowa, Griffin's more personal career began (figs. 102–3). The forms are solid and heavy, the mass, though horizontals predominate, conveys no sense of lateral movement (as at the Carter house), and the porch and garage are appendages rather than being inseparable extensions of the building itself. The similarities with the Emery house (fig. 29) are striking,

FIG. 102 Walter Burley Griffin. B.J. Ricker house, 1510 Broad Street, Grinnell, Iowa, 1911. Garage added by Barry Byrne. Photo by H.A. Brooks

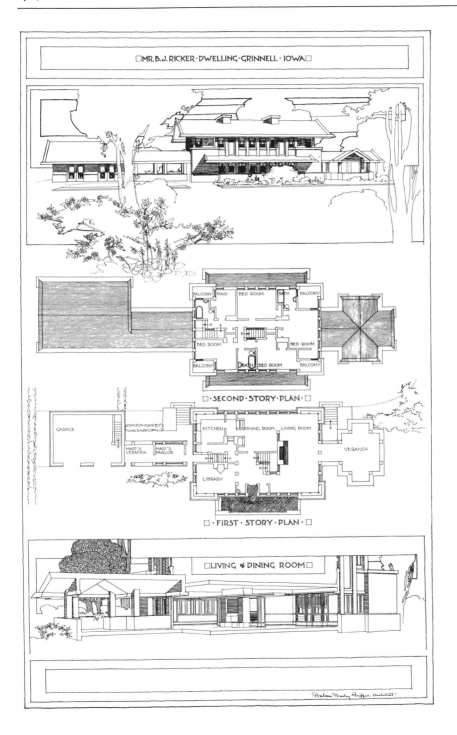

□MR. B.J. RICKER · DWELLING · GRINNELL · IOWA□

□ · SECOND · STORY · PLAN · □

□ · FIRST · STORY · PLAN · □

□LIVING & DINING ROOM□

FIG. 103 Walter Burley Griffin.
B.J. Ricker house. Plan. Courtesy
Northwestern University

FIG. 104 Walter Burley Griffin. Solid
Rock, 82 Essex Road, Kenilworth,
Illinois, 1911. Rendering by Marion
Mahony Griffin. Courtesy North-
western University

especially in the corner piers (which serve as sleeping porches), rows of windows, flaring eaves, and gable roofs, except that in the Ricker house all are lower, heavier, and more solid.[12] The shelf roof over the entrance and general massing also recall the Jenkins, Lewis, Dickinson project of 1906 (fig. 56), further indicating that Griffin was returning to his own past for inspiration. The paired decorative panels are of tile, brick, and plaster, abstract in design, and related to those at the Robert Mueller house. Probably they were designed by Marion Mahony Griffin.

Locally the house is sometimes called 'the Sullivan house,' undoubtedly because of the architect's nearby bank which is the town's chief claim to architectural fame. Yet there is perceptivity in this remark; the Ricker house has that solid and quiet dignity expected of Sullivan, and it is the kind of house one might expect that architect to design.

Spaciousness and freedom of movement typify the interior, where the axial arrangement of the earlier Orth, F.W. Itte, and Sloan houses is rejected in favor of an L-shape relation between the living and dining rooms (fig. 103). Openness exists without destroying the enclosing box. Corner

12 A splendid detail at the Emery and Ricker houses is the attic windows which are slits against the underside of the gable roof. Seen from the outside they make a clear demarcation between the wall and roof; from the inside they convey a marvelous sense of weightlessness, as though the roof were floating rather than pressing down (as at Ronchamps). At the Ricker house there are skylights between the chimney flues, flues which join only near the peak of the roof. Below they spread like an inverted Y so that one walks between the converging flues. But, alas, these details are little appreciated in an attic.

FIG. 105 Walter Burley Griffin. Solid Rock. Photograph showing house before remodeling. *Craftsman* 1913

13 The house was published under three different names, or four if one includes 'Solid Rock.' The original working drawings, dated March 1911, call it the Frank Pallma house (thus the most valid name), the *Western Architect, 18, 9*, September 1912, entitles it the E.L. Springer house, while the *Craftsman, 24*, 1913, 533, merely termed it 'A Monolithic Concrete [sic] Structure.' It is also called the William F. Tempel residence and at the Chicago Architectural Club exhibition of 1910 Griffin entered two projects (#213 and #219) for Tempel, neither of which was illustrated, so it is impossible to identify them. One was called a residence and the other a bungalow; both were listed for Kenilworth. How much should be read into the words 'bungalow' vs. 'residence' is questionable, but as there is a drawing in the Northwestern University collection for a two- to three-storey William F. Tempel 'Dwelling' – which is entirely unrelated to 'Solid Rock' – it is not impossible that the bungalow listed in 1910 was the initial project for Solid Rock. This is important for the date. It means that the design for Solid Rock may have been conceived early in 1910. The fact that the working drawings are dated 8 March 1911 (and these would have been completed only several months after the initial design stage) tends to place the actual design date of the house in 1910.

The occupant's name, according to Barry Byrne, was William F. Tempel,

but Tempel might have bought the house after it was finished instead of building one of his own. When Byrne remodeled the house Tempel was the owner. For Byrne the name Frank Pallma had no significance; perhaps he

was a generous father-in-law or a client who moved away. In any event Solid Rock was the name given to the house when exhibited in 1912, and it seems the most appropriate name of all.

piers confine the interior, and within their depth contain cabinets and bookshelves faced with ornamental leaded glass; thus secluded corner nooks are formed in visual contrast to the rows of windows in between. The double-pitch ceilings (like the underside of a gable roof) of the bedrooms give an amazing sense of spaciousness – weightless like a tent and high above the head.

Construction of the Ricker house began in the spring of 1911 (the design, therefore, may date from late in 1910), but millwork and labor difficulties delayed completion until 1912. The garage, although planned from the start, was added later by Barry Byrne, who redesigned it with the gable facing forward (the plan shows Griffin's arrangement with the roof ridge the same as the house).

More acclimated to the rugged Southwest than to the prairies of the Midwest is Solid Rock, an imposing, almost awesome design (figs. 104–5).[13] The intended material was concrete, but concrete blocks covered with a rough cement plaster were used instead; this therefore, was one of the first instances where he used this material. Details, appropriately, are minimized, with the only overt decoration being I-shaped motifs between the windows and on the corner piers. The severity is intensified by the absence of a traditional roof, although part of the roof terrace is covered with an open trellis, and great flower boxes adorn the corners. The roof, however, leaked, and some years later Byrne remodeled the house by adding a hipped roof, a porch at the front, and, with Alfonzo Iannelli, redecorating the interior. The house is situated at 82 Essex Road, Kenilworth; the working drawings at Northwestern University are dated 8 March 1911.

The plan of Solid Rock is exceptionally efficient for a small, one-storey home. The shape is a truncated T with the entry, corridor, and stairs centralized at the crossing (fig. 104). The bedrooms are isolated and each has corner windows because of the T-shaped plan; the dining, living, and kitchen area is open, yet compact.

Other work by Griffin at this time included the G.B. Cooley house at Monroe, Louisiana, a much larger, more refined version of the Ralph

Griffin house. The original design was exhibited at the Chicago Architectural Club in 1910, but construction was long delayed. For the same town Griffin later designed a clubhouse, the Monroe Club, a project of 1913 that was based on the Niles Club of 1909 but never built.[14] These buildings,

FIG. 106 Willatzen and Byrne. C.H. Clarke house, The Highlands, near Seattle, Washington, 1909. Entrance front, original drawing. Courtesy *Prairie School Review*

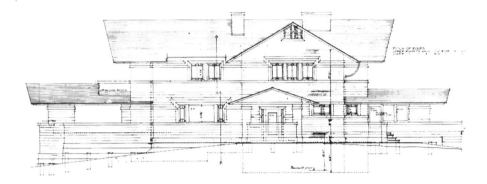

14 For his former Evanston client, Mrs Mary H. Bovee, Griffin built a small beach cottage at Ludington, Michigan (contract for $1076.25 dated 5 May 1911), and also prepared projects, with working drawings, for Dr Karl Stecher of Maywood, Illinois (drawings in Northwestern University collection dated April 1910), and F.P. Marshall of Kenilworth (drawings in Avery Library collection dated July 1910). For Harry E. Gunn he built a house in 1911 important for its progeny, but this will be discussed later.

FIG. 107 Willatzen and Byrne. C.H. Clarke house (old photograph, prior to remodeling)

however, represent the past; it was the Ricker house and Solid Rock that set the stage for Griffin's future.

Griffin's future associate, Byrne, was working in Seattle with Willatzen. The latter had left the Studio in 1906, moved west in 1907, and been joined by Byrne during the winter of 1908–9. Byrne, fresh from Griffin's office and

FIG. 108 Willatzen and Byrne. C.H. Clarke house. Plan. *Country Life in America* 1914

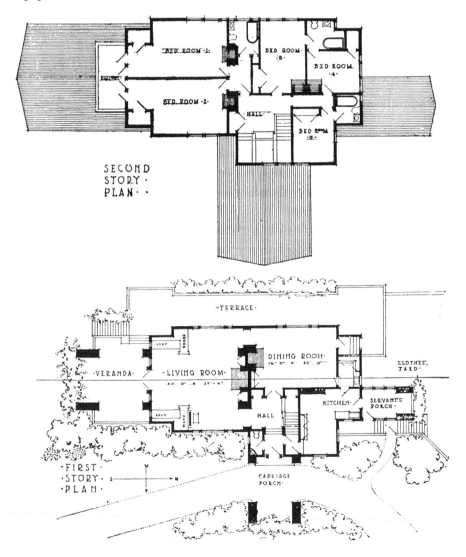

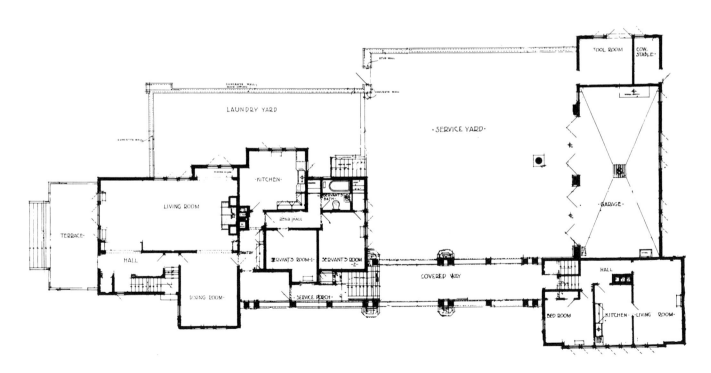

HOUSE·

FIRST FLOOR PLAN

·GARDENERS LODGE·
A·S·KERRY ESQ· OWNER
WILLATZEN & BYRNE
ARCHITECTS

FIG. 109 Willatzen and Byrne. First project: A.S. Kerry house, The Highlands, near Seattle, Washington, 1909. Courtesy *Prairie School Review*

FIG. 110 Willatzen and Byrne. A.S. Kerry house, The Highlands, near Seattle, Washington, 1910–11. Plan. Courtesy *Prairie School Review*

with seven years of experience under Wright, found himself artistically and temperamentally different from Willatzen and after four years, in February 1913, the partnership was dissolved and Byrne departed for California. Exactly what role each played in the firm is difficult to ascertain, especially because they had similar experience under Wright. Stylistic comparison with Byrne's later work is complicated by his intervening experience in California, yet there is a distinct relation between the Willatzen and Byrne designs and those which Byrne did alone after his return to Illinois. One is, therefore, inclined to credit him as the major designer.

The C.H. Clarke house at The Highlands, north of Seattle, was built by Willatzen and Byrne during their first year of partnership (figs. 106–8). Its long gable roof and extending porches present a silhouette typical of the prairies, a horizontality which is emphasized by the wood sheathing, string courses, and the band of plaster under the broadly overhanging roof. As an early work it demonstrates considerable facility in design.

For A.S. Kerry a large home, with grounds landscaped by Olmstead Brothers, was projected for The Highlands in 1909 (fig. 109). The long, varied massing with extensive servants' quarters, service yard, and gardener's lodge, indicated an estate of considerable size, while the design suggests a hybrid between certain midwestern features and the more severe, smooth, plaster-surfaced buildings of the Southwest. To these the design owes its solid, respectful dignity yet the detailing – except for the arch-topped French doors of the living room – is more characteristically midwestern. The casement windows, with dividing piers extending down over

FIG. 111 Willatzen and Byrne. A.S. Kerry house. View from the rear. Frank Calvert ed., *Homes and Gardens of the Pacific Coast* Seattle 1913

the wall, specifically recall Griffin's Philip Itte house of 1908 (fig. 58), which was on the drafting boards during Byrne's brief stay in Griffin's office.

The project was evidently too ambitious. It was resigned in 1910 by reducing in size the living quarters without curtailing the service area. When built in 1911 the main house lacked the grandeur originally intended, yet retained the basic architectural treatment (figs. 110–11). In shape and detail it was more akin to the work of Spencer and Griffin than to Wright, and in compactness and solidity it indicated the direction taken by Byrne a few years later.

Other designs by the firm included the George Matzen house in Seattle, reminiscent of the prairies but more block-like in shape, and a project published in 1910 for a 'Proposed Catholic Church.'[15] The latter is undistinguished architecturally, but interesting as another indication that the designers were conscious of old California architecture; it is also the first of Byrne's life-long series of Catholic churches.

Taylor Wooley also went west, returning to his native Salt Lake City after helping Wright prepare the Wasmuth drawings at Fiesole. He entered the partnership of Miller, Wooley and Evans, where any recollection of his Oak Park years was entirely submerged in the work of the firm. Perhaps one Salt Lake building, however, bears his mark, the Technical High

15 The George Matzen house was published by Robert C. Spencer, Jr in the *Architectural Record*, *33*, 1913, 162. A rendering of the church project appeared in *The Seattle Architectural Club Year Book 1910*, Seattle, 1910, n.p., the author being indebted to James F. O'Gorman for this information.

FIG. 112 Taylor Wooley (?) for Cannon and Fetzer. Technical High School, 264 N. 3rd Street W., Salt Lake City, Utah, 1911. *Brickbuilder* 1917

16 The Salt Lake City Board of Education writes that 'Taylor Wooley was associated with the firm of Miller, Wooley and Evans and was not involved in the design of the [Technical High School] building' (letter dated 26 April 1961).

17 For preliminary projects of the Larkin Building in Buffalo see Grant C. Manson, *Frank Lloyd Wright to 1910*, New York, 1958, p. 148.

18 Published in *A Brick House* (Building Brick Association of America), Boston, 1910, p. 71

School at 264 N. 3rd West which was opened in 1912 and apparently designed in 1911 (fig. 112). The architects were Cannon and Fetzer, and although no documentary evidence exists to support the conclusion, stylistic evidence suggests that Wooley prepared the design – perhaps prior to entering into partnership.[16] The date coincides with his arrival, and the design itself points to an intimate rather than casual knowledge of Wright's work. The source is the Larkin Company Administration Building, imaginatively recast, yet the large pier sculptures recall the heraldic figures represented in Wright's early drawings of the building rather than the atlas figures actually executed by Richard Bock.[17]

The last apprentice to leave the Studio was Van Bergen, who had worked successively for Griffin and Wright, and next entered Drummond's employ where he remained the year between June 1910 and June 1911 while studying for the Illinois licensing examinations, which he passed in 1911. In 1910 he had entered the competition sponsored by the *Brickbuilder* for a $4000 brick house, his published design being a well-studied variant of a prairie house, albeit rather awkwardly drawn.[18]

Drummond left the Studio at an opportune moment. Departing in 1909, prior to Wright's exodus, he went into practice just as clients who otherwise would have solicited Wright were seeking other architects. For Mrs Avery Coonley he built a house and a kindergarten, and on her recommendation

FIG. 113 William E. Drummond. Brookfield Kindergarten, 3601 Forest Avenue, Brookfield, Illinois, 1911. *Western Architect* 1913

Dexter M. Ferry, Jr, her brother, asked Drummond to design a magnificent six-acre estate at Grosse Pointe, Michigan, which, unfortunately, was not built. Thus there was no painful period of building a clientele; work was almost immediately available and some of it on a grand scale.

'Thorncroft' was constructed near the Wright-designed Coonley house at 283 Scottswood Road, Riverside. This stucco and wood frame house had a boldness and stockiness often characteristic of Drummond's designs, while the detailing of the veranda was most inventive. More important, however, was the Brookfield Kindergarten at 3601 Forest Avenue, Brookfield, Illinois, built in 1911 (figs. 113–14). This is the most Wrightian of Drummond's early work and may, therefore, follow some stipulation of the client. The plan is T-shaped with the open wings facing a large fireplace at the head of the T – a plan, incidentally, adapted for Wright's more famous Coonley playhouse at Riverside of 1912. The continuous sweep of unbroken horizontals lends unity to the design, both inside and out, and the dark voids of grouped windows create a striking contrast against the broad areas of stucco walls. The building still stands but is remodeled internally as a house.

Other commissions from this period include the A.W. Muther house

FIG. 114 William E. Drummond. Brookfield Kindergarten. Interior. *Western Architect* 1913

19 'Thorncroft,' the A.W. Muther house, and the C.J. Barr house are all illustrated, with interior views, in the *Western Architect, 21, 2,* February 1915; recent exterior photographs will be found in the *Prairie School Review, 1, 2,* 1964.

(1910) at 560 Edgewood Place, across from Drummond's own River Forest home, and the Charles J. Barr house at 7234 Quick Street in the same town.[19] Similar to the Barr house is the Curtis Yelland house, 37 River Height Road, Mason City, Iowa, of 1911, long unattributed but surely the work of Drummond (fig. 115). The high waisted board and double batten siding is now painted gray and the porch screened, but otherwise the house is in excellent condition. The second-storey windows, set close to the plane of the wall and enclosed in a panel bounded by wood trim, have that stark, bold quality so typical of Drummond's work.

The greatest opportunity of Drummond's life came in 1910 with a magnificent commission to design the lakeshore estate of Dexter M. Ferry, Jr at Grosse Pointe, Michigan. Two alternate schemes were prepared and presented to the client in eleven beautiful renderings in brown ink and colored pencil. For each project there was a plot plan, two perspectives (front and rear), and two floor plans (first and second storey), plus one drawing which served as the title page. It was dated 9 August 1910. Whether the two projects were prepared and presented simultaneously or successively is not known, yet internal evidence suggests that the second

FIG. 115 William E. Drummond. Curtis Yelland house, 37 River Heights Road, Mason City, Iowa, 1911. Photo by H.A. Brooks

FIG. 116 William E. Drummond. First project: Dexter M. Ferry, Jr house, Grosse Pointe, Michigan, 1910. Front elevation. Courtesy W.H. Ferry, photo by Joseph Klima, Jr

FIG. 117 William E. Drummond. Dexter M. Ferry, Jr house. Rear elevation. Courtesy W.H. Ferry, photo by Joseph Klima, Jr

FIG. 118 William E. Drummond. Dexter M. Ferry, Jr house. Plans. Courtesy W.H. Ferry, photo by Joseph Klima, Jr

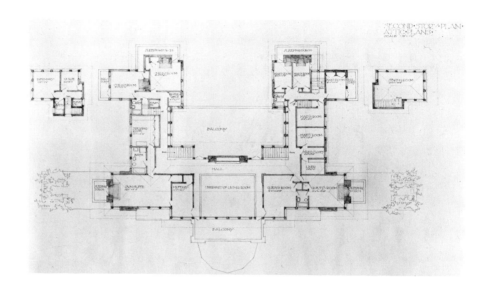

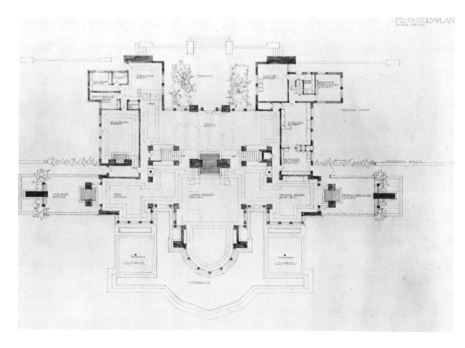

was designed after the first, the later rendering being simply added to the original set of six.[20]

The first project, that dated 9 August 1910, is a brilliant concept (figs. 116–19). Paired towers dominate the symmetrical scheme, and at the center, near the rear of a deep terrace, is the entrance – silhouetted against the massive chimney that stands at the middle of the house. The focus is therefore down and inward, denying the traditional arrangement of a

his initial suggestion was rejected – probably as too grandiose and too un-orthodox. Finally, there is a difference in rendering technique between the projects. The first is done with a lighter, more delicate touch and the trees are more slender and leafy; the perspectives are entirely inked and lightly tinted. They were probably drawn by Mahony. In the second set the inking is not complete, the trees are a mass of foliage, and the colors are strong.

20 The reasons for proposing a different date are these: There are two perspectives on the title page but both represent the same project. The project which lacks a separate title page is for a smaller, much more conservative house and is possibly a compromise scheme offered by the architect after

FIG. 119 William E. Drummond. Dexter M. Ferry, Jr house. Plot plan. Courtesy W.H. Ferry, photo by Joseph Klima, Jr

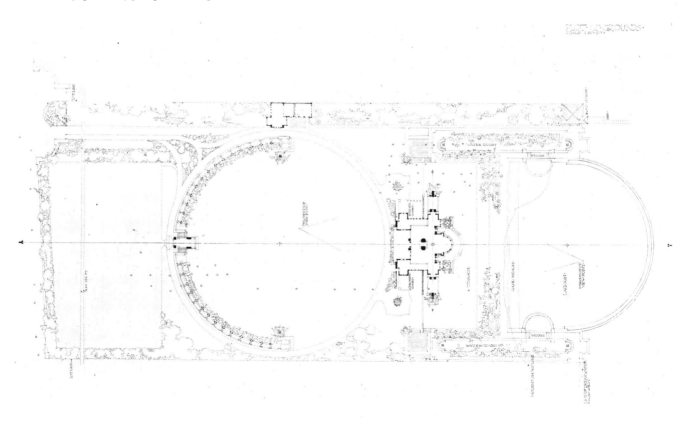

FIG. 120 William E. Drummond. Second project: Dexter M. Ferry, Jr house, Grosse Pointe, Michigan, 1910. Front elevation. Courtesy W.H. Ferry, photo by Joseph Klima, Jr

FIG. 121 William E. Drummond. Dexter M. Ferry, Jr house. Rear elevation. Courtesy W.H. Ferry, photo by Joseph Klima, Jr

high central mass. Horizontals and verticals interpenetrate; poised roofs are pierced by chimneys to create a lively yet balanced sense of order.

The progression of verticals, and the exterior space which they define, leads in toward the entrance. One enters a great hall (17 x 66 feet) which stretches out on either side; covered by skylights, it is like an inside extension of the outside terrace. Opposite the door stands a large, two sided fireplace which is flanked by staircases. By circumambulating the fireplace one enters the living room, two storeys in height and laid out symmetrically with the dining room and den on either side. On axis with the entrance and fireplace a great bay window overlooks the lake. The plan is formal, axial, and bilaterally symmetrical. The order and grandeur of a Beaux-Arts scheme is successfully combined with expressive forms which are as original as they are effective.

FIG. 122 William E. Drummond. Dexter M. Ferry, Jr house. Plan. Courtesy W.H. Ferry, photo by Joseph Klima, Jr

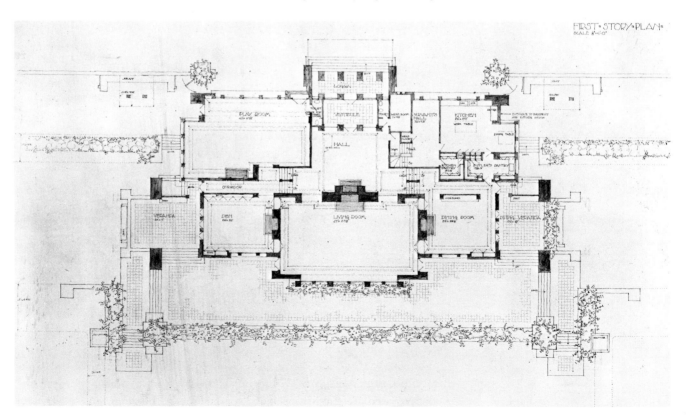

21 Wright's work has understandably influenced this design, yet it has been thoroughly assimilated in an imaginative and personal way. The idea for the twin towers certainly stems from the Mason City hotel, and in the second project the lake front façade bears comparison with the B.J. Westcott house. On the other hand, an admittedly small detail such as perforating the slab roofs (over the lateral terraces) appears first in Wright's 1912 design for the Coonley playhouse but not in his 1911 project; Drummond's design was exhibited at the Chicago Architectural Club in April 1912 and thus was available to Wright.

22 Dexter Ferry's son, W. Hawkins Ferry, writes the author: 'The general concept did not meet with [my father's] approval, so the house was never built. I believe he thought the scheme was too elaborate and impractical. Instead he employed Trowbridge and Ackerman of New York to build his house, which was completed in 1915 and only recently torn down' (letter of 23 August 1965).

The rear or lake-front elevation is less dramatic because the towers and chimneys of the entrance front are largely obscured behind the long, low roof. The symmetrical design is balanced on either side by broad terrace roofs while the center is accentuated by the projecting bay window of the living room.[21]

The second project for Dexter Ferry is related to the first, but is more compact and conservative, less imaginative and personal (figs. 120–2). The entrance front is entirely redesigned with a deep loggia set in the dominating central pavilion. The detailing is busy and not well studied; it lacks the simplicity and integration of the earlier scheme. The lake-front façade, while less changed, lacks repose. The plan has been compartmentalized. The layout is nearly the same, but the rooms are now closed volumes of space; axes and vistas no longer exist. The free-standing fireplace is all that remains, and even that has lost its open-through hearth. One is tempted to conclude, therefore, that this was a compromise project: the heart and soul of the young architect had gone into the first design. It was unappreciated, so, without rethinking the problem, the designer merely altered the existing scheme – making it more compact, replacing the unorthodox façade, and doing away with several extravagances. This design did not win acceptance either; the architect was dismissed and a New York architect hired to build the house.[22] Drummond had lost the greatest opportunity of his career.

Although Drummond, Griffin, Mahony, Wooley, Willatzen, Byrne, and Van Bergen had all at some point worked for Wright, there were others who had received their training elsewhere. Elmslie, as we have seen, was one of these. For some 20 years he worked for Sullivan, his employment dating back into the 1880s when Adler and Sullivan were still busy with the Auditorium Building. His friendship with Purcell began in 1903 when he obtained work for the Cornell graduate in Sullivan's office; from that time onward he occasionally assisted the younger man with designs. In 1909 it became official; Elmslie left Sullivan's inactive office and joined Purcell and his engineer classmate in the firm of Purcell, Feick and Elmslie. This occasioned no real change in the character of the firm's work, as Elmslie's participation was not really new. Their employment then consisted mainly of small houses; not until 1911 did more exciting commissions come in. Yet Purcell and Feick had already built a church and designed two banks, and banks soon became a specialty.

The small Exchange State Bank and Office Building (1910) on Main Street in Grand Meadow, Minnesota, was not a very propitious beginning. Order existed in the simple rectangular block, but not much life and

FIG. 123 Purcell, Feick and Elmslie. First National Bank Building, West Davenport and Stevens Street, Rhinelander, Wisconsin, 1910–11. *Western Architect* 1913

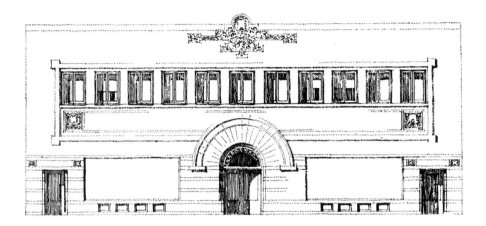

FIG. 124 Purcell, Feick and Elmslie. Project: St Paul's Methodist Episcopal Church, Cedar Rapids, Iowa, 1910. P&E Archives, courtesy David Gebhard

23 This podium scheme derives from the office wing behind the National Farmers' Bank at Owatonna, which Elmslie certainly had something to do with when it was designed.

vitality. More distinguished, however, was the First National Bank Building at Rhinelander, Wisconsin, begun later the same year (fig. 123). Nearly square in plan and occupying a corner site, the building had a recessed banking chamber entered through an imposing central arch. Illumination was admitted by a skylight, and by windows along the side. Rentable store space was thereby made available on the main street, with desirable office space above. The lower storey of cut stone came no higher – except at the archway – than the top of the plate glass windows of the shops, and had the appearance of a base or pedestal.[23] From a distance, therefore, the second storey – which was of brick highlighted with terra cotta ornament – was predominant. This effect was emphasized by a raised brick band that framed the windows and dropped so low as to add apparent size to the height of the second floor – and also to add greater dignity and monumentality to the entire design.

In 1910 the firm entered a closed competition for St Paul's Methodist Episcopal Church at Cedar Rapids, Iowa, with a bold cruciform design that had a square clerestorey rising up through the center (fig. 124). Brick with terra cotta ornament were the intended materials; a separate bell tower was to stand at the side. The award, however, went to Sullivan, who proposed a semicircular church with a rectangular block of Sunday-school rooms behind the altar end. The solution was eminently practical and

FIG. 125 Purcell, Feick and Elmslie. E.L. Powers house, 1635 26th Street W., Minneapolis, 1910. *Western Architect* 1913

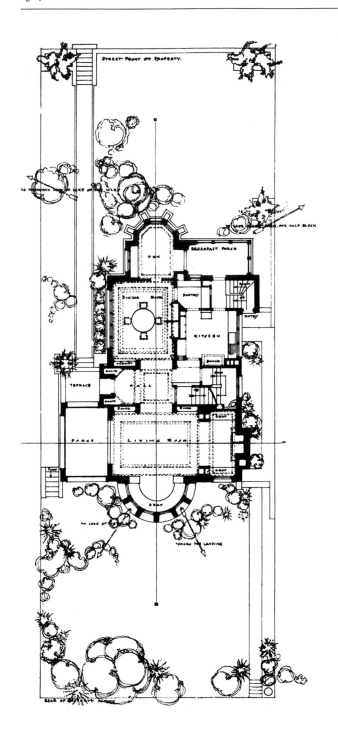

FIG. 126 Purcell, Feick and Elmslie. E.L. Powers house. Plan. *Western Architect* 1913

24 Willard Connely, *Louis Sullivan as he lived*, New York, 1960, pp. 251–2

25 David Gebhard, in the *Journal of the Society of Architectural Historians*, *19*, 1960, 66, says that the preliminary plan for this bank was worked on by Elmslie prior to leaving Sullivan's office. This would explain the similarity in the clerestorey concept between the bank and Purcell, Feick and Elmslie's project for St Paul's church.

Illustrations of Sullivan's bank and church at Cedar Rapids will be found in Hugh Morrison, *Louis Sullivan, Prophet of Modern Architecture*, New York, 1935, plates 75 and 76 and figure 16.

26 Among the smaller houses with basically similar plans built in 1909 or 1910 are the W.E. Baker (Minneapolis), A.B.C. Dodd (Charles City, Iowa), E. Goetzenberger (Minneapolis), H.E. Hineline (Minneapolis), T.W. McCosker, and E.C. Thompson (Bismarck, ND) houses.

For a complete listing of extant Purcell and Elmslie buildings, including street address and comments concerning present state of preservation, see David Gebhard, *A Guide to the Architecture of Purcell and Elmslie*, Roswell Museum and Art Center, Roswell, New Mexico, 1960. This list has been republished in the *Prairie School Review*, 2, 1965, 1.

appropriate – almost like a Roman theater. The curve was expressed on the exterior, with twin stair towers as entryways. Sullivan, however, resigned as architect because of financial disagreements and, as Willard Connely vividly recounts,[24] the church board retained the drawings and gave them to another architect with instructions to use cheaper materials and make minor modifications in the design. This was mishandled and ultimately – just prior to construction – Elmslie revised the drawings to annul the worst injustices to the design (this gratis) and then the church was built.

Simultaneous with his project for St Paul's Church, Sullivan was building in Cedar Rapids the People's Savings Bank. This, his second bank, is a completely different solution from that at Owatonna. A low one-storey structure fronts on the corner of two streets, and rising from its core is the high clerestorey of the central banking chamber. The form follows the space requirements, as numerous offices were needed off the public hall. In spite of these planning advantages, however, the Cedar Rapids bank is no match for its predecessor. The forms are gaunt and somewhat ill-proportioned, and the resulting building is not one of Sullivan's most pleasing designs.[25]

In spite of their activity designing churches and banks, Purcell, Feick and Elmslie were mainly concerned with small houses. These varied considerably in outward appearance, although most were two stories in height with a gable (perhaps crossed) or hipped roof, and with tinted stucco walls and casement windows grouped together but not necessarily symmetrical in arrangement. The plans, however, were sufficiently uniform to categorize the type. Square, or nearly so, with living and dining rooms set at an angle to one another, and with a large central chimney, the type is seen in the now remodeled T.W. McCosker house in Minneapolis of 1909 or the earlier house for Catherine Gray. These examples pre-date Elmslie's official entry into the firm, but the type continued in use for many years and the plans remained pretty much the same, while the elevations became more ordered and symmetrical.[26]

Larger in scale and different in plan is the E.L. Powers house (1910) at 1635 26th Street W., Minneapolis (figs. 125–6). Brick is here combined with stucco as at the earlier Charles Purcell house (1909) by Purcell (fig. 70), but the design lacks the light, thin quality of its predecessor. By comparison it is more solid and heavy and the buttressed forms, including the octagonal and semi-circular windows, recall the Babson and Bradley houses (figs. 78, 80, and 82), thereby suggesting that these characteristics or forms were Elmslie's contribution to the Powers house design. The color and combination of materials, typical of the firm's houses, were described by the partners as of 'greenish-brown texture brick, brown woodwork and a floated surface buff plaster with a decidedly pink tone.'[27] Colors, particularly the warmer ones, were often used to tint the stucco walls.

The plan of the Powers house has an entrance hall at the center with living and dining rooms at either side (fig. 126). The arrangement is common enough in American architecture, but distinctive here is the strong axial order and the openness of the scheme. It was a favored plan for medium sized houses by the firm and was used earlier at the P.E. Byrne and H.P. Gallaher houses (although they are of radically different exterior design) and utilized as late as 1916 in the Louis E. Heitman house at Helena, Montana.

Tallmadge and Watson, like Purcell and Feick, had no experience under Wright. Initially they built mostly houses, but later they developed a specialty in church design where they followed a more traditional course – as at the First Methodist Church in Evanston with its simplified Gothic forms.

FIG. 127 Tallmadge and Watson. H.H. Rockwell house, 629 N. Oak Park Avenue, Oak Park, Illinois, 1910. Photo by H.A. Brooks

27 *Western Architect, 19*, 1, 1913, pl. 8

28 Certain additions have been made to the house which are not shown in the photograph or drawing. The author is indebted to Frank Mezzatesta, owner of the house, for preparing the plan from the original blueprints.

Their houses were less orthodox. Bold but not uncharacteristic was the H.H. Rockwell house of 1910 built at 629 N. Oak Park Avenue in Oak Park (figs. 127–8).[28] The vertical pier-like forms on the façade became the

FIG. 128 Tallmadge and Watson. H.H. Rockwell house. Plan. Courtesy Frank Mezzatesta

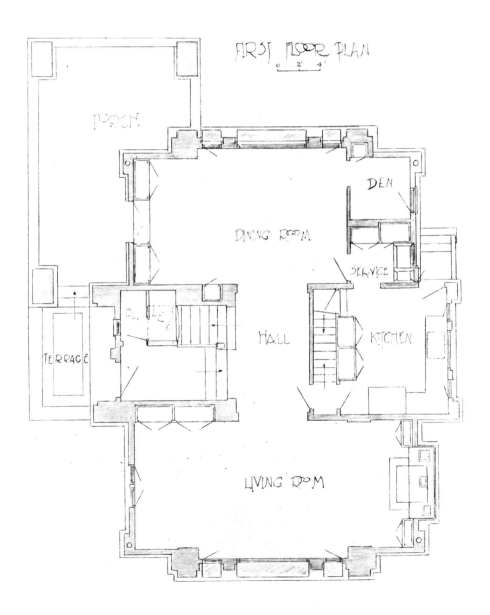

FIG. 129 Nimmons and Fellows. James R. Chapman, 547 Roslyn Road, Kenilworth, Illinois, 1910. Front elevation, detail of entrance, and plans. *Brickbuilder* 1913

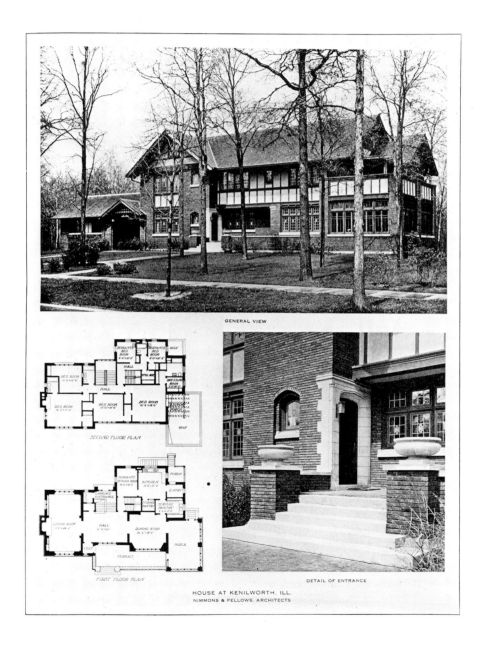

GENERAL VIEW

SECOND FLOOR PLAN

FIRST FLOOR PLAN

DETAIL OF ENTRANCE

HOUSE AT KENILWORTH. ILL.
NIMMONS & FELLOWS. ARCHITECTS

29 Illustrations of the Hauberg and Smith houses will be found in the *Western Architect, 20,* April 1914, an issue devoted to the work of Spencer and Powers. The Hager house is illustrated in the *Western Architect, 18,* July 1912.

dominant theme. They are not, however, without a functional purpose, being hollow ducts which circulate air between attic and cellar – thus, according to the occupants, keeping the house comfortable in the heat of summer.

The narrow end of the Rockwell house faces the street (fig. 127); the longer, more restful elevation turns sideways to utilize the depth of the lot. The rooms – living room, hall, and dining room – are open from front to rear with the entry located mid-way along the side. The exterior is rough stucco tinted gray, the trim is wood, and the high foundations are concrete. Watson was probably primarily responsible for the design.

In 1909 and 1910 Tallmadge and Watson exhibited over twenty buildings at the Chicago Architectural Club. Add to this the work done by other architects, previously discussed, and the number is impressive – for such a restricted period of time. But this production, it should be noted, was largely achieved by those who had recently entered practice; among the former stalwarts from Steinway Hall most, like Perkins, Garden, and Spencer, had sought an alternate course. The brilliant design for the Grover Cleveland Public School of 1909–10 (fig. 54) marked the end, not the beginning, of Perkins' more inventive career. So too with Garden's work as designer in the firm of Richard E. Schmidt, Garden and Martin. The Dwight Building (1911) bespoke the same structural logic, predominant horizontality, and disdain for historicism as the Montgomery Ward Warehouse, but it marked the end of a line. That same year Garden designed what he called a Georgian apartment house for Samuel T. Chase. It was not his first revival design, but from this time onward he did little else.

Actually Perkins and Garden had never renounced historical styles, nor had Spencer. His work had continued to vacillate between English influences and a more independent course, and his 1903 Adams house in Indianapolis (fig. 18) was indicative not of what he rejected but rather of what he ultimately came to accept. The O.J. Hager house at Waukon, Iowa, c. 1910, was a personal design, but more typical of the period were the Mrs J.H. Hauberg house, Rock Island, Illinois, 1909–10, and the Fred B. Smith house, Allendale, Indiana, 1910, with their strong Anglicized tendencies.[29] In spite of his personal inclinations, however, Spencer as author remained sympathetic to the Prairie School and continued to publicize their work.

One design of 1910 clearly indicates what was occurring – that is the James R. Chapman house at 547 Roslyn Road, Kenilworth, Illinois, by Nimmons and Fellows (fig. 129). We may ask: is it inspired by Tudor Gothic design, or a work more characteristic of the Prairie School? One can argue either way; the distinction is not precise. The favored materials of the Prairie School are here, brick with raked horizontal joints and plaster with wood trim. The build-up of gable roofs, including the cross gable, is also typical as are the casement windows, arranged in rows, with leading in the glass. Brick piers accentuate the corners; there are even flower urns at the entry. Despite all this, the design *is* basically Tudor; only the plan has no essential similarity with the work of the Prairie School. There is, therefore, something foreboding in the Chapman house design, a demonstration of how easily the prairie architects could slip into a traditional guise. With Spencer's work this is what had happened.

So too in England. The more unorthodox work of Baillie Scott, Voysey, and Ashbee had already given way to greater conformity with the norm, and Ashbee could still write – partly in retrospection – 'The "School of the Middle West" and we architects of the arts and crafts movement in England are working toward the same goal ... '[30] That he felt in continuing sympathy with midwest work, in view of what has just been said, is entirely understandable. But Ashbee's visit to the Midwest in 1908, which occasioned these remarks, injected no new impetus into the Arts and Crafts Movement. On the contrary, a check of the Chicago Architectural Club catalogues indicates that the current favorite was the American Academy in Rome. In 1911 it sent 75 exhibits to Chicago and was featured in the catalogue by an article discussing its history and objectives.

Nor was the waning Arts and Crafts Movement aided by Gustav Stickley's appalling confession of 1910. Under pressure from his readers, Stickley admitted he was guilty of deception – he had never built the Craftsman Houses which he designed and published, and therefore had never realized their grievous faults. This indiscretion was bad enough, but shortly thereafter Stickley also acknowledged that the Craftsman Houses which he advertised as being inexpensive were in fact more expensive to build than comparable homes. The cheapest, he confirmed, cost $3000–$5000 with the price more likely to reach $6000–$8000.[31] This admission came as the *Craftsman*'s circulation reached its peak – approaching 60,000 – from which figure it soon began to retreat.

The really significant publication of 1910, of course, was *Ausgehührte Bauten und Entwürfe von Frank Lloyd Wright*; it altered the course of European design. Yet at home it hardly caused a ripple. Admittedly Wright's designs were already well known, but it is unfortunate that this splendid work should attract so little midwest notice. Only the *Architectural Record* published a worthy review, that by the noted critic Mont-

30 C.R. Ashbee, 'Man and the Machine,' *House Beautiful*, 28, 1910, 56

31 *Craftsman*, 17, 1910, 430, 683. For a discussion of the financial collapse of Stickley's Craftsman empire see John Crosby Freeman, *The Forgotten Rebel, Gustav Stickley and his Craftsman Mission Furniture*, Watkins Glen, NY, 1966.

32 Montgomery Schuyler, 'An Architectural Pioneer: Review of the Portfolios Containing the Work of Frank Lloyd Wright,' *Architectural Record*, *31*, 1912, 427–35, quotation from p. 435

33 McLean wrote an article, full of insight, about Richardson, Sullivan, Root, and others in the *Inland Architect and News Record* (vol. *28*, #6) of 1897.

34 'A Departure from the Classical Tradition,' *Architectural Record*, *20*, 1911, 326–38

gomery Schuyler, whose nine-page discourse on the work of Wright revealed an author of two minds. He realized, on the one hand, that Wright was a great designer, or at least had that potential. Yet he was displeased with Wright's recorded progress and believed that Wright had not yet reached maturity as an architect. Although he did not say it, one senses that Schuyler's concern was over ornament – without such ornament as Sullivan would supply, Wright's architecture was too severe. Schuyler wrote: 'The stark unmodelled transitions [in the designs] give an air of something rude, incomplete, unfinished. The buildings seem "blocked out," and awaiting completion rather than completed.'[32] This 'deficiency' the reviewer ascribed to 'lusty growth' of a style which still awaited maturity.

That Wright's monograph was slighted by the midwest architectural press comes as no surprise. Since 1900, when his work *had* reached maturity, his designs – and to a lesser extent those of the entire Prairie School – had been excluded from the two midwestern architectural journals. Robert Craik McLean, editor of the *Inland Architect and News Record*, had enthusiastically supported Sullivan and the other architects of the Chicago School,[33] yet Wright and his contemporaries were ignored. The completeness of this exclusion suggests that animosity, and not mere disapproval of designs, was the underlying reason.

The second journal was the *Western Architect*, founded in 1902 and published by Edward A. Purdy in Minneapolis. Although avowedly dedicated to midwest architecture, the editor sought to appease his eastern advertisers by publishing eastern-style architecture as found in the Midwest; the Prairie School, it seems, did not exist, and the Chicago School, by 1902, was sufficiently passé to be forgotten.

In 1905 McLean left the *Inland Architect and News Record* (which ceased publication in 1908) to become editor, under Purdy, of the *Western Architect*. Editorially both men agreed concerning the Prairie School. That 'style' was not their criteria for exclusion may be inferred from the fact that Greene and Greene and Irving Gill in California were being published by 1908, but not their midwest counterparts.

In November 1911 the situation came unexpectedly to a head. Editorially the *Western Architect* lashed out against Wright. The pretext was flimsy and obviously contrived. The *Architectural Record* had published a fascinating article comparing Sullivan's Babson house with Wright's Coonley house, an ideal contrast because both houses were contemporary, of nearly equal size, and built close to one another in Riverside, Illinois.[34] Choosing the rather unorthodox procedure of writing an article to 'review' an article in another magazine, the *Western Architect* – under the suggestively biased title of 'A Comparison of Master and Pupil Seen in Two Houses' – completely falsified its representation of what had been said. It reported that 'between the lines' in the *Architectural Record* one could read that 'the house by Mr Wright ... is practically a freak.'[35] The writer (probably McLean) concluded that 'None have gone so far into the realm of the picturesque, or failed so signally in the production of livable houses as Frank Lloyd Wright.'[36]

But Purdy and McLean had misjudged their readers; the reaction was lightning swift. Although no letters to the editor were published, the next issue – December 1911 – outdid itself in superficial praise of Wright, but underneath there was reserve. By devoting the lead article, profusely illustrated, to Wright's City National Bank at Mason City, the editor was able to break the ten-year silence because to praise a bank required no retraction of what was said about a house the month before.

However, the storm did not abate; Purdy next removed editor McLean (only temporarily, it turned out). He then consulted Purcell who, always an author at heart, was quick to respond with advice and help. Soon the *Western Architect* began to change until by 1915 some 50 per cent of its pages were devoted to the Prairie School. At last the group had won midwestern recognition.

Purcell's influence became apparent in 1912. H.P. Berlage, for whom Purcell had arranged an American lecture tour (which began in October 1911),[37] contributed to three issues beginning in August 1912.[38] The same year Purcell wrote an article about Griffin, and Griffin wrote about the 'Commonwealth of Australia Federal Capitol Competition.' In January 1913 the entire issue was devoted to the work of Purcell, Feick and Elmslie, the architects themselves writing the text, arranging the layout, and devising the border decorations (designed by Elmslie). In 1914 one monograph issue went to Maher and another to Spencer and Powers – with part of the text written by Purcell. And in 1915 five of the monthly issues were devoted to the architects of the Prairie School: January to Purcell and Elmslie, February to Guenzel and Drummond, April to Van Bergen, July to Purcell and Elmslie (their third),[39] and December to Tallmadge and Watson. In addition to these special issues the *Western Architect* regularly published one or more buildings by various prairie architects – a policy which continued for many years.[40] One architect, however, was never accorded a

35 'A Comparison of Master and Pupil Seen in Two Houses,' *Western Architect, 17*, 1911, 95

36 Ibid.

37 Regarding this tour see Leonard K. Eaton, 'Sullivan and Berlage,' *Progressive Architecture, 37*, 1956, 138–41 ff.

38 H.P. Berlage, 'Art and the Community,' *Western Architect, 18*, 1912, 85–89, and a fascinating theoretical discussion by Berlage entitled 'Foundations and Development of Architecture,' which was published in two successive issues of the *Western Architect, 18*, 1912, 96–9 and 104–8.

39 The three issues devoted to Purcell and Elmslie have been reissued by the Prairie School Press as a single book with an introduction by David Gebhard (*The Work of Purcell and Elmslie, Architects*, Park Forest, 1965).

40 Barry Byrne, who lacked sufficient oeuvre for publication in 1915, had his work presented in February 1925 with some of his residential designs also illustrated the previous March (volumes 34 and 33 respectively).

monograph issue of the *Western Architect*: Wright. Obviously the old animosity was not dead.

In retrospect, therefore, the aftermath of Wright's departure provided few of the potential pitfalls and dangers that were expected – and are by some still thought to have occurred. Difficulties were surmounted; the movement did not collapse. Nor did it suffer depletion in its ranks – for each that fell aside several took his place. Productivity increased, as did the quality of the work. Wright's designs continued as a principal source of inspiration, but there was increasing independence and the beginnings of several strongly personal expressions. Griffin's was most notable, its transition clearly recorded in the Ricker and Solid Rock designs of 1911. Marion Mahony, who that year became his wife, had her one real fling as a nearly independent designer, producing several highly personal works under the guise of von Holst. Drummond, practicing alone, prepared his masterpiece in the project for Dexter Ferry but, alas, a project it remained. Byrne, working in far-off Seattle with Willatzen, was defining what later became the characteristics of his style. And as the Oak Park Studio closed, Elmslie left Sullivan to join Purcell in what became the single most important firm within the Prairie School.

The period about 1910 was thus a turning point, but not a retrogression. It was the moment before fulfillment as the school proved itself – showing its strength, growing independence, and power of expansion. The stage was being set for a great leap forward, for the consolidation and confirmation of what now seemed so close at hand.

At last, but only after surmounting obstacles primarily associated with Wright, the group obtained a voice, and a strong one too, in the midwest architectural press. The *Western Architect*, after its belated conversion of 1911, served to publicize the school at its strongest, most vital moment, and to record it for posterity.

Wright's departure from Oak Park (judged in its short-term effect) proved a favorable factor in the unfolding history of the Prairie School. It strengthened the hand of those he left behind, taught them to stand alone, and prepared them for the final pre-war years – the most prosperous and prestigious years of all.

DIVERSITY, DECENTRALIZATION, AND THE FINAL FULFILLMENT

The most significant years for the Prairie School were 1912–14, years made memorable by the quality, quantity, and diversity of the work produced. The greatest number of architects was then practicing, fifteen or more in all, only a few of whom had been vital contributors a decade before. Wright, Sullivan, and Maher (the latter always somewhat on the sidelines) were still active, although Garden, Perkins, and Spencer were not. Others, notably Byrne, Drummond, Elmslie, Griffin, Mahony, Purcell, Tallmadge, and Watson, had been students or apprentices ten years before, while the youngest men – Percy Dwight Bentley, Parker Berry, Francis C. Sullivan, and John S. Van Bergen – had not begun their training, and only about 1912 did they begin to practice.

Wright was executing relatively few commissions, a fact partly obscured by the size or importance of those he completed, such as the Coonley play-

1 The work of the Prairie School, as well as its influence, was not entirely limited to the Midwest. Wright's activities were widely scattered, Purcell and Elmslie built houses from California to Massachusetts and planned projects for China and Australia, Byrne built in Washington and New Mexico, Griffin in Louisiana, Australia, and India, Maher in California, New Jersey, and Ontario, and Francis Sullivan from Manitoba to Quebec. Taylor Wooley, as previously noted, settled in Salt Lake City, and Andrew Willatzen in Seattle. R.M. Schindler, after a brief sojourn with Wright, migrated to California where Wright's two sons, Lloyd and John, were also practicing; if this book were more encompassing, the work of these men would be considered in some detail. (A monograph on Schindler by David Gebhard will soon be published; Gebhard is also preparing an exhibition of Lloyd Wright's work.) F.D. and C.J. Wolfe in southern California came under the influence of the Prairie School, as did Bugenhagen and Turnbull in Saskatoon, Saskatchewan, and Antonin Nechodoma in far-off San Juan, Puerto Rico. His William Korber house, now a synagogue, is based on Wright's 1903 Dana house as perhaps known through the Wasmuth folio. Trost and Trost in Tucson, Arizona, and later El Paso, Texas, have recently been the subject of study, especially by Marcus Whiffin (*American Architecture Since 1780: A Guide to the Styles*, Cambridge, Mass., 1969), by Lloyd C. Engel-

house, the Imperial Hotel, and Midway Gardens – but none of these, it should be noted, were houses. While his own work was tapering off, that of the other Prairie School architects was increasing. They, not he, were receiving the major publicity in professional journals and they, not he, were awarded the lion's share of new commissions. Although still identified as a fountainhead, he was no longer in the forefront, and events were beginning to pass him by. The influence of his earlier work (rather than his current work) was still great, yet Griffin, Drummond, and Purcell and Elmslie were beginning to exert an influence of their own.

Increasingly important at this time was the decentralization of the movement. This resulted largely from a cultural time-lag during which ideas that initially won acceptance in suburban Chicago spread outward – usually westward. No longer were Chicago's suburbs the greatest source of new commissions, but rather the small towns of the Midwest, those Minnesota, Iowa, and Wisconsin towns immortalized by Sinclair Lewis in *Main Street*. Their place names were rich and descriptive, and often suggested the importance of water – as Eau Claire, Jump River, Cedar Rapids, Fountain City – or the splendid legacy of Indian names – Owatonna, Sioux City, Keokuk, Winona, and Lake Minnetonka – or, occasionally, the name of an early settler – Adams, Mitchel, or Le Roy. None of these, we should note, indicate a romantic yearning for another time or place; they are names of the moment, free and independent of the past. How different from upper New York state – Troy, Rome, Ithaca, Utica, Attica, Syracuse – with its accompanying classical revival architecture, or further east in New England – Boston, Cambridge, Portsmouth, New Haven, New London – with its early architectural dependence on the mother country. The young Midwest, initially without cultural servitude, was what the Prairie School depended on.[1]

Typical of these midwestern centers was Winona, Minnesota, a one-time mill and lumbering community which became, after the depletion of the forests, a manufacturing site and center for the surrounding agricultural district. Situated on the west bank of the Mississippi, and also connected with the outside world by rail, the business of this town was carried on through several rival banks. In 1907 Purcell and Feick had prepared a project for the First National Bank, cubic in form with great engaged piers

brecht ('Henry Trost: The Prairie School in the Southwest,' *Prairie School Review*, 6, 4, 1969, 5–29), and in the

unpublished researches of Gorden Heck. It is evident, therefore, that much research still needs to be done.

rising to support the thin slabs of the roof (fig. 77). The scheme was eminently appropriate, yet rejected by the directors who wanted, and from
another architect obtained, a classical design.

The firm, soon augmented by Elmslie's able hand, *did* build a bank in
Winona, this in 1911 for the rival Merchants Bank, where no committee
appeasement was required. William P. Tearse, president, gave the architects a free hand. The result was a brilliant design, one largely determined

FIG. 130 Purcell, Feick and Elmslie. Merchants Bank of Winona, Third and Lafayette, Winona, Minnesota, 1911–12. P&E Archives, courtesy David Gebhard

by the space-enclosing steel frame which supported the great multicolored walls of glass (figs. 130–2). This frame, with its broad metal spandrels across the top, was sheathed in brick – the verticals and horizontals of these piers and lintels establishing an abstract interplay of forms that was in itself dramatic. The enclosure read as four superimposed planes: the most deeply recessed was the glass screen, further forward was a one-storey wall (adjusted to human scale) with its entrance and small office windows, then

FIG. 132 Purcell, Feick and Elmslie. Merchants Bank of Winona. Interior. *Western Architect* 1915

FIG. 131 Purcell, Feick and Elmslie. Merchants Bank of Winona. Detail of corner. *Western Architect* 1915

FIG. 133 George W. Maher. J.R. Watkins Medical Company, Administration Building, Winona, Minnesota, 1911. Photo by H.A. Brooks

FIG. 134 George W. Maher. Winona Savings Bank, Winona, Minnesota, 1914. Photo by H.A. Brooks

2 The Administration Building was extensively illustrated in the *Western Architect*, 20, March 1914. Lamp standards similar to those in front of the Northwestern University Gymnasium originally stood in front of the building. Maher built several buildings for the J.R. Watkins Co. in other cities, with the biggest concentrations being in Memphis, where the firm had extensive operations.

the monumental corner piers and, finally, the almost free-standing paired piers which support the broad steel core lintels. The precision and clarity is striking. It is a dynamic design, springing from the earth, and thus radically different from Sullivan's bank at Owatonna with its static, cohesive shell of brick resting high upon a pedestal (fig. 75).

Ornament was important to Purcell and Elmslie and often was incorporated in their buildings. It served to accentuate major features such as the entrance or a prominent window, or it might emphasize a structural member such as the corner piers at the Winona bank (fig. 131). The designs, inevitably by Elmslie, were inspired by the concept of organic growth, but often they lack the vitality and spontaneity characteristic of his best work under Sullivan. For houses the ornament was usually sawed or carved in wood or stenciled on plaster; in masonry buildings it was normally of terra cotta as here at the bank where its tan color is reiterated by the raked-joint Roman brick and stone sills and coping. The only exterior color contrast exists in the mottled blue-green glass. This color scheme is repeated on the interior, where the same Roman brick is combined with tinted plaster (fig. 132). Veined marble, oak, and dull bronze are used for the desks, counters, and tellers' windows which, in their simple linear design, contrast sharply with Sullivan's more sensuous forms (fig. 76). Opposite the window-walls are two scenic murals by Albert Fleming. The interior of this splendid banking chamber still retains much of its original character.

The largest single manufacturer in Winona was the J.R. Watkins Medical Company, producer of patent medicines which were peddled from door to door. In 1911 Maher designed for them an Administration Building, and in 1913 added a ten-storey Manufacturing Building at the rear (fig. 133).[2] The earlier building recalls those at Northwestern; the plan is an imposing, axial Beaux-Arts scheme. Three great pavilions are united by glazed galleries, the floor inside being ranged with desks for the clerical staff. The central, or entrance, pavilion is crowned by a dome, and a cool gray tonality is established by the smooth marble surface of the exterior.

The Winona Savings Bank, which was controlled by the Watkins Company through an interlocking directorship, commissioned Maher in 1914 to design a bank. Planned as a long, two-wing building to accommodate the dual functions of a savings and a national bank, it was symbolically linked by common offices at the middle (fig. 134). As described by Maher, 'The center is monumentalized by a pylon treatment heroic in scale and representing strength and conservatism ... [and] the large exterior wall surfaces typify strength and solidity, necessary for a monumental building.'[3] The monolithic columns, 37 feet high and each weighing 32 tons, were of North Carolina granite; the ornamental motif was the American lotus plant. The interior was plain yet rich in its materials. Polished marbles from Greece and Italy veneered the walls, floors, and counters, and the window glass, bronze fixtures, and other fittings were by Tiffany of New York.

The design, like that of the Watkins Administration Building, was atypical of the Prairie School; it rather exemplified Maher's personal search for an independent expression, one based on a synthesis (not unlike Viollet-le-Duc's method) which was closer in spirit to the work of Olbrich and Hoffmann in Vienna. The result, while a laudable effort, did not result in works of great distinction.

Concurrent with their work at Winona, Purcell, Feick and Elmslie designed their best-known house, the shingled Harold C. Bradley bungalow on the Crane Estate at Woods Hole, Massachusetts.[4] The plans were

3 *Architectural Record, 41*, 1917, 38. This reference is part of an article (pp. 36–50) by Peter B. Wight in which the bank is profusely illustrated.

4 The term bungalow is contemporary with the design and signified that it was a summer residence and not intended for year round use. Such usage was common in late nineteenth-century New England. The word also served to distinguish this dwelling from the Bradley house at Madison.

FIG. 135 Purcell, Feick and Elmslie. Harold C. Bradley bungalow. Crane Estate. Woods Hole, Massachusetts, 1911–12. Photo by Frank R. Sweet

FIG. 136 Purcell, Feick and Elmslie. Harold C. Bradley bungalow. Plan. *Western Architect* 1913

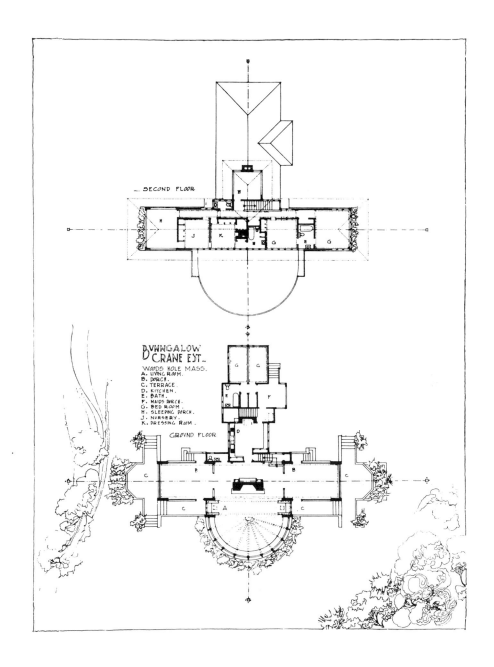

drawn in 1911–12 with construction completed the following year. The site was a high, grass-covered peninsula jutting out into the sea, a dramatic setting fully exploited by the splendid design (figs. 135–7). The semi-circular living room crowns the knoll, thus commanding a spectacular view

FIG. 137 Purcell, Feick and Elmslie. Harold C. Bradley bungalow. Detail of woodwork in living room. P&E Archives, courtesy David Gebhard

FIG. 138 Purcell, Feick and Elmslie. Edward W. Decker house, Holdridge, Lake Minnetonka, Minnesota, 1912–13. P&E Archives (c. 1913), courtesy David Gebhard

FIG. 139 Purcell, Feick and Elmslie. Edward W. Decker house. Side view and service buildings. *Architectural Record* 1915

of the shoreline; the horizontal sweep of the elevated bedrooms makes them appear to hover, almost like a sea gull, above the point of land (this effect is now somewhat dulled by the glazing of the originally open porches underneath). The broad, continuous surfaces, the interplay of solids and voids, and the imposing order and symmetry of the design, make this one of the most outstanding works by the firm.

The cruciform plan is bilaterally symmetrical with its dominant axis passing behind the chimney and linking the lateral porches; the living room extends forward, locked into position by a massive brick fireplace – its great arched opening echoing the shape of the room. Wood prevails throughout the interior, with beams, purlins, and rafters exposed. The casement windows are set in rows and glazed with leaded glass; sawed decorative panels abut the beams.

The majestic Edward W. Decker house at Lake Minnetonka, Minnesota (1912–13) is a further development of the Bradley scheme (figs. 138–41). With its long hipped roof, raised to command the view, rows of casement windows, and semi-circular extension of the living room, this house on the hill clearly indicates its parentage. Yet the exterior materials have changed – brick below and smooth plaster under the broad eaves – and the layout

FIG. 140 Purcell, Feick and Elmslie. Edward W. Decker house. Dining room. *Western Architect* 1915

FIG. 141 Purcell, Feick and Elmslie.
Edward W. Decker house. Plan.
Architectural Record 1915

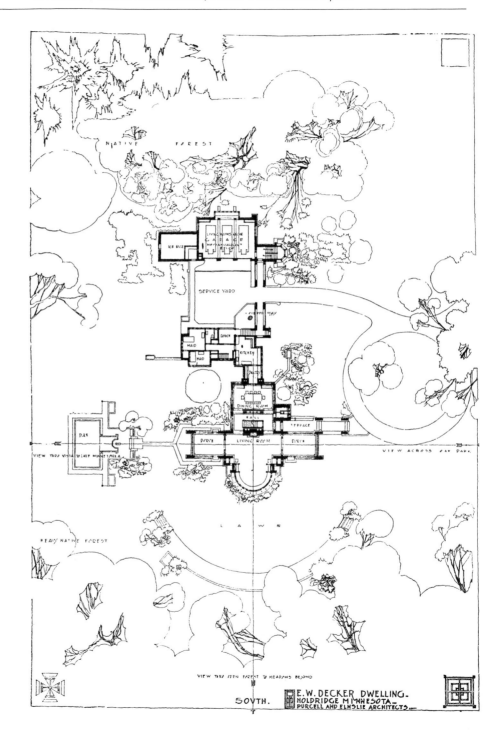

is modified to permit greater accommodation. It differs from the earlier Steven and Bradley plans because the chimney mass has been moved back from the lateral axis to create a large, multi-purpose living area with the dining room behind. A service wing, attached at the rear, surrounds a service yard with the garage and caretaker's lodge situated opposite the kitchen and servants' quarters. These are on the down-slope, thus creating a lower, less dominant silhouette as the various wings cascade down the hill (fig. 139). It is from the side that one approaches the building so that the entire sweep of this extensive complex is seen before reaching the entrance. Steel was incorporated in the structure to make possible the dramatic cantilever, and concrete was used extensively. Yet these materials did not find expression in the design, a characteristic previously noted with regard to the Prairie School.

The architects designed many of the furnishings, including the dining room set which repeats the long lines and abrupt angles of the architecture (fig. 140). Boards and battens sheath the walls, at the top of which is Elmslie's stenciled frieze. This magnificent house was willfully demolished when later owners wanted the site for a so-called traditional house; only the service wing was spared.

Another variant of the Bradley-Decker designs was the E.S. Hoyt house, 300 Hill Street, Red Wing, Minnesota, of 1913 (fig. 142). Spread across a broad, sloping lot overlooking the town, the house seems to lift itself almost clear of the ground in order to improve the view. The central upper section projects slightly forward, supported by two brick piers, giving a sense of lightness and vitality to the design. The sleeping porch (now cheaply glazed, as is the porch beneath it) is partly cantilevered on great carved beams; the materials are a deep red brick for the lower storey with red-tinted plaster above. A heavy, exposed wood sill serves as a clear line of demarcation. Horizontality is further emphasized by the low pitched roof and the bands of casement windows, the casements white, and the glazing ornamented with colored leaded glass. The Hoyt house plan differs radically from its predecessors as the living and dining rooms both face the downhill view. Separated by a fireplace they share the row of windows which are set back under the projecting section of the second floor. The kitchen, service, and entry areas are located at the rear in the off-center stem of the ⊤-shape plan. A covered walkway and garage were added by the architects in 1915. This fine house remains in excellent condition, both inside and out.

The most brilliant spatial planning achieved by the firm was at the 1913

FIG. 142 Purcell, Feick and Elmslie. E.S. Hoyt house, 300 Hill Street, Red Wing, Minnesota, 1913. Photo by H.A. Brooks

FIG. 143 Purcell, Feick and Elmslie. Edna S. (or William) Purcell house, 2328 Lake Place, Minneapolis, Minnesota, 1913. P&E Archives, courtesy David Gebhard

Edna S. Purcell house, 2328 Lake Place, Minneapolis, a relatively small house initially occupied by William Purcell (figs. 143–6).[5] Situated on a deep, narrow lot, the plan is organized on a single axis and open from end

FIG. 144 Purcell, Feick and Elmslie. Edna S. (or William) Purcell house. Writing nook. P&E photo

[5] The house was sold to the Cutts family when Purcell moved to Pennsylvania during the war. It has long been maintained by them in perfect condition.

to end. Variety is introduced by varying the floor level, but not the ceiling height, and by expanding and restricting the width. Openness and intimacy are ingeniously combined. The high-ceiling living room nestles below ground level, with its window wall of glass overlooking the garden and pool at the front. The dining room, its pointed prow jutting into the room below, is a half storey above the living room which it overlooks. Yet visual privacy is maintained; when one stands in the living room, or sits in the dining room, the people and furnishings in the adjacent room are screened

FIG. 145 Purcell, Feick and Elmslie. Edna S. (or William) Purcell house. Entry area from dining room. *Western Architect* 1915

from view. Only the ceiling and upper walls of the other room are visible. From the dining room the direct view is over the living room and out through the end wall of glass. Continuing this axis to the rear, there is a short passageway that connects the dining room to a porch overlooking a distant lake. Between the level of the two principal rooms, and situated at their side, is the entry with steps leading up and down. Behind, and to the rear, is the kitchen.

The furnishings and numerous ornamental details were designed by Elmslie to produce a unified, harmonious whole. This is most evident in the ingeniously designed writing nook, a space carved from the corner of the living room where it joins the low dividing wall of the dining room; the common ceiling is seen overhead with its continuous stenciled frieze (fig. 144). The verticals, horizontals, and pointed forms found in the furniture are repeated in the leaded glass of the bookcase doors, and in turn echo similar forms in the house, such as the sharp prow butting into the living room and the tent-shaped ceiling. The wood trim is stained, not painted, and the plaster walls and ceiling are a sandy yellow-brown hue. The embroidery was executed by Louise Elmslie from George Elmslie's design and the curtains were worked by Mrs Edna S. Purcell. The statue was by Richard Bock and the fireplace mural (not visible) was painted by Charles Livingston Bull. George M. Niedecken of Milwaukee built the furniture.

FIG. 146 Purcell, Feick and Elmslie. Edna S. (or William) Purcell house. Plan. P&E Archives, courtesy David Gebhard

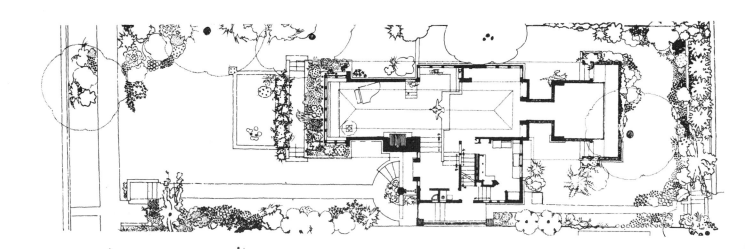

FIG. 147 Purcell and Elmslie. C.T. Bachus house, 212 W. 36th Street, Minneapolis, Minnesota, 1915. Photo by H.A. Brooks

FIG. 148 Purcell, Feick and Elmslie. Ward Beebe house, 2022 Summit Avenue, St Paul, Minnesota, 1912. Plan. *Western Architect* 1913

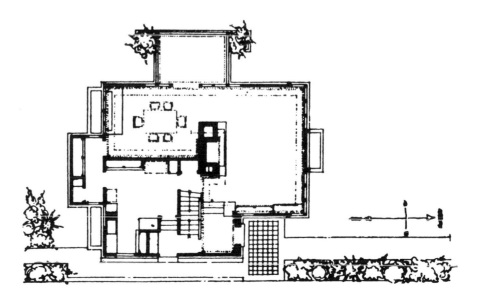

FIG. 149 Purcell, Feick and Elmslie. Ward Beebe house. Photo by H.A. Brooks

FIG. 150 Purcell, Feick and Elmslie. Harry S. Parker house, 4829 Colfax Avenue S., Minneapolis, 1912–13. P&E Archives, courtesy David Gebhard

6 The Owre house (1911) is located at 2625 Newton Avenue S., Minneapolis, the Beebe house (1912) at 2022 Summit Avenue, St Paul, and the Bachus house (1915) at 212 W. 36th Street, Minneapolis.

The Owre house, except for enclosing the porches, remains in its original condition as does the Beebe house where, however, the exterior stucco has been painted white and the wood trim dark. This destroys the intended harmonious color scheme of the exterior surfaces and has the unfortunate effect of making the windows and their casements look like dark holes against the white walls. The Bachus house has long remained in near perfect condition both inside and out. The original tinted plaster (a light rose, almost orange, tone), stained wood trim, and white window casements have not been touched; the resulting tonal relations are clearly evident even in a black-and-white photograph (see fig. 147).

Exterior details were designed with the same loving care. Unnoticed from a distance, they offer a rich variety of visual enjoyment when seen closer. There is the carved beam end at the entrance, the slender piers set between each of the large front windows, and the stenciled frieze under the eave. Yet the total exterior effect is that of a direct, almost harsh design due to the emphatic, flush-to-the-cornice second-storey wall which is abruptly severed by the chimney mass. A broader, more obvious roof – as at the Hoyt house – would have softened the appearance by creating a shadow line at that point. The unplaned, stained woodwork bears the rotary marks of the miller's saw, while the tinted plaster repeats the interior color scheme.

In 1913 George Feick, Jr left the firm. His participation the previous two years had been nominal, and never had he played a decisive role. Trained as an engineer, he returned to his native Ohio and his father's construction business. The firm, known as Purcell, Feick and Elmslie from 1909 to 1913, became simply Purcell and Elmslie – or P&E as they called themselves – until dissolved in 1922. As a convenience, however, the name Purcell and Elmslie is often applied to the entire period after 1909.

Elmslie, after joining the firm in 1909, moved to Minneapolis, but in 1912 returned to Chicago and opened an office of which he remained in charge. The drafting and supervision continued to be done in Minneapolis with Fred A. Strauel (who joined the staff in 1913) as chief draftsman; he continued to draft for the principals even after the dissolution of the firm. Purcell, always the inveterate traveler, co-ordinated the diverse activities and, during the war, did so from Philadelphia, where he was advertising manager (and a design consultant) for Alexander Brothers, prior to their bankruptcy in 1919. This strenuous life, however, led to a deterioration in his health, so in 1920 Purcell moved to Portland, Oregon, and entered semi-retirement. In spite of – or because of – his constant traveling, he and Elmslie continued to function as a design team and not as separate individuals.

Inexpensive houses for small city lots typified the firm's endeavors, not large summer dwellings such as the Bradleys' and Deckers'. Essential, therefore, was a simplicity in massing, a corresponding compactness of plan (yet, if possible, without suggesting constriction), and the use of inexpensive materials. The successful achievement of these goals is well exemplified by three houses built between 1911 and 1915 in Minneapolis–St Paul for Dr Oscar Owre, Dr Ward Beebe, and C.T. Bachus (figs. 147–9).[6] Each is a variation on the planning scheme introduced earlier at the Catherine

Gray and T.W. McCosker houses (discussed in chapter 6), which ultimately derive from Wright's 1906 project for 'A Fireproof House for $5000,' as well as from the midwest vernacular. The Bachus house is the latest (1915) and most compact of the series, being an almost perfect cube topped by a low-pitched roof (fig. 147). Built for less than $3000, this ultra-simple form is given vitality by a lively arrangement of the fenestration, which is grouped in broad bands and balanced against the off-center doorway. Surface, not plasticity, is emphasized by placing the windows close to the plane of the wall. The resulting thin, crisp character recalls the much earlier Charles A. Purcell house in River Forest (fig. 70). The walls are a smooth-floated plaster, rose-orange in color, the wood trim a natural stain, and the window casements painted white. The latter practice was standard with Purcell and Elmslie, as was the use of leaded glass, where finances permitted.

The plan of the Bachus house, like those of the Owre and Beebe houses (fig. 148), was organized with the living room (approximately one-half of the floor area) and the dining room set at right angles – an L-shaped arrangement with no partition in between. A common exterior wall (with a row of windows) united these rooms and, because each seemed to participate in the area of the other, an added sense of spaciousness was achieved. Next to the dining room was the kitchen. This scheme remained constant in all three houses, the only variables being the entry area and the location of a porch. At the Owre house, to conform to the narrowness of the lot, the porch was placed in front, and an extra bedroom at the rear. Its exterior appearance, therefore, was different from that of the Bachus house, and totally distinct from the Beebe house, which has a cross-gabled roof. The latter was the most formal of the three, its windows arranged symmetrically under the strong inverted v of the gables, gables which gave the house somewhat the character of an English cottage (fig. 149).

The Bachus, Owre, and Beebe houses were typical of numerous small houses constructed by the firm. Larger variants were also built, such as the Harry S. Parker house at 4829 Colfax Avenue S., Minneapolis (1912–13). Here a single gable (the dormers were added later) established the dominant theme, its crisp leading edge emphasizing the thinness of the tinted stucco wall (fig. 150). Windows are close to the wall plane and placed so as to create a balanced pattern with the door; the entryway is topped by a distinctive fan-shaped ornament by Elmslie of sawed wood. Similar large gables were also characteristic of the J.W.S. Gallager house at 457 Broadway, Winona (1913), the parsonage of the First Congregational Church, 403

FIG. 151 Purcell and Elmslie. Mrs T. Lewis Waller (Margaret Little) house, 392 Shattuck Avenue, Berkeley, California, 1914. *Western Architect* 1915

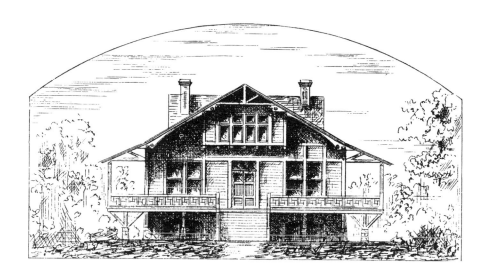

FIG. 152 'The Planter's House' from E.C. Gardner, *Illustrated Homes*, Boston, James R. Osgood & Co., 1875, p. 171

FIG. 153 Purcell and Elmslie. Henry Einfeldt house, 1010 Forest Avenue, River Forest, Illinois, 1914–15. Photo by H.A. Brooks

FIG. 154 Purcell and Elmslie. Harold C. Bradley house, 2914 Oxford Road, Shorewood Hills, Madison, Wisconsin, 1914–15. Photo by H.A. Brooks

7 Located at 382 Shattuck Avenue in Berkeley, the house has been extensively remodeled. The design date is 1914.

8 Located at 4845 Bryant Avenue S., Minneapolis, the Mueller studio and office of 1910–11 has a hipped roof with board and batten siding below, and plaster above the line of the window sills.

Third Street, Eau Claire, Wisconsin (1913–14), or the earlier Gardener's Cottage on the Crane Estate at Woods Hole, Massachusetts (1911).

The American tradition of the wood frame house has already been mentioned as a source for Purcell and Elmslie's designs, designs not unlike those represented by the Parker house. This is dramatically evident in the Mrs T. Lewis Waller (Margaret Little) house, Berkeley, California, the original architect's drawing of which is illustrated in figure 151.[7] A comparison of this elevation with the Planter's house published in E.C. Gardner's *Illustrated Homes* of 1875 suggests the latter as the source (fig. 152). Both have a dominating, rather thin-edged gable roof which sloped to the top of the first-storey windows. Also comparable are the symmetrically placed dormers, continuous bands of windows, and exposed wood members which screen certain areas of the wall.

Lower, essentially one-storey buildings were also popular with Purcell and Elmslie, the Henry Einfeldt house (1914–15) at 1010 Forest Avenue, River Forest, Illinois, being representative (fig. 153). The long, low massing is emphasized by horizontal boards and battens, grouped windows, accentuated string courses, and boldly overhanging gable roofs, all of which add to the unity of the design. Purcell and Elmslie, unlike Wright, frequently combined two materials on the outside walls. Tinted stucco was the most prevalent and, if not applied to the entire surface, was used only for the upper portion. Below would be brick, as at the Charles Purcell, Powers, Hoyt, and Decker houses, or wood, as here at the Einfeldt house, the Owre house, or the single-storey studio for Paul L. Mueller.[8] Houses entirely of brick were not built; this material was reserved for more monumental structures such as banks, courthouses, and churches. Houses completely sided in wood were rare, and when built always were of two different textures, the division occurring between the storeys or, in a one-storey house, at the window sill. The texture variation at the Bradley bungalow, Woods Hole, for example, was achieved by doubling each fourth row of shingles to create a striated effect on the lower storey, while laying the upper-storey shingles in the normal manner (fig. 135). At the one-storey C.I. Buxton house (1912), 424 E. Main Street, Owatonna, horizontal boards and battens sheath the walls to the height of the window sills with shingles above. Thus for Purcell and Elmslie there was an apparent hierarchy among building materials: brick the most prestigious, wood the least, and plaster rated in between.

The rich assortment of house designs produced by Purcell and Elmslie speaks volumes in behalf of their creative ability. There are consistent personal characteristics that typify their work, and clearly distinguish it from that of Wright, Sullivan, and other members of the school. The most striking of these is the treatment of the wall as a thin, almost skin-like membrane which encloses the form of the house. The vigorous plasticity of Wright is rejected in favor of other values, values which anticipate the aesthetic of the International Style of the nineteen-twenties and thirties. This is clearly evident in the third house for the Harold C. Bradleys, that built at 2914 Oxford Road in the Shorewood Hills area of Madison, Wisconsin, in 1914–15 (fig. 154). The slightly tinted plaster – such as Le Corbusier might use a decade later – is punctuated by rows of windows held flush against the wall, while a lively interplay of roof slabs and small balconies project somewhat tentatively from the wall. With its crisp angularity and strong horizontals, this house seems raised above its sloping site because of the dark, recessive brickwork used below. The entry, and originally the inside garage, are located on this lower level, the living and dining rooms with the cantilevered eating porch are on the second floor, and the bedrooms above.

Commercial work undertaken by Purcell and Elmslie during the period 1912–14 is well represented by the Chicago Edison Shop (1912), the Madison (Minnesota) State Bank (1913) and the First State Bank, Le Roy (1914), as well as the Merchants Bank of Winona, which was completed in 1912. All were constructed of brick. The Babson Brothers Building, better known as the Edison Shop, involved rebuilding an extant structure at 229 S. Wabash Avenue for Henry Babson (whose patronage had been withdrawn from Sullivan when he learned that Elmslie was in practice on his own). The building contained business and executive offices and a street level lounge intended for the display and sale of phonographs (figs. 155–6).

Architecturally this tall, narrow four-storey building is treated as a single unit with the Roman brick wall rising from sidewalk to coping. Spandrels are only slightly recessed and overt ornament is restricted to capitals, coping, and a large Sullivanesque – though less exuberant – foliate ornament on the attic. In essence this single-bay wide design is a series of superimposed Chicago windows with the dividing mullions expressed as piers. It is a further development of the post and lintel theme of the Merchants Bank of Winona, except that the plasticity of the forms is reduced; perhaps this was a necessity in view of the existing structure underneath. Strong and dignified, this brilliant design stood in sharp contrast to its busy surfaced neighbors – stood, that is, until recently when, during a brief period in which Chicago's landmark preservation law was not in effect, speculative

FIG. 155 Purcell, Feick and Elmslie. Edison Shop, S. Wabash Avenue, Chicago, Illinois, 1912. Demolished. P&E photo

FIG. 156 Purcell, Feick and Elmslie. Edison Shop. Interior. *Western Architect* 1913

FIG. 157 Purcell and Elmslie. First State Bank, Main Street, Le Roy, Minnesota, 1914. *Western Architect* 1915

FIG. 158 Purcell and Elmslie. First State Bank. Architects' rendering. P&E Archives, courtesy David Gebhard

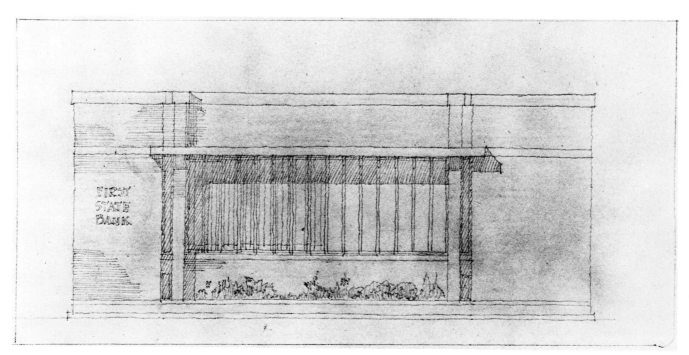

9 Several illustrations, including plans of both of these banks, are published in the July 1915 *Western Architect* (vol. 22) or its reissue, *The Work of Purcell and Elmslie, Architects*, Park Forest, 1965, pp. 72–4 and 88. Illustrations of the four Edison Shops will also be found in this source.

builders speedily demolished this historic structure.

The Edison Shop was entered through a deep loggia (flanked by show cases) into a large, comfortable lounge arranged more like a living room than a shop (fig. 156). The furnishings, including the carpet which repeated the decorative strip-patterns of the wall, were the collaborative work of the architects and George Niedecken, the Milwaukee furniture designer and manufacturer. What distinguishes this interior from those previously discussed is the thinner and lighter, less Wrightian, character of the design. Surfaces are stressed rather than the multifarious wood components in the furniture and the walls.

This interior apparently pleased the clients because in 1914 Purcell and Elmslie remodeled three other shops for the company. These were the Minnesota Phonograph Company at Minneapolis, the Edison Shop at Kansas City, Missouri, and the Edison Shop at San Francisco, California.

Smaller and less monumental than the Merchants Bank of Winona were those at Madison and Le Roy, Minnesota, built in 1913 and 1914 respectively. The Madison State Bank was located at mid-block with only a single façade facing the street. And, as in the Edison Shop, the architects created a frame of brick, like a broad inverted u, and filled the intervening space with a row of windows in polychromatic glass. The entrance and flanking windows were treated like those at Winona – as a separate plane that was placed slightly forward from the building. The interior was domestic in scale and finished in plaster and wood trim with quartered oak and bronze for the tellers' cage.[9]

The First State Bank at Le Roy is an essay in simplicity (figs. 157–8). Only 25 feet wide, 60 feet long, and costing $10,000 to build, it is shaped like a long, thin, machine-wrought safety deposit box. Its enhancement exists in the abstract interplay between verticles and horizontals enframing the window and in the thin, precise Richardsonian arch which accentuates the entrance. Below the coping three courses of brick define the cornice.

The years 1912–14 had been richly rewarding for Purcell and Elmslie and by comparison the few commissions received by their former employer seem insignificant. Yet for Sullivan these were his busiest years between 1900 and his death in 1924. A slight increase in work offered encouragement, and allowed his Auditorium Tower office and skeleton staff to be retained. But the roster of work was short: in 1912 an unexecuted house project for Carl K. Bennett, in 1913 the little Adams Building, the ill-fated St Paul's Church, and the Van Allen Store, and in 1914 three banks of which only that at Grinnell was of much significance.

Sullivan's interest did not lie in houses, and in more prosperous times he let others assist in this responsibility. Yet the Carl K. Bennett house was apparently his own conception and so ranks among the few houses that he designed after the 1880s (figs. 159–60).[10] It is, therefore, of more than ordinary interest. The plan is related to the earlier Babson and Bradley houses (figs. 79, 81) except for the more rigidly enforced symmetry, a symmetry which often has little to do with function. It is cruciform, with a major east-west axis entirely open except for the kitchen. The dining room, reception hall, living room, and music room are arranged en suite with only an Adamesque placement of paired piers to suggest a differentiation of space. Not a single window on this floor faces the street; the opposite wall is amply glazed. The octagonally-ended crossing axis contains the entry and stairs with, opposite, a garden-facing den. On the second floor five bedrooms are set in a row and connected by a corridor along the front (north) side. The small, square windows of this corridor are the only apertures along this outside wall.

The exterior has the same high-perched detachment from the ground already noted at the Babson and Bradley houses yet it is much more formal,

10 A complete set of working drawings for the Bennett project are recorded on roll #12 of the Burnham Library–University of Illinois Architectural Microfilming Project.

FIG. 159 Louis H. Sullivan. Project: Carl K. Bennett house, Owatonna, Minnesota, 1912. Courtesy Burnham Library

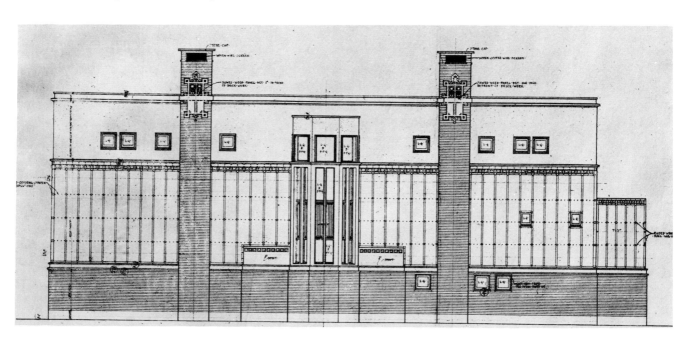

formidable, and non-domestic than its predecessors. In this respect it bears comparison with Nimmons and Fellows' Julius Rosenwald house (fig. 13). Yet the materials are essentially domestic, with brick for the basement and the pair of chimneys, board and batten siding laid vertically for the walls (with sunken nail holes to create a horizontal pattern), and plaster surfacing above the high dado-like belt course. Otherwise it is an uncompromising design which seems to imply that the earlier Babson and Bradley houses were a compromise between Sullivan and Elmslie, with the latter's

FIG. 160 Louis H. Sullivan. Carl K. Bennett house. Plan. Courtesy Burnham Library

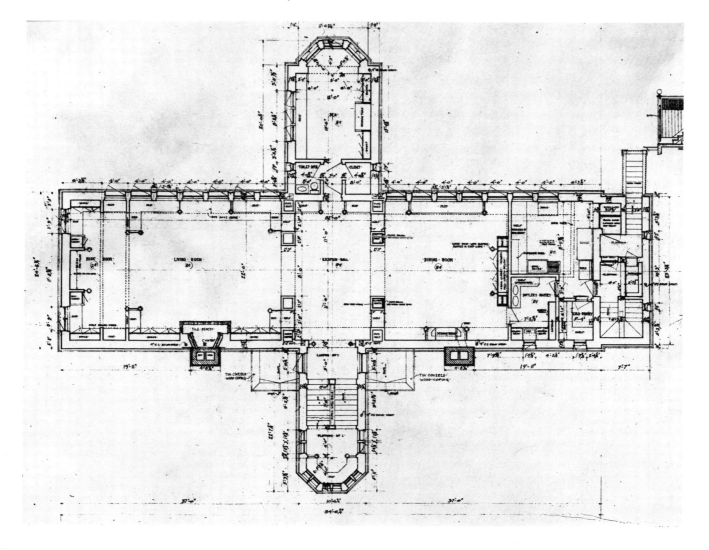

responsibility being the more home-like touches of gable roofs, balconies, porches, and porte-cochère. The almost windowless façade is severe and monumental, a characteristic favored by Sullivan and perhaps requested by the client. The house was not built, which is not necessarily a reflection on the design because Bennett later asked Purcell and Elmslie for designs that he also rejected.

The handsome detailing and fine proportions of the Henry C. Adams Building at Algona, Iowa, distinguish this unpretentious building from its neighbors (fig. 161). Long and rectangular and located on a corner lot, its simple mass clearly suggests the enclosure of space. This effect is achieved by deeply recessing the windows which, with mottled glass, seem like an inner membrane set against the thick brick shell. The glass, diapered brickwork with inset colored squares, and terra cotta capitals are almost the only ornament in this restrained yet dignified design. Built as a bank, which, however, failed to receive its charter, the building has since served as an office.

Unlike Sullivan's masterpiece at Owatonna, the Adams Building more nearly recalls the small Exchange State Bank at Grand Meadow by Purcell, Feick and Elmslie. The entrance in particular is similar, as well as the diapered pattern in brick. That this could have served as Sullivan's guide is possible since it was published in the January 1913 *Western Architect*.

Larger and more monumental is the Merchants' National Bank at Grinnell with its broad expanse of richly colored brick walls (figs. 162–3). A forty-foot window of mottled glass is precisely cut into the side and inset are a row of slender, gilded columns, their thinness emphasizing the apparent thinness of the enclosing brick walls. The eye-catcher, however, is the great outburst of ornament above the door, an overlay of squares and circle interwoven with foliate forms and cast in a gray terra cotta highlighted with areas of gold. Often criticized for its overbearing presence and lack of relation to the basic design of the building, this window frame nevertheless reads clearly as something applied or attached to the surface, something free and unrelated to, but ornamenting, the structure.[11]

More harmonious is the interior, surely the finest bank interior which Sullivan ever designed (fig. 163). Stylistically, and chronologically, it stands midway between the richness of Owatonna and the stark severity of the Columbus bank. Precise, angular shapes predominate except for the focal point opposite the entrance where a frieze of ornamental gilded terra cotta emphasizes the location of the vault; as one leaves the bank the great circular window comes into view. The burnished bronze of the tellers'

11 For a perceptive analysis of Sullivan's ornament, particularly as related to his banks, see Vincent Scully, Jr, 'Louis Sullivan's Architectural Ornament,' *Perspecta*, 5, 1959, 73–80.

FIG. 161 Louis H. Sullivan. Henry C. Adams Building, Algoma, Iowa, 1913. Photo by Richard Nickel

FIG. 162 Louis H. Sullivan. Merchants' National Bank, Grinnell, Iowa, 1914. Photo by Richard Nickel

cages sets the color key. Counters are of brick, topped with blackish-green marble; the walls of this dignified, unified rectangular space are of brick with tan-tinted plaster above. Oak and bronze are used for the trim and

FIG. 163 Louis H. Sullivan. Merchants' National Bank. Interior. Chicago Architectural Photographing Co

12   In February 1912 the *Western Architect* began a year-long project of publishing Harvey Ellis' drawings. The lead article for the series, entitled 'A Revival of Pen and Ink Rendering: The Work of Harvey Ellis,' said that 'we need not go back to Angelo, Piranesi, or Hogarth for examples of line drawing' when the work of Ellis is at hand (*Western Architect, 18*, 1912, 36). The Security Bank drawing appeared in the issue of March 1912.

furnishings. A rich, soft light filters through the yellow and lavender glass window along the side.

Compared with Sullivan's earlier buildings the relative restraint of this interior is striking and may in part be due to the work of Purcell and Elmslie, specifically the Merchants Bank of Winona (fig. 132). The similarity is remarkable and, except for the tall lamp standards in the Winona building and the more uniform and sophisticated proportions throughout the Grinnell design, the two interiors could almost be by the same hand. While the interior of the Owatonna bank was still in the tradition of the McVicker's Theater or Golden Doorway at the Transportation Building, the interiors at Grinnell and in all later banks were not. This dramatic change, it would seem, resulted from the effect of Purcell and Elmslie on their teacher.

The question of influences, however, is most complex and involves several architects. Wright's Mason City bank probably originated certain features in the Winona building, such as the tall lamps and the particular character of the brick-faced vault, items, incidentally, which were rejected by Sullivan at Grinnell. The exterior post and lintel theme at Winona has Wrightian antecedents, as does the box-like massing common to most of these banks – yet this characteristic was known from Harvey Ellis' Security Bank project of 1891, which was republished by the *Western Architect* in 1912 and may have inspired the arched entry of the 1914 Purcell and Elmslie bank at Le Roy.[12] Thus these banks indicate a lively interchange of ideas among several men and come closer to representing stylistic unity and common expression than did the contemporary residential work.

The Purdue State Bank in West Lafayette, Indiana, and the Home Building Association Bank in Newark, Ohio, both of 1914, number among Sullivan's smallest and least distinguished designs, although the interior of the latter before remodeling must have been impressive. Sullivan's project, subsequently pirated, for St Paul's Church, Cedar Rapids (see p. 189–91), dates from this period as does the four-storey dry goods store for John D. Van Allen and Son Company in Clinton, Iowa. The latter – a sufficiently large problem for Sullivan to grasp intellectually – is dignified and well proportioned, but lacks the harmonious unity characteristic of the architect's best work. The four storeys seem almost detached from one another, while the bright green, blue, and white three-storey high terra cotta ornament, repeated thrice, of tall stems with bursting foliate tops seems irrelevant to the building, nor does it register as an independent decoration. At the Gage Building (Chicago, 1898) a somewhat similar motif was effective;

here it is not. What Sullivan apparently attempted to create was a super-bay, and thereby a monumental building: to do for a three-bay building what Purcell and Elmslie had so brilliantly achieved, by different means, at the single-bay Edison Shop in Chicago.

A project for a State Bank at Spring Green, Wisconsin, was exhibited by Wright in 1914.[13] It was a nearly square building of inordinately heavy forms with grilled windows that suggest a jail more than a bank. It was set, like a house, back from the street on a landscaped plot of land. Although neither influential nor particularly pleasing, the design indicates the direction Wright's work was taking – a preference for the heavier, more massive forms soon seen in the A.D. German Warehouse and Aline Barnsdall house and theater. Wright was seeking greater monumentality, a monumentality that he recognized in pre-Columbian architecture.

At the Chicago Architectural Club exhibition in April 1914, Wright was well represented by models, drawings, photographs, and even educational toys. These included not only the Spring Green bank project but plans, sections, and elevations for the Imperial Hotel in Japan which indicates, incidentally, that as early as the spring of 1914 the initial design for this

13 Illustrated in Arthur Drexler, *The Drawings of Frank Lloyd Wright*, New York, 1962, pl. 46

FIG. 164 Walter Burley Griffin. Hurd Comstock house (no 1), 1416 Church Street, Evanston, Illinois, 1912. Photo by H.A. Brooks

14 *Architectural Record*, 35, 1914, 405

15 Ibid., p. 409

16 Iannelli (1888–1965), Italian by birth, was raised in Newark, New Jersey, where he first apprenticed as a jeweler before winning a scholarship to the Art Students League in New York and turning to commercial art for his livelihood. Disapproving of what fellow students were learning in Europe, he traveled west to California, where he made his living designing posters. Those for the Orpheum Theatre in Los Angeles caught the attention of John Lloyd Wright, then in the employ of Harrison Albright; he introduced Iannelli to his employer, who needed sculpture for the Workingman's Hotel that John had designed in 1912. When John Lloyd Wright was called to manage his father's Chicago office in 1913, Iannelli was recommended for the Midway Gardens job. Thus the sculptor came to the Midwest.

For an excellent critical biography emphasizing Iannelli's pre-1916 years see Joseph Griggs, 'Alfonzo Iannelli, the Prairie Spirit in Sculpture,' *Prairie School Review*, 2, 4, 1965, 5–23.

Also active at Midway Gardens was the sculptor Richard Bock, whom Wright had met while working with Adler and Sullivan on the Schiller building (1891–2) and had first employed at his own Studio in 1895. For a discussion of Bock's work see Donald Parker Hallmark, 'Richard W. Bock: Sculptor for Frank Lloyd Wright and the Architects of the Chicago School,'

building was complete. Midway Gardens, then under construction, was well depicted, and there were several residences including Wright's own Taliesin, so soon destroyed by fire by an insane servant who also murdered seven members of the household – a tragedy that profoundly influenced Wright's professional as well as his personal life.

Earlier in 1914 Wright had written his famous diatribe against 'disciples, neophytes, and quacks,' whom he accused of stealing his ideas, saying that 'the so-called "movement" threatens to explode soon in foolish exploitation of unripe performances ...'[14] Wright was never one to approve of another architect's designs, but this attack hit close to home as, under the title 'In the Cause of Architecture, Second Paper,' his damnation included those who six years before, in the first paper, he had spoken of with such fondness and confidence. Then Wright had been at the height of his local prestige, the center of activity, surrounded by a group of young and admiring apprentices. By 1914, although internationally renowned, his home ties were broken, the Studio closed, and professionally he was being rapidly eclipsed by a younger generation, men building on the foundations that he had so largely laid. In spite of his bitterness, however, he did pay those he condemned a back-handed compliment: 'I think the worst of them do better,' he admitted, 'than nine-tenths of the work done by average architects who are "good school".'[15]

To assist at Midway Gardens (1914) Wright invited his son John and Alfonzo Iannelli to Chicago; the latter settled in the Midwest where he frequently collaborated with Byrne and occasionally with Purcell and Elmslie.[16] As a sculptor it was Iannelli's task to design and execute, under Wright's direction, the so-called sprits and other figurative pieces for Midway Gardens. This he did, and with such success that Wright eventually claimed the designs as his own, saying that Iannelli had only cast the figures. Nearly 40 years passed before the sculptor received his due – but never from the architect.[17] Wright, always the jealous guardian of his fame,

unpublished MA thesis submitted to the University of Iowa, May 1970.

17 When Wright exhibited models of these figures at the Chicago Architectural Club exhibition in 1914 he listed Iannelli as the sculptor. But that was before Midway Gardens opened. Once the building was completed and na-

tionally published, Iannelli's name was omitted; at first by inference and finally by declaration, Wright claimed himself as the sprites' designer. John Lloyd Wright, who was on the scene, and more recently historians, have finally set the record straight.

could neither accept Iannelli's rival creativity nor admit that his former apprentices were making a viable contribution to the cause of architecture.

Before Iannelli met John and Lloyd Wright and Barry Byrne in Los Angeles, his poster style was typified by large simple forms and sweeping Art Nouveau curves. Once familiar with Frank Lloyd Wright's work, however, including the late (1909–10) renderings illustrated in the Wasmuth folio (simultaneously he was also studying the paintings and murals of Gustav Klimt), Iannelli's style modified to one of closed, angular forms, even for figure designs. That Wright responded to this work is understandable. By 1915, however, Iannelli abandoned this angular manner in favor of the more continuous, flowing forms seen in the mural at the Franke house (fig. 208) and in the terra cotta relief over the entry of the Woodbury County Courthouse (fig. 212).

Announcement that Griffin had won the Canberra competition was made in May 1912, but before moving to Australia early in 1914 he undertook time-consuming trips to Australia and Europe and carried on an extremely active practice at home. His newly acquired renown obviously enhanced his reputation, and in addition to designing homes he planned many subdivisions, of which six were illustrated by the *Western Architect* in 1913.[18] For several of these he intended to serve as architect. None, however, was completed, and few were even begun. The two most significant were the nine-acre Trier Center Neighborhood in Winnetka, Illinois, for which Griffin planned his own home, and the eighteen-acre Rock Crest–Rock Glen subdivision in Mason City, Iowa, for which five houses were built

18 The *Western Architect*, *19*, 1913, 67–80 illustrated, along with a text by Griffin, the Trier Center Neighborhood; Ridge Quadrangles, Evanston (5 acres); Emory Hills, Wheaton, Illinois (20 acres to be divided into 5 farms); Clark's Resubdivision, Grinnell, Iowa (57 lots); Idalia, Lee County, Florida; Rock Crest–Rock Glen, Mason City, Iowa; and Canberra. The original drawings for most of these subdivisions are in the collections at the Burnham Library, Northwestern University, and the Avery Library respectively.

FIG. 165 Walter Burley Griffin. Hurd Comstock house (no 2), 1631 Ashland Avenue, Evanston, Illinois, 1912. North elevation. Historic American Building Survey

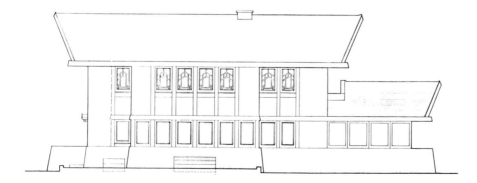

FIG. 166 Walter Burley Griffin. Hurd
Comstock houses (1, 2). Perspective
and plan. Rendering by Marion
Mahony Griffin. Courtesy Northwestern University

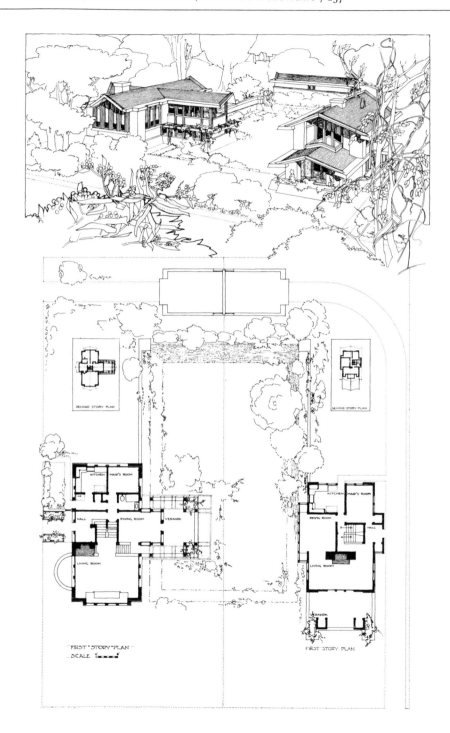

before Griffin turned his practice over to Byrne. The architect also found time to present his work at the Chicago Architectural Club in 1912 and 1913, and made ready an exhibition for shipment to Paris in 1914. Undoubtedly his wife prepared the renderings.

For Griffin's development as a designer the year 1911 had been decisive. The B.J. Ricker house marked his strongest attempt thus far to break bonds with his training under Wright and establish a more personal expression of his own. His life-long predilection for heavy, compact forms here found expression, though still in combination with gable roofs and laterally extending appendages (fig. 102). At Solid Rock, however, the last reminiscences of the past were gone and severity reigned supreme (figs. 104–5). Personal maturity was gained and the type of design that Griffin introduced into Australia was established.

In 1912 he consolidated his position and demonstrated his ability to achieve a rich variety in his newly created mode. This is evident at the Melson house and the project for Griffin's own home (fig. 168). That he did not immediately reject his previous work, however, is witnessed by the pair of Hurd Comstock houses in Evanston that he exhibited in April of 1912 (figs. 164–6). Located at the south-east corner of Church and Ashland, these budget-built homes shared a visually unified garden but otherwise were of independent design. The corner house, often referred to as #1, is larger and developed around a split-level plan. A full one-and-a-half storey living room is set half a level above the ground-storey hall, kitchen, and dining room and overlooked by the bedroom wing. One senses the spatial expansiveness while mounting the living room stairs; there also exists a fascinating spatial interplay between the master bedroom and the well-lit living room below. The house is small yet full of variety; it is unfortunate that Griffin had no opportunity to work out his multi-level ideas in a house where economy was not a major factor.

The roof-height corner piers on the exterior visually confine the house, while the window-wall of the living room is cantilevered slightly forward under the projecting gable roof. The entrance is sheltered by a partially cantilevered bedroom which balances the dining room and veranda on the garden side. Sand-toned plaster and stained wood are the principal materials inside and out.

The companion house, #2, is smaller and more characteristic in its prairie plan. But the vigorous plasticity of the piers and the thinness and greater breadth of the gables (which rest on flat, narrow soffits) impart a lightness and delicacy to this design not often found in Griffin's work.

FIG. 167 Walter Burley Griffin. Project: Trier Center Neighbourhood, Winnetka, Illinois, 1912–13. Courtesy Burnham Library

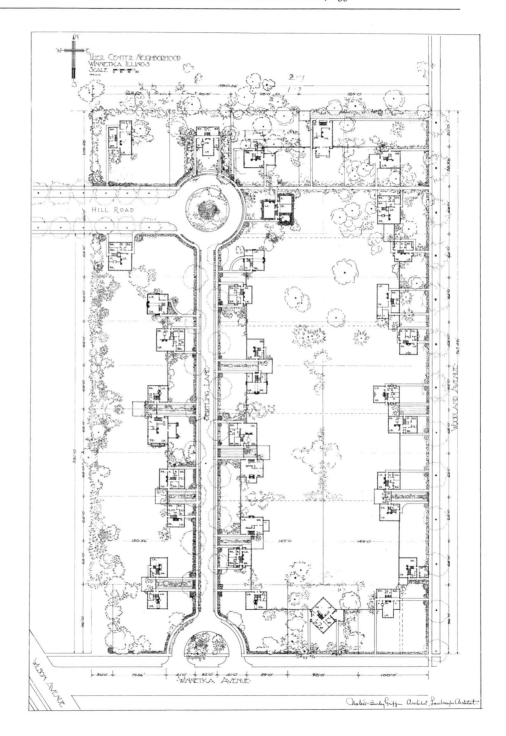

FIG. 168 Walter Burley Griffin. Project: Walter Burley Griffin house, Winnetka, Illinois, 1912. Rendering by Marion Mahony Griffin. Courtesy Northwestern University

19 The precise source of this motif is not immediately apparent, although it relates to Griffin's fondness for piers. Sullivan that same year intended to use paired chimney-piers at the Carl Bennett house, but better known were the paired semi-detached chimneys at the Homewood Country Club at suburban Flossmoor, Illinois, by Howard Shaw. Bruce Price used the motif at Tuxedo Park, New York, which could have been the midwesterners' source.

Speculation arises, therefore, as to whether Marion Mahony Griffin contributed to the design, a most plausible suggestion when comparison is made with the Adolph Mueller house and its heavy battered base and almost playful use of piers.

The type of plot planning Griffin achieved for Hurd Comstock – including both common and private gardens and a shared garage – was what he intended for such subdivisions as Trier Center Neighborhood in Winnetka, where 30 houses were to be arranged in pairs (fig. 167). With the street pattern set out of phase with the neighboring grid, and no roads leading directly across the nine-acre plot, Griffin eliminated through traffic, a farsighted concern in 1912. Here the streets were straight, but in larger subdivisions he preferred sweeping curves and frequent cul-de-sacs. And for monumental schemes such as Canberra or a university campus his preference ran toward radial planning and diagonal arteries.

Griffin's own house was to be at the head of the principal street deep within the Trier Center Neighborhood. Complete working drawings, dated 1 October 1912, were prepared, but the house was never built. The plan was a stunted T as at Solid Rock, but modified as a two-storey, split-level scheme (fig. 168). The stairs and entry divided the house at mid-point with the hall, conservatory, dining room, and kitchen at ground level, over which were the bedroom, studio, and balconies. Between these levels, in the stem of the T, was the one-and-a-half storey living room (with basement underneath).

Dominating the exterior were pairs of great chimney-like piers that flanked both front and rear entries and which, like Griffin's corner piers, were primarily decorative as only one contained a flue.[19] The basic shape of the house was rectangular, since the T-plan did not extend above the lower level. This form was articulated by large diamond-shaped mullions set in an alternating rhythm between the window sills and roof cornice, thereby creating an imposing, rather monumental design. As these mullions are similar to those at the Henry Ford project (fig. 95), again the possibility exists that Marion Mahony Griffin participated in the design.

Griffin's major American work as architect and planner was at the Rock Crest–Rock Glen subdivision in Mason City, Iowa, begun in 1912 (fig. 169). The eighteen-acre site, bypassed during the city's expansion, followed sluggish Willow Creek on its crescent course. One side cut sharply into a limestone bluff – Rock Crest – while the opposite bank sloped gently from the water's edge and was called Rock Glen; it was serviced by a right-angle street (as at Trier Center) bearing the subdivision name. Along these streets were built houses which shared the landscaped, creek-side park upon which they faced – an excellent planning scheme which is still in use.

The circumstances surrounding this commission are incredibly complex because so many Prairie School architects became involved. The chronicle of events is this: In 1908 Wright built the G.C. Stockman house and later that year designed the City National Bank and adjoining Park Inn Hotel, an undertaking for which J.E.E. Markley, as bank director and attorney, apparently selected the architect. Markley's eldest daughter had studied at the Lloyd-Jones' Hillside Home School in Spring Green, Wisconsin, and during Wright's visit to Mason City he stayed at the Markley home. Wright

FIG. 169 Walter Burley Griffin. Rock Crest–Rock Glen, Mason City, Iowa, 1912. Rendering by Marion Mahony Griffin. Courtesy Burnham Library

was also asked to design Joshua Melson's house, a drawing of which is published in the 1910 Wasmuth folio where it is miscaptioned the Isabel Roberts house, which it closely resembles (fig. 173). Why it was not built is not known, unless because of Wright's departure for Europe in the autumn of 1909 (Griffin later built the Melson house as well as the Page house for which Purcell and Elmslie had submitted drawings in April 1912). When Wright left America the bank and hotel were still not finished, and for uncertain reasons it was Drummond who completed the supervision. This brought him to Mason City and the Curtis Yelland commission, already discussed (p. 181, fig. 115), was the result. The Yelland lot was bought from Melson in 1909 and the house was completed in 1911 – dates which coincide with Drummond's presence. The bank and hotel were finished and being occupied in August-September 1910.

Griffin's involvement occurred in the following manner. In 1912 Melson

was still without a new home. Rather than continuing negotiations with Wright, however, he sought out Marion Mahony, whose acquaintance he presumably made at the Studio. She declined, claiming to be too busy, but she did convince Melson that her husband should lay out the Rock Crest–Rock Glen subdivision. Griffin subsequently visited Mason City, proposed a plan, and on 30 July 1912 the four interested parties – Melson, Blythe, Markley, and W.J. Holahan – signed an agreement which guaranteed the preservation of the natural site and regulated the placement of buildings along only its outer fringe with each facing inward toward the open park (fig. 169). Once this was done the house designs also fell to Griffin.[20]

By mid-1912 Griffin was in full command at Mason City. Yet almost immediately he began traveling to Australia and Europe, and in 1914 he permanently left the United States after taking on Byrne as an associate to look after his American work. Before leaving he had designed and built the Melson, Rule, Page, and Blythe houses (figs. 170, 175, 177, 179), and prepared drawings for four others – two were never built and two were redesigned and built by Byrne. In addition, he designed the Schneider house; it was slightly modified and built by Byrne. Byrne also constructed the Melson mausoleum.

In conclusion, therefore, only two of the Rock Crest–Rock Glen houses involved a single architect – the Blythe and Rule houses by Griffin (although even here his wife's role must be considered). Griffin built the Melson house, for which Wright prepared a design, and the Page house, for which Purcell and Elmslie had submitted drawings. Griffin designed the Gilmore and Franke houses, but Byrne redesigned and built them at a later date. The Schneider house was built by Byrne largely to Griffin's design. Thus the whole Mason City affair was an architect's version of musical chairs.

Melson had a most dramatic site. His lot was atop the limestone cliff which dropped off abruptly into Willow Creek, the embankment being called Rock Crest. Wright, in keeping with his predilection for level sites, located his projected house well back from the natural cliff (fig. 173). Griffin, by contrast, turned the cliff to his advantage; he wedded the house to the outcropping rock (fig. 171), and utilized the rugged natural materials of the site to construct the house (Wright proposed the use of smooth plaster trimmed with wood).

Griffin's design was a master stroke. Partly hewn, and partly growing, from the striated cliff, the house is poised over the dammed stream where its image is reflected (figs. 170–2). The limestone of cliff and house are one,

20 For much of the documentation in the last two paragraphs I am indebted to an important article by Robert E. McCoy, MD, 'Rock Crest/Rock Glen: Prairie School Planning in Iowa,' *Prairie School Review*, 5, 3, 1968, 5–39. Therein are quoted (pp. 16–17) excerpts from Marion Mahony Griffin's 'The Magic of America,' in which she discussed the Melson commission.

FIG. 170 Walter Burley Griffin. J.G. Melson house, 56 River Heights Drive, Mason City, Iowa, 1912. Rendering by Marion Mahony Griffin. Courtesy Northwestern University

FIG. 171 Walter Burley Griffin. J.C. Melson house, 1912. Photo courtesy Hugh Gilmore and Robert E. McCoy

FIG. 172 Walter Burley Griffin. J.G. Melson house. North and east elevations from original working drawings dated 7 September 1912. Courtesy Northwestern University

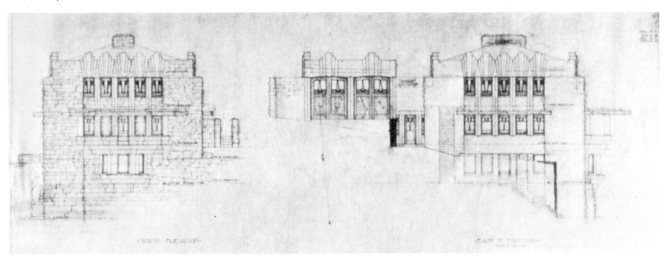

and the window voids appear as caverns wedged open by great voussoirs. From the nearby street the house seems to sink below the cliff and disappear into the ravine beyond. The very roughness of the stone blurs both the outline of the building and its plan, and only by careful observation does one notice Griffin's characteristic corner piers and typical square plan in which the dining and living rooms are juxtaposed at right angles. A large fireplace, built of limestone, half divides these rooms, between which a balcony-porch extends out over the ravine. A pool room, partly hewn from the living rock, is situated below, and the two-car drive-through garage rests on the level plateau facing toward the street. The cramped feeling so often experienced in Griffin's earlier houses is not found here.

Marion Griffin's role in this design is open to question, but she knew Melson and so presumedly took a more than average interest. The beautiful rendering bears her monogram (fig. 170), and the rough limestone, embankment site, and diamond-shaped window mullions all recall her earlier work. The corner piers and plan, however, seem to be Griffin's. Therefore the basic scheme was probably his, while the details, choice of materials, and final execution may have been left to her. The blueprints are dated 7 September 1912, with revisions through 9 October.

A project for William J. Holahan, another partner in the Rock Crest enterprise, was prepared for a sloping site with the main floor carved into the embankment so that the hexagonal veranda and living room were

FIG. 173 Frank Lloyd Wright. Project: J.G. Melson house, Mason City, Iowa, 1908. *Ausgeführte Bauten und Entwürfe von Frank Lloyd Wright 1910*

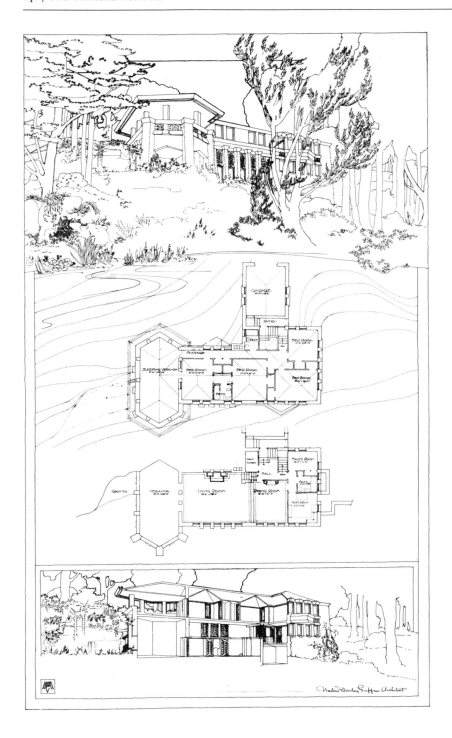

FIG. 174 Walter Burley Griffin. Project: William J. Holahan house, Mason City, Iowa, 1912 or 1913. Perspective and plan. Rendering by Marion Mahony Griffin. Courtesy Northwestern University

lower, and overlooked by, the contiguous dining room (fig. 174). Griffin intended to depress the living room into the ground (as at the Ralph Griffin house) in order to gain height, rather than to raise the ceiling into the second storey. This arrangement recalls the Edna (William) Purcell house (figs. 143–6) by Purcell and Elmslie. The exterior masonry has an almost primitive crudeness and the near-absence of a sloping roof enhances this effect. The design, which was intended for the lower end of Rock Crest, dates from 1912, or at least earlier than April 1913 when it was exhibited at the Chicago Architectural Club.

The most modest, yet one of the best, Griffin houses at Mason City was commissioned by Blythe for occupancy by Arthur Rule; the blueprints are dated 4–19 November 1912 (fig. 175). The ancestor of this design is patently Wright's 1906 project for the Curtis Publishing Company (fig. 62), yet Griffin has so substantially refined, improved, and personalized the design that it constitutes virtually a new work. The plan is particularly revealing. Corner piers, quite similar in size and height to those at the 1902 Emery house (fig. 29), define the space within (see the first-floor plan, fig. 175). Built into these apparent piers are cabinets and bookshelves – as though in the thickness of the wall – which add to, without subtracting from, the usable space of the rooms. Between the piers walls give way to windows, while the pier tops serve as window boxes in front of the bedroom windows. The cube-like, boxy shape of Wright's interior is here negated by numerous surfaces that define the various areas rather than precisely enclose them. The sense of variety and spaciousness thus gained is remarkable; it is an extremely pleasant place in which to be. The rich, warm tone of gumwood – used also in the ceiling beams – prevails on the interior, while leaded glass doors add a decorative note to the cabinets and French doors. The veranda, originally open, has since been enclosed and obtrusive bedrooms added overhead. The large, simple forms that dominate on the exterior are given scale by the cypress fascia of the roof and the broad trellises over the windows and (originally) around the veranda. The windows of the second-storey fold around the corners; those at ground level are banded together at the center. The exterior material is tinted stucco.

In Griffin's own work the immediate prototype for the Rule house was the now demolished Harry E. Gunn house (1911–12) formerly at 10559 S. Longwood Drive, Tracy (now Chicago), Illinois. The earlier building had an enclosed sun porch (not an open veranda) which extended out between the living and dining rooms; the fireplace and beam ceiling at both houses were much the same. Fortunately an old photograph of this interior exists, showing the original Morris and Craftsman type of furnishings, and it is illustrated here (fig. 176).[21]

Next to the Rule house, and built at about the same time (1912), is the Harry D. Page house at 21 S. Rock Glen (fig. 177). This rather stiff and awkward design is the least pleasing of the group, yet in one major respect it is the most important. The walls are built with a reinforced concrete frame, a frame which is directly expressed on the exterior. This is of the utmost significance because it is the first time that a prairie architect allowed the concrete (or steel) in a house to have a clear and direct expression in the design. Wright was probably the first of the group to use concrete extensively within a house (Martin house, Buffalo, 1904) but neither he nor the others had actually built a house wherein it was evident and basic to the design. In Griffin's scheme the structural grid of closely spaced verticals, and lintels atop the windows, is eminently apparent because it projects slightly forward from the infilling of stuccoed clay tile.

The Page house rests on a prominent platform-like base of limestone, the texture of which contrasts sharply with the smoother walls above. The low-pitched gable roof, with flaring eaves, seems thin and almost delicate by comparison, as perhaps it should. The plan, in the shape of a truncated T, is arranged with the living room overlooking the sloping community park. The garage is a later addition; the house interior was recently redecorated, at which time the concrete pier between the two center living room casements was demolished to create a picture window.

21 This photograph was mistakenly identified as the Rule house interior when published in the *Western Architect*, *19*, August 1913.

Walter Burley Griffin. Arthur Rule house

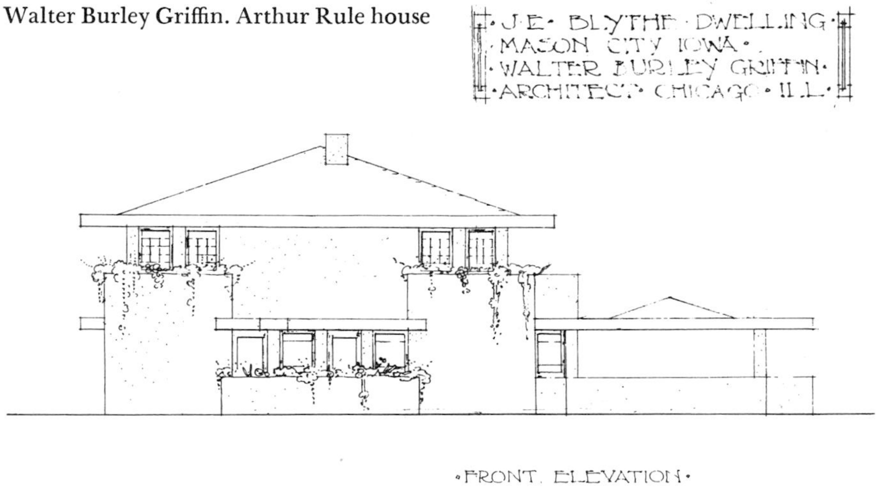

· J·E· BLYTHE · DWELLING ·
· MASON CITY IOWA ·
· WALTER BURLEY GRIFFIN ·
· ARCHITECT · CHICAGO · ILL ·

· FRONT · ELEVATION ·

FIG. 175 Walter Burley Griffin.
Arthur Rule house, 11 S. Rock Glen,
Mason City, Iowa, 1912. Courtesy Dr
J.S. Westly

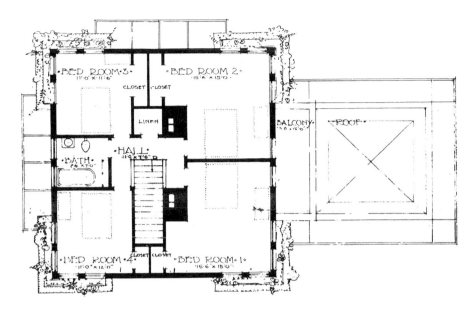

·SECOND FLOOR PLAN·

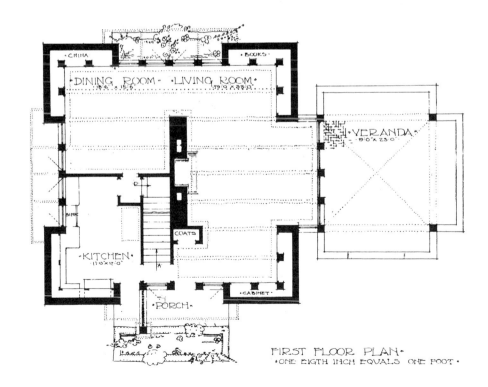

·FIRST FLOOR PLAN·
·ONE EIGTH INCH EQUALS ONE FOOT·

As with other executed designs, the Page house raises the question of Marion Mahony Griffin's contribution to her husband's work, a question complicated by their similar training under Wright and shared predilection for rather heavy forms. The structural innovations at the Page house are certainly Griffin's, and for this reason he probably exercised a more complete control over the design than was usual. The exterior proportions lack sophistication and refinement (in spite of my somewhat flattering

FIG. 176 Walter Burley Griffin. Harry E. Gunn house (demolished), Longwood Drive, Chicago, Illinois, 1911–12. Interior. *Western Architect* 1913

22   In contrast to the Ricker house (fig. 102), Solid Rock (figs. 104–5), Comstock house No. 1 (fig. 164), Mess house, and Rule house (fig. 175) which seem to represent only a negligible contribution from Marion

photograph, fig. 177), but this may in part be excused by the experimental nature of the design. Griffin lacked an innate sense of proportions, but then his wife's were not unerring. Perhaps each judiciously criticized the other for what he could not always do alone.

Therefore the Page house is probably by Griffin without much aid from his wife while certain earlier designs – the second Hurd Comstock house (figs. 165–6), the Griffin project (fig. 168), and the Melson house (figs. 170–2), for example – perhaps represent a direct contribution on her part.[22] Each of these, as well as the Stinson Memorial Library (figs. 182–3), has certain characteristics in common with her Evanston church (fig. 28), Adolph Mueller house (fig. 91), or Henry Ford project (fig. 95) such as materials, their use, or a preference for specific forms. Marion's contribu-

FIG. 177 Walter Burley Griffin. Harry D. Page house, 21 S. Rock Glen, Mason City, Iowa, 1912. Photo by H.A. Brooks

FIG. 178 Walter Burley Griffin. J.E. Blythe house, 431 First Street S.E., Mason City, Iowa, 1913. Roof construction being examined by James Blythe. In the background is the already completed Page house. Courtesy Hugh Gilmore and Robert E. McCoy

FIG. 179 Walter Burley Griffin. J.E. Blythe house. Photo courtesy Barry Byrne

FIG. 180 Walter Burley Griffin.
J.E. Blythe house. Plan, section, and
elevation of first project. Courtesy
Northwestern University

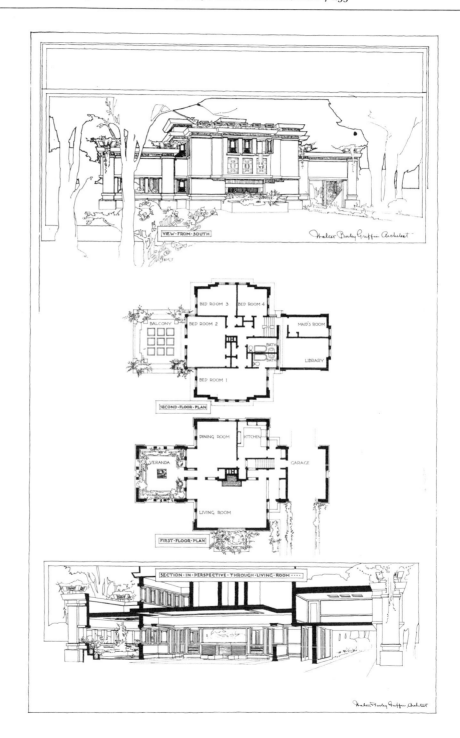

tion may have been as critic (verbal suggestions and recommendations) or as actual assistant with the design (pencil in hand) or, most likely, as a combination of the two. It is significant that what we earlier defined as her typical house plan does not appear among Griffin's designs; this absence implies that she did not formulate the initial scheme. It should be noted also that she did not claim participation in her husband's work, although when with von Holst she insisted on recognition as designer. Her beautiful renderings often bore her monogram, yet only Griffin's signature appeared as architect. These splendid drawings, executed in India ink on linen but sometimes transferred to satin and tinted, enjoyed international acclaim and were exhibited at the Musée des Arts Décoratifs in Paris from 20 June to 13 July 1914, an exhibition deprived of further European showings by the war.[23]

In summation, therefore, it would seem that Griffin was usually responsible for the basic concept of the designs – their plan, massing, and general character – and that his wife contributed only to the later stages of this process. Her role might be limited to designing some decorative panels or preparing the perspective rendering, or she might take over her husband's initial scheme and bring it to completion – refining the plan and massing, determining the materials and how they should be used, and designing such details as windows and doors, fireplaces, and any exterior or interior decoration.

James E. Blythe (Markley's business partner) was the most active of the Rock Crest–Rock Glen sponsors since it was he who actually commissioned the Rule, Schneider, Gilmore, and Franke houses as well as his own at 431 First Street for which the blueprints are dated 24 July 1913, with revisions to 20 August (figs. 178–80). It was the last building for which Griffin supervised construction. The house was built entirely of reinforced concrete – floors, walls, and roof – and as such it represents a milestone in Griffin's endeavor to effectively utilize this new material and find for it an appropriate expressive form. And to the extent that he succeeded, the Blythe house stands today as a significant monument in the annals of American architecture.

The broad, hard surfaces of wall and precise, heavy mouldings of the Blythe house explicitly convey the impression of solidity and mass. The design clearly could not have been built of wood, stucco, brick, or stone although its cruciform plan with lower extending wings recalls the interior spatial scheme of earlier prairie houses. Built on the same sloping site as the Page house, the building is supported on the lower side by a terrace

23 The exhibition, with catalogue by Louis Bonnier, was listed as an 'Exposition d'esquisses d'architecture de l'architecte américain Walter-Burley Griffin.' From Paris the drawings were apparently being sent to Vienna, where Otto Wagner was assisting with exhibition arrangements, when the war intervened. Assuming that Griffin later retrieved the renderings, it is probable that they now constitute part of the splendid collection of Griffin drawings at the Avery Library.

24 The original drawing is at Northwestern University, a tinted version at
the Avery Library. This earlier design
is without stone foundations and shows
a carport in the wing at the right; it was
intended for a more level site.

foundation of rough limestone which also sheathes the living room wall to
the height of the window lintel, thereby effectively diminishing the apparent height of the house. Over the broad picture window are three
decorative panels cast in concrete; these were probably the contribution
of Marion Griffin. They, and the cast railing of the terrace, imply acquaintance with pre-Columbian design which was increasingly to become a force
in Griffin's work. An earlier project for this house envisioned an ornamental cast cornice which also owed much to pre-Columbian design (fig.
180).[24]

FIG. 181 Walter Burley Griffin. Project: Franke, Gilmore, and Schneider houses on
State Street, Rock Glen, Mason City, Iowa, 1913. Schneider house on right built
under supervision of Byrne. Courtesy Northwestern University

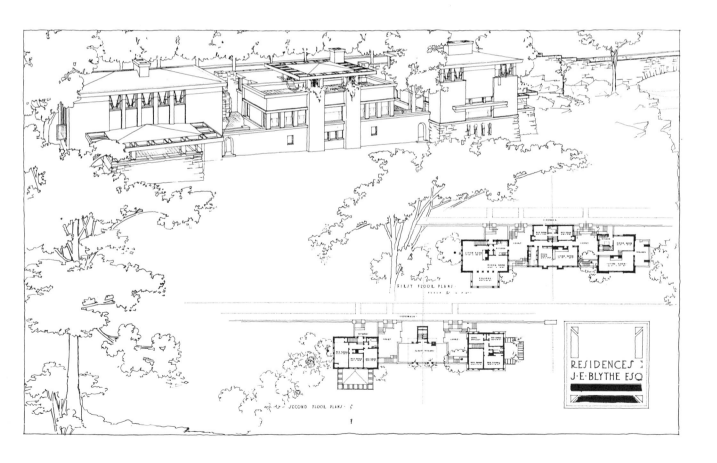

The plan of the Blythe house was modified both before and after construction. In the earliest scheme (fig. 180) the garage was to be of the drive-through type but this was later changed, while over the garage was built a poolroom with tent-like ceiling. Some of the light came from 10-inch high, by 13-foot long, strip windows that were placed under the cornices (a window so narrow as to be all but invisible in the photograph) to provide lateral, clerestorey light – a lighting arrangement popularized by Wright in his Usonian houses. The opposite, south-facing wing, contained a veranda that was soon enclosed, and later a bedroom addition was placed on the veranda roof, thereby destroying the symmetry and clean silhouette of the house. A living room stretched across the front, while the dining room stood at right angles behind the fireplace mass. Patterned tile decorated the fireplace wall and all cabinet doors were of leaded glass. The window mullions, as was Griffin's preference, were of wood and set in bilaterally symmetrical patterns.

The Sam Schneider house at 525 E. State Street was built after Griffin left for Australia, and therefore speculation has arisen that the designer was Byrne (fig. 181, house at the right). Yet extant plans, dated 24 July–4 September 1913,[25] as well as the style of the design, discount this possibility. Close inspection of the house reveals only minor changes after Byrne took charge, except in the second storey where an additional sleeping porch was added for the second owner, Hanford MacNider. The heavy foundations and window-topped corner piers are Griffin hallmarks, as is the low-pitched, seemingly flat roof. The spatial organization of the interior is an interesting variant of the square plan combined with divided levels. At the entry one overlooks the living room from a bridge-like corridor that passes behind the central chimney to the dining room beyond, a room which shares the same high view across the living room of the neighborhood park. A few steps connect this corridor with the area below in a spatial arrangement full of variety and interest. In this, as in the other interiors, it is evident that Griffin – in contrast to Wright – was not concerned with the lateral flow of space but rather with the relation of interconnected vertical spaces, spaces which are made partly visible, partly hidden, from one another by changes in level, by right-angle juxtaposition of rooms, and by spur walls (which might be the fireplace mass). Such spatial themes did not require obliteration of the basic, most economical house shape – the rectangle or the square – and were in keeping with Griffin's predilection for solid, contained forms. The excitement and richness of these spatial experiences was often quite remarkable – they prefigure the vertical space concepts of the

25 These dates overlap Griffin's trip to Australia yet this does not necessarily affect the question of design authorship because working drawings are not usually prepared until several weeks or months after the actual design is made. Beginning with the set of drawings dated 1 August 1914, Byrne is listed as associate architect.

26 Quite similar to the middle house of these three is a project for J.G. Melson bearing the date 23 April 1914, which lists the architects as 'Walter Burley Griffin Francis Barry Byrne, Associates.' The date is a few weeks prior to Griffin's final departure for Australia, and the design, now in the Northwestern University collection, may be attributed to Griffin.

27 On the same side of Willow Creek, at 28 S. Carolina Avenue, there is a well designed house which stylistically owes much to the Griffins (the Rule house, especially). Long of unknown authorship, it has recently been documented by Robert McCoy (*Prairie School Review*, 5, 3, 1968, pp. 37–8) as the work of Einar Broaten of Mason City. It was built in 1914–16 for Samuel Davis Drake, who had earlier approached Griffin, or more likely Byrne, but some friction developed and Drake gave the commission to Broaten.

28 The H.M. Mess house at 928 Pine Street, Winnetka, relates to, but was not part of, the Trier Center Neighborhood. Chronologically it precedes Griffin's house project as the blueprints are dated 15 June 1912. The much remodeled two-storey building was almost as massive as Solid Rock, its distinction lying more in its unusual character than in its intrinsic merit as a design.

present day, such as are perhaps best seen in the work of Moore, Lyndon, Turnbull and Whitaker at the Sea Ranch, California, and elsewhere.

The Schneider house was but one of three planned by Griffin as an integrated unit along State Street between Willow Creek and the Rule house.[26] They were set close together and close to the street so as to leave maximum area for the park. Although each design was apparently well formulated, judging from Marion Griffin's rendering illustrated as figure 181, the two other houses were completely redesigned before being built by Byrne. Thus Griffin's architectural contribution consisted of five houses – Melson, Rule, Page, Blythe, and Schneider – plus projects for at least four more. Byrne added two houses for a total of seven, far short of the number originally intended. Griffin's planning scheme fared no better. Rock Glen is substantially as he intended and has remained so except for the recent addition of a house between the Rule and Page premises, a house at least sympathetic to the site plan and the other buildings. But little or no planting was done and the creek bank was never fully developed – it is now entirely neglected. Nevertheless, this remains the best extant example in America of Griffin's work as planner. On the Rock Crest side of Willow Creek only the Melson house was built by Griffin.[27]

Concurrent with his Mason City work Griffin was busy with his own house and the Mess house,[28] a project for the Monroe Club, Monroe, Louisiana (a design dated September 1913 and based on the earlier Niles Club of 1909, but never built), several house commissions that later went to Byrne, the Clark Memorial Fountain built at Grinnell, Iowa, in 1914, and the Stinson Memorial Library at Anna, near the southern tip of Illinois, for which the blueprints are dated 28 March 1913.

The Stinson Memorial Library is a brilliant design and a fitting climax to Griffin's American career. Its simplicity of concept is striking; it is a rectangular mass consisting of only three basic parts: masonry base, continuous band of windows, and paired pylons flanking the entrance (figs. 182–3). Rough-quarried limestone, laid without apparent mortar joints, rises from the ground to the high band of windows. These battered walls are actually tremendous piers, cyclopean in scale, separated only enough to allow for doors or windows. Upon these walls (and above a slight indentation) rests the band of windows, heavily scaled yet smooth-surfaced by contrast with the wall beneath. The roof is inconspicuous, its battered cornice doubling as a lintel, and its shape, inverted, serving also as the sill. Similarly the small window dividing piers, shaped like those at Solid Rock, have interchangeable tops (capitals) and bottoms (bases). Ornamental leaded glass fills the windows. The third feature of the exterior are the entrance pylons which repeat the L-shape motif of the windows. These monumental forms emphasize the cave-like entrance and, internally, define the area of the vestibule, from which steps lead down to the auditorium or up to the library. The high windows illuminate the reading rooms and stacks, but leave space for continuous bookshelves underneath.

The design of the Stinson Memorial Library embodies many of the characteristics of Griffin's maturity – rugged masonry base, huge piers, horizontal rows of windows held close against the roof, and a quiet silhouette. Symmetry and solidity are prized; forms are heavy and robust.

Small yet monumental, this excellent design makes an interesting comparison with Henry Hobson Richardson's Crane Memorial Library at Quincy, Massachusetts. Griffin's library is implanted in the ground, not placed on it; a band of windows, not a steep roof, determines the silhouette. Abstract, non-historical forms are used throughout. Symmetry and the right angle predominate, while pylons mark the entry, not a tower, gable, and an arch. Both are massive, static, and emphatically horizontal, but Griffin's design has less polychromy and fewer constituent parts.

The Stinson Memorial Library stands at the height of Griffin's American career and along with the Melson, Blythe, and other Mason City

FIG. 182 Walter Burley Griffin. Stinson Memorial Library, Anna, Illinois, 1913.
Photo by Robert Kostka

FIG. 183 Walter Burley Griffin. Stinson Memorial Library. Rendering by Marion Mahony Griffin. Courtesy Northwestern Library

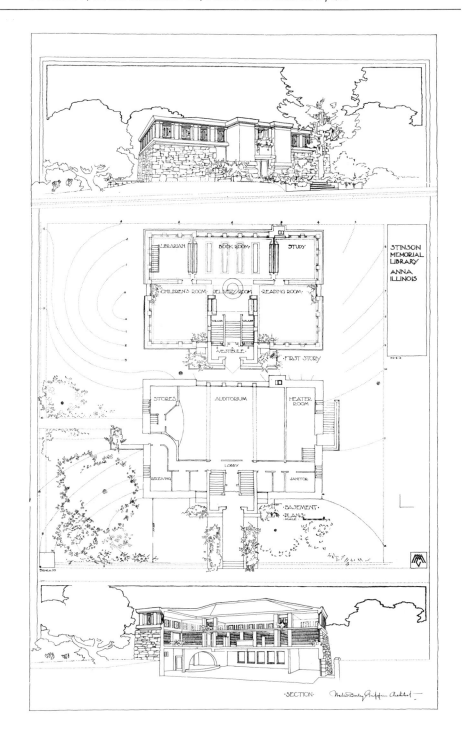

houses represents his maturity. His achievement had been considerable, even when measured against his former teacher Wright. He had pioneered the development of vertical space in contrast to Wright's concern for horizontal flow. He had exploited the use of concrete and its structural expression in residential architecture at a time when Wright was still proposing, but not building, houses of concrete. And soon thereafter Griffin developed a workable system of concrete blocks (Knitlock) which was patented in 1917 – long before Wright's more publicized concrete block experiments of the 1920s (Millard house, Pasadena, etc.).[29] In terms of planning and urban design Griffin's work was more respectful of nature and has proved more realistic and enduring. In 1909 Wright laid out the ill-fated Como Orchards by imposing a bilaterally symmetrical, patterned grid of buildings on an uneven landscape, a (decorative) grid idea that he later proposed for Broadacre City. Griffin, in 1912, laid out Rock Crest–Rock Glen, which has demonstrated its worth for over half a century; his town and city plans, moreover, were not merely expansions of smaller unit schemes (cf. Canberra). And not least significant is the fact that Griffin had achieved a viable architectural expression which, though initially based on that of his teacher, had continued to evolve and develop as the architect added his own ideas to those which he had learned. All this Griffin had accomplished in only eight years of independent practice (1906–13), a time-span comparable to that of 1893–1900 in Wright's independent career.

We may only speculate what the future would have held in store had Griffin remained in America. But by winning the competition to design Canberra his contacts and career were disrupted and for many years he was as active in fighting political battles as in practicing his profession. His mature style, however, was of immense significance for Australia, where already by 1915–16 he was building Newman College at the University of Melbourne. Down under he laid the foundations for the modern movement and by some has been called the 'father of modern architecture in Australia.'[30] His immediate influence there certainly equalled, and may have exceeded, Wright's in the United States. The dominant water body at Australia's federal capital has recently been renamed Lake Burley Griffin (imagine the Potomac being renamed after L'Enfant or Wright!), and in 1963 a large commemorative postage stamp was issued in his honor. But Griffin's Australian, and later Indian, careers lie beyond the scope of this discussion.

Walter and Marion Griffin, indeed all of the architects previously con-

29 Wright apparently knew of Griffin's experiments before designing his own block houses in California. Both systems utilized pre-cast concrete blocks of special design in combination with metal reinforcing rods, but Wright's textile blocks formed a cavity wall in contrast to Griffin's knitlock blocks which interlocked back to back by means of grooves through which the metal rods also passed. Wright's rods passed along the edge of each block, Griffin's along the back – with a resulting wall thickness of only 2½ inches. See Donald Leslie Johnson, 'Notes on W.B. Griffin's "Knitlock" and His Architectural Projects,' *Journal of the Society of Architectural Historians*, 29, 1970, 188–93.

30 For a discussion of Griffin's influence on Australian architecture see Robin Boyd, *Australia's Home, Its Origins, Builders and Occupiers*, Carlton, 1952. For more detailed studies of his work see James Birrell, *Walter Burley Griffin*, Brisbane, 1964, and Mark L. Peisch, *The Chicago School of Architecture*, London, 1964.

sidered, shared certain experiences in common, whether it be an association in Steinway Hall, working for Wright or Sullivan, or merely a deep involvement with events in Chicago or Oak Park. Not so, however, with Percy Dwight Bentley (1885–1968), whose contact with Chicago was brief and who never personally knew or studied with any of the prairie group. He represents, therefore, a fascinating example – and there may be unknown others – of how a man could be inspired by the work and assimilate enough knowledge and feeling for it to successfully adapt it in his practice. Yet equally significant was his ability to introduce these ideas into a new locale, develop an appreciative clientele, and within a few short years, virtually to transform the architectural image of a region.

This occurred in La Crosse, Wisconsin, a prosperous manufacturing and brewing town on the east bank of the Mississippi below Winona. Since the mid-nineteenth century La Crosse had accumulated a rich architectural heritage, rare outside the immediate sphere of a metropolitan center, and one eminently worthy of note by architectural historians.

Bentley was born in La Crosse on 30 January 1885, the son of a local

FIG. 184 Percy Dwight Bentley. Edward C. Bartl house, 238 S. 17th Street, La Crosse, Wisconsin, 1910. Photo by H.A. Brooks

banker. He was educated at the public schools, graduated from Ohio Wesleyan University in 1907, and attended Armour Institute. 'Our mornings,' Bentley writes, 'were spent at the Art Institute and afternoons out at Armour. The office of Frank Lloyd Wright was in a building almost directly across Michigan Avenue from the Art Institute so I frequently saw him with his cape, cane and low crowned broad brim hat. Louis Sullivan ... [was] in an office not far from Wright's. I became very much indoctrinated with both, so when I opened my office in La Crosse it plainly showed in most of my work, which was mostly residential.'[31] Without completing his studies, Bentley returned to La Crosse, where he hired Otto A. Merman as an assistant. Later, when Bentley left La Crosse, Merman assumed his practice.

The 1910 Edward C. Bartl house at 238 S. 17th Street, La Crosse, is perhaps Bentley's first executed work; its antecedents and inventiveness combine to make it a fascinating design (fig. 184). As Wright before him ('A Fireproof House for $5000'), Bentley accepted the vernacular which in turn was modified, refined, and infused with a vitality of its own. That his source was not entirely Wright's prototype is evidence from the small square windows at the center of the upper storey; common to Midwest architecture, they are absent in Wright's design. A most interesting feature is the prow-shaped stair tower which projects out under the broad hipped roof, breaking the confines of the box and establishing a vertical element precisely where interior space moves upward. The windows (compare Spencer's Magnus stair tower, fig. 36) emphasize this upward movement and impart to the interior a brightness and spaciousness which belie its small dimensions; ascending the stairs is a delightful experience.

One is tempted to ascribe the corner piers to a knowledge of Griffin's Gunn and Rule houses yet Bentley's design is earlier, thus indicating his extraordinary ability to synthesize, in this case presumably from Griffin's previous work. Also personal is his disposition of materials – lap boards over the piers, set off against smooth, light plaster. The porch, now enclosed, was originally open; on the interior a wooden screen once separated the living and dining rooms which abut at right angles. A huge, arched brick fireplace contrasts the delicate leaded glass covering numerous built-in cupboards and cabinets. The Bartl house is a small (35 x 30 feet) yet choice design. Soon after completion it was visited by Mr and Mrs Alois A. Fix who were determined to have a house like those being published by the Midwest school. They were impressed, and as Bentley was well recommended, he was commissioned to build a similar house in brick.[32] In 1912

31 Letter of 24 August 1965 addressed to Robert Warn and quoted with the writer's permission.

32 Conversation with Mrs Alois A. Fix, 17 May 1966

33 Letter to the author dated 16 January 1963

34 Information obtained in conversation with Mrs D.S. Brown, September 1956

35 A rendering of the Salzer house (published in the *Western Architect*, *18*, 12, December 1912) was delineated by Otto A. Merman in a style closely resembling that of Marion Mahony Griffin. There can be no doubt, therefore, that the Griffins' work was well known in Bentley's office.

it was constructed at 1403 Kilbourn Avenue in nearby Tomah, Wisconsin.

That same year, 1912, Bentley built a large house for a local seed merchant; it stands today as a fascinating document in the history of taste. 'Mr Salzer,' Bentley recalls, 'had clipped two or three house sketches from magazines, in the Wright trend, which seemed to meet his fancy. Of course being a great admirer of Wright I was very pleased and used my influence to encourage him with the result that, after several sketches, a sketch following the Wright pattern was adopted.'[33] Mrs Salzer, however, disliked the design; her preference was for something colonial. A compromise was therefore reached with her will prevailing on the interior and her husband's on the exterior. Thus the house has a typical colonial plan with a central hall and staircase, and with the living room located on the opposite side from the dining room and kitchen. The interior woodwork is mahogany, and the carpets, curtains, and furnishings were designed and manufactured by George Niedecken in collaboration with the architect.

The Salzers' predicament was by no means unique. What is remarkable, however, is that these divergent views remained so distinct in the design – a split-personality house reflecting one personality on the exterior, another on the interior. Yet this was not an isolated phenomenon. At almost the same moment the rambling D.S. Brown house was built at 1316 W. Moss Avenue, Peoria, Illinois. Wright had been rejected as the architect (he was the husband's choice) because Mrs Brown insisted on a traditional design as a setting for her antiques.[34] A compromise architect was therefore hired who modeled the exterior on Wright's Francis W. Little house in Peoria, while creating an interior that met with Mrs Brown's approval. Such instances as this were not without relevance to the longevity of the prairie movement.

The Henry Salzer house is a strong, dignified design of amazing maturity for a young man of twenty-seven (fig. 185). Located at 1634 King Street, corner of 17th, in La Crosse, it is less Wrightian than the architect's description would lead us to believe. Griffin's work seems equally, or more, important here, especially his Jenkins, Lewis, Dickinson project (fig. 56) and his preference for corner-and-entrance-flanking piers.[35] The end chimney, of course, is a concession to the colonial plan. But most striking is the horizontal unity achieved by the broad hipped roof, the unbroken rhythm of second-storey windows, and the careful alignment of all horizontal elements in the design. The fireproof construction is of hollow tile for walls and floors, the exterior being surfaced with plaster and painted deep tan-cream with string course and trim stained brown; the roof was

FIG. 185 Percy Dwight Bentley. Henry Salzer house, 1634 King Street at 17th, La Crosse, Wisconsin, 1912. Photo by H.A. Brooks

FIG. 186 Percy Dwight Bentley. Dr H.H. Chase house, 221 S. 11th Street, La Crosse, Wisconsin, 1913. Photo by H.A. Brooks

36 *Western Architect, 18,* 1912, 129

37 Seldom did Bentley date his plans, so design dates are difficult to ascertain. The Wahlhuter property was purchased on 19 December 1911 and the Assessor's Office records indicate that the twin houses were built in 1914. Thus the design date is probably 1913.

38 Dates ascertained from listings in the Lakeside City Directory of Chicago and the catalogues of the Chicago Architectural Club

39 Drummond's own copy of the *Western Architect* for February 1915, annotated by him, is in the author's collection. On the cover the words 'Guenzel and Drummond' have been struck and replaced by 'William Drummond 1600 Monroe Building Chicago' (which, incidentally, was the address of Griffin and Byrne). And with the same red pencil the caption 'Louis Guenzel Archt.' has been added to the following plates: #12, bottom, the White City College Inn, Chicago; #14, the Healy and Bigot Apartment, Chestnut Street, Chicago, and the Office Building for the Chicago Mill and Lumber Company, Chicago. The inference, which is born out stylistically, is that all other plates represent the work of Drummond.

of cypress shingles stained moss green.[36]

Contemporary with the Salzer house are two residences built by Bentley for Dr H.H. Chase and Henry G. Wohlhuter at 221 and 223 S. 11th Street, La Crosse (fig. 186).[37] These adjacent one-storey bungalows are virtually identical in plan, except reversed, with a common service area in between. Horizontal lap boards, exposed 8″ to weather, sheathe the walls below the windows, while rough plaster with wood trim is used above. The low, broadly overhanging roofs were originally shingled, with four triple courses establishing forceful horizontal lines. In both scale and proportions these buildings are most pleasing, their repetitive horizontals lending strength and unity to the design. The plans, of necessity, are compact, with the porch of the Chase house, but not that of its neighbor, enclosed and integrated with the living room. Unfortunately the present storm sash obscures the delicate leading of the windows. The initial inspiration for these houses may well be the Paul L. Mueller studio in Minneapolis, designed by Purcell and Elmslie, or possibly the W.A. Glasner house by Wright.

Bentley's earliest designs were created during his first few years of active practice, at a time when he taught himself what he could not learn in school and had not learned from working with others. One expects that these designs will show indebtedness; what is unexpected is how well studied, brilliantly evolved, and well proportioned these designs really are – works of considerable inherent merit.

In turning to the work of William Drummond and Louis Guenzel, it should be noted that, in spite of published references to the contrary, their partnership did not begin until 1912. It terminated in 1915.[38] The misunderstanding undoubtedly derives from the February 1915 publication of 'The Work of Guenzel and Drummond' in the *Western Architect*, where no attempt was made to differentiate between works done individually and those done in partnership. The illustrations dated back to 1908, and although several were published or exhibited previously under Drummond's name alone, historians have usually assigned all of Drummond's pre-1915 work to the partnership.[39] This is particularly unfortunate since the partnership had so little design significance; Guenzel was not an Adler, a Purcell, or a Marion Mahony Griffin.

The arrangement was purely a business convenience. Guenzel (1860–1956) was an older man with money, connections, and business ability, all of which Drummond lacked. It relieved Drummond of the (for him considerable) worries of running a business and left him free to design. But from the outset there was friction, and with the mounting anti-German sentiments engendered by the war the partnership was quietly dissolved in 1915.[40]

Built under the aegis of the firm, yet designed entirely by Drummond, was the River Forest Woman's Club at 522 Ashland Avenue of 1913 (fig. 187). In layout and shape it owes much to Drummond's earlier church at Austin (fig. 66) including the divided floor level which allows for ample illumination in what otherwise would be a darkened basement. Yet the horizontal boards (rough and showing saw cuts) and battens, and the dramatically cantilevered roof slabs, impart a less monumental but nevertheless dignified character to the design.[41] The corner towers, because they

40 Guenzel was German by birth, having immigrated to America in 1892.

41 Originally the entire porte-cochère was open; the section closest to the building is now enclosed but without detriment to the design. The exterior was stained, but is now painted dark green.

FIG. 187 Guenzel and Drummond. River Forest Women's Club, 526 Ashland Avenue, River Forest, Illinois, 1913. Photo by H.A. Brooks

rise above the clerestorey, are prominent on the exterior but are little noticed on the interior where they serve (at the front) as committee rooms and (at the rear) as dressing rooms and stairs on either side of the stage. The stage is at the end of the large, clerestorey-illuminated auditorium.

Intrinsically less interesting are three churches of this period, the Maywood Methodist Episcopal Church at 6th Avenue and 5th Street in Maywood (1912), the Lorimore Memorial Baptist Church at 600 E. 73rd Street in Chicago (1914), and the River Forest Methodist Church located at 7970 Lake Street (1912). These lack the bold, positive character of the earlier First Congregational Church in Austin, though the octagonal plan developed for the church at Maywood is a splendid solution to the needs of an auditorium-type building.

Unexecuted projects from these years abound, including an office building for the architects, a Danish Old Folks Home (in collaboration with Jensen), and a project for the Oak Park Country Club. The latter (fig. 188), with its rigid symmetry and interplay of flat roof slabs and vertical chimney masses, re-employs the theme so brilliantly evolved for the Dexter Ferry project.

Residential work includes the Ralph S. Baker house at 1226 Ashland

FIG. 188 Guenzel and Drummond. Project: Oak Park Country Club, Oak Park, Illinois. *Western Architect* 1915

Avenue, Wilmette, of 1914, with its long rectangular forms (figs. 189–92). These redevelop ideas expressed in Drummond's square-shaped house (fig. 67) with its slab roof, rows of casement windows, and plaster walls tinted and trimmed with wooden strips. The sharp, angular quality is characteristic of Drummond's work. The interior is open and bright; the trim is painted and the plaster is light in tone – very different from Wright's interiors of the period. A balcony surrounds three sides of the two-storey living room. The fourth side is dominated by a clerestorey glass

FIG. 189 Guenzel and Drummond. Ralph S. Baker house, 1226 Ashland Avenue, Wilmette, Illinois, 1914. *Western Architect* 1915

wall, below which ornamented glazed doors open into the sun porch. Similar doors to the left of the fireplace screen the dining room; balancing this latter room is the reception room and entry. The interior is bright,

FIG. 190 Guenzel and Drummond. Ralph S. Baker house. Section and east elevation. Historic American Building Survey

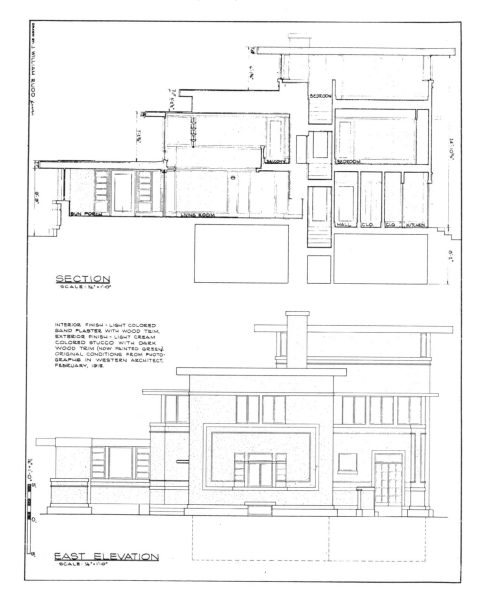

open, and airy; the exterior crisp and precise with the successive roof slabs adding variety and interest to the design.

Drummond and Griffin both benefited from extensive training at the Studio, yet for Francis C. Sullivan (1882–1929) the situation was different. Born of Irish parents in Kingston, Ontario, where he remained the first eighteen years of his life, Sullivan worked as a carpenter, a cabinet maker in a woodworking shop and then, when in his early twenties, as a draftsman in the office of Moses Edey with whom he was later (about 1908) to associate briefly in practice. It was perhaps in 1907, while on a trip to California, that he first met Wright; in any event he knew Wright by 1911, at which time he spent several months in his employ. The friendship, for Sullivan, was to dominate his future life and career.[42]

By the autumn of 1911 Sullivan was back in Ottawa and was named

42 The author is much indebted to Martin Birkhans, and his very useful thesis, for information pertaining to Sullivan. See his 'The Life and Work of Francis C. Sullivan, Architect, 1882–1929,' unpublished thesis for the degree of Master of Architecture, University of Toronto, 1964. As a more accessible source of illustrations see Birkhans, 'Francis C. Sullivan, Architect,' *Journal of the Royal Architectural Institute of Canada*, 39, 1962, 32.

FIG. 191 Guenzel and Drummond. Ralph S. Baker house. Living room, view toward sun porch. *Western Architect* 1915

43 The Wright project is illustrated in Drexler, *The Drawings of Frank Lloyd Wright*, plate 41; the Banff pavilion is illustrated on the same page. Birkhans believes that Wright's project was among those submitted by Sullivan to the library board (Birkhans, 'The Life and Work of Francis C. Sullivan,' p. 22).

architect for the Pembroke (Ontario) Public Library (with whose board Edey and he had first made contact in 1908); the following day Sullivan resigned his post at the Department of Public Works. He had submitted three library schemes, one of which went to tender but was re-designed after the bids (which exceeded the budget) came in. Unfortunately the initial schemes have not been preserved. They would demonstrate what part, if any, Wright played in the original submissions and whether his project, exhibited at the Chicago Architectural Club in 1914, was among them – of which there is a real possibility.[43] In any event the executed design was not Wright's although its slab-like roof, casement windows, and symmetrical, cruciform massing owe much to him and the architecture of the American Midwest. The building, now remodeled with new entrance doors and an additional wing, was Sullivan's first inde-

FIG. 192 Guenzel and Drummond. Ralph S. Baker house. Living room. *Western Architect* 1915

pendent commission and the beginning of his direct architectural involvement with Wright.

Other Canadian projects exhibited by Wright in 1914 were a double house for Ottawa, a post office, and a pavilion for Banff, Alberta. All were presumably designed in association with Sullivan but only the latter was built. The commission was obtained by the Canadian through his connections in the Department of Public Works and the original drawings, still preserved, list 'Frank Lloyd Wright and Fras. C. Sullivan Associate Architects Ottawa Ontario.' The plan of this 200-foot long park shelter is based on that of the River Forest Tennis Club (1906), although the symmetrical elevation presents a more imposing, monumental view because of its broad clerestorey, which continues throughout most of the building's length. The design, with its horizontal wood siding and massive stone chimneys, was certainly Wright's and, somewhat modified, it was built in 1913 for the Canadian government. Regrettably this, the only significant Wright building in Canada, was demolished in 1939.

Sullivan's bold, vigorous style is easily distinguished from that of Wright.

FIG. 193 Francis C. Sullivan. Edward P. Connors house, 166 Huron Street, Ottawa, Ontario, 1914–15. Courtesy National Capital Commission

His massing was more solid, his forms were heavier, and often he combined decisive verticals with lighter, thinner, and at times almost playful, horizontals. Frequently these verticals, as piers, chimneys, and the basic proportions of the building, predominate, resulting in an awkward conflict between a mass that is striving for height, and details that are stressing breadth. Within Sullivan, this was perhaps an unconscious compromise between the verticality of the Victorian Gothic which lingered in his native Ontario and the acquired horizontality he learned from Wright. In any event, no historicism appeared in his work; the square and the rectangle were his chosen shapes.

These characteristics are most evident in the Edward P. Connors house (1914–15) at 166 Huron Street, Ottawa, where the side walls, interrupted

FIG. 194 Francis C. Sullivan. Francis C. Sullivan house, 346 Somerset Street E., Ottawa, Ontario, 1913–14. Courtesy National Capital Commission

FIG. 195 Francis C. Sullivan. Post Office, Stonewall, Manitoba, 1914–15. Front and Jackson Avenue elevations from Sullivan's original working drawings. Courtesy National Capital Commission

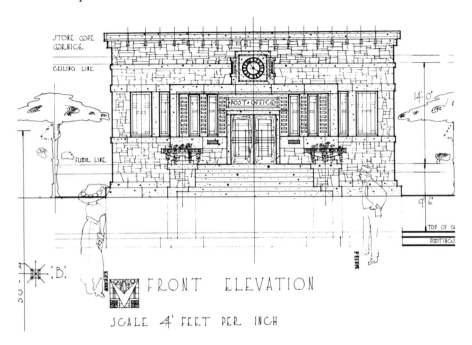

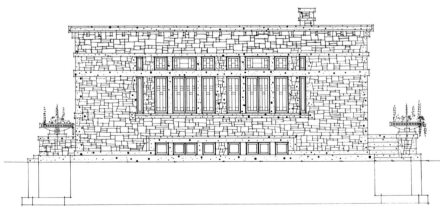

by chimneys, extend forward to become massive piers (topped with urns) – their bulky shape being reiterated in the needlessly heavy piers of the porch (fig. 193). Everything which is thick, massive, and heavy is vertical and of brick; even the chimneys are exposed throughout their entire height to add to the vertical emphasis. The horizontals, of which there are many, are generally thin, light, and constructed of wood; although continuous (as the high belt course and the eaves) they play a secondary theme – one which does not predominate.

Sullivan's own house was built on a narrow lot with a limited budget in 1914. It still stands, although remodeled internally, at 346 Somerset Street E. in Ottawa (fig. 194). It looks small (it *is* small) and is rather awkwardly upright. This impression is conveyed by a façade which, instead of being treated as a single mass, is divided vertically, so that each section has vertical proportions (rather than square, or static, ones) which even the broad roof, strong cornice, and horizontal wood banding cannot annul. Sullivan's interiors reveal the work of a craftsman-architect, a characteristic which is even apparent from the exterior woodwork. Wooden blocks set in patterns

FIG. 196 Francis C. Sullivan. Sainte-Claire de Goulbourne, (near) Dwyer Hill, Ontario, 1915. Courtesy National Capital Commission

adorn the banding where it turns an angle, and the entrance porch has a slat screen of great delicacy.

The variety of Sullivan's output was truly remarkable, and was matched by few, if any, of his Midwest counterparts. In less than six years of practice (1911–16) he built a library, hospital, fire hall, pump house, exhibition building, several homes, two schools, two churches, and at least two post offices. The latter were for the Department of Public Works. One still stands in Shawville, Quebec (1914–17), and another – the more interesting – in Stonewall, Manitoba (1914–15, fig. 195). This one-storey masonry building is among Sullivan's finest. It is more ordered and disciplined than most of his work and as a result the heaviness of the stone construction does not seem at variance with other aspects of the design.[44]

Among Sullivan's extant works the Horticulture Building (1914) in Lansdowne Park, Ottawa, is probably the best known – if only by virtue of its location. Partly remodeled, and now painted white, this multi-purpose structure owes much to the Pembroke Public Library in its cruciform shape with symmetrical wings, yet here the central pavilion dominates because of its greater height. Also somewhat of a local landmark is the Patrick J. Powers house (1915) at 178 James Street, corner of Bay, which Sullivan remodeled about 1911–12. It is a design in which the architect's love of crafted woodwork is most evident.

At Dwyer Hill, some distance from Ottawa, Sullivan built the church of Sainte-Claire de Goulbourne in 1915 (fig. 196). It is one of his most individualistic expressions and, like most of his work, was built on a minimal budget – $6600. The long gable roof rests low over the walls, flaring eaves emphasizing shelter and solidity. Banks of windows create voids in the walls while a bell tower, slender and emphatically vertical, soars above the roof at the side. The size is small, suggesting a hall of domestic scale. The interior is simple and severe, with an arch-shaped, white-stuccoed ceiling.

In 1916, at the age of 34, Sullivan found himself suddenly without work. He had always been a good salesman in spite of being quick tempered and an extrovert. It was the early war years, 1914–15, which had been his most productive, and the period of his best designs, but early in 1916 he closed his office and so began the decline which lasted until his death. He commenced to roam and to seek temporary employment. His marriage, never too happy an affair, came to a separation. His health also failed, and he

44 Does this imply, therefore, that the design was based upon one initially submitted by Wright?

45 Biographical data from Birkhans. (See note 42.) For a list, with addresses, of Sullivan's work in the Ottawa area, see Courtney C.J. Bond, *City on the Ottawa*, Ottawa, 1961, p. 113.

took increasingly to drink. In 1916 he had revisited Taliesin, where he worked on the drawings for the Imperial Hotel, but by 1917 he was back in Ottawa without work. About 1918 Wright invited him to Japan as an assistant – but to no avail. Ultimately he obtained work with the Military Hospitals Commission designing hospitals, but finally lost his job. In 1921 he moved to the United States and eventually settled in Chicago for some five years while working for himself, for the Board of Education, and for others. At Eagle River, Wisconsin, he built (1925–6) the Edward J. Kelly estate – a residence, caretaker's quarters, garage, and boathouse. The large, arch-windowed house has little in common with his earlier work although the utilitarian boathouse is imbued with a simple dignity and fine proportions.

Again Sullivan's health broke; he was operated on for throat cancer. Later Wright, himself beset with problems, mercifully took Sullivan to his winter camp, Ocatillo, in Arizona, and for over a year he remained with Wright until his death in 1929.[45]

Other architects active during the years 1912–14 included John Van Bergen, who worked successively for Griffin, Wright, and Drummond before entering private practice in 1911. His earliest houses were profoundly indebted to Wright and, although such later works as the Alfred Bersbach and C.R. Erwin houses are more personal, Van Bergen came close, perhaps closer than anyone, to actually imitating Wright's designs. And because so many of these were built in his home town of Oak Park where pilgrims go to seek out Wright's work, the impression has been

FIG. 197 John S. Van Bergen. Houses for Floric Blondeel, 426, 432, and 436 Elmwood Avenue, Oak Park, Illinois, 1913. *Western Architect* 1915

fostered that Wright's contemporaries were generally imitators of the master. 'A Fireproof House for $5000' and the later American System-Built House were the source of many Van Bergen designs, and his intimate knowledge of the Drummond house would have abetted him in this direction. His excellent sense of proportions was much to his credit, yet because of this his houses look so well designed that they more readily pass for the work of Wright.

Best known among his Oak Park houses are three (1913) for Floric Blondeel at 426, 432, and 436 Elmwood Avenue, corner of Chicago Avenue, (fig. 197).[46] The outer two are identical but reversed, while the middle house is smaller and more compact. It is similar to the Mrs Charles Yerkes house at 450 Iowa Street (across from Wright's Fricke house of 1902), except that the Yerkes house is sheathed with clapboards to the height of the second-storey windows. At 106 Grove Street is another variation on the theme.

Closer to Drummond in feeling was the William M. Webster house (1913), now demolished, at 5730 Sheridan Road, Chicago (fig. 198).[47] This very angular, flat-roofed design was far more severe than the hipped-roof houses in Oak Park.

The C.P. Skillin house (1914), at 714 Ashland Avenue, Wilmette, was certainly derived from Wright's Ward Willits house, as is particularly evident in the plan. But is lacks the same lateral extension, and has a rather agitated movement along the cornice lines and string courses. In sum, it lacks unity and repose (fig. 199).[48]

Only with the nearby Alfred Bersbach house at 1120 Michigan Avenue, Wilmette, of 1914, does Van Bergen's work come into its own (figs. 200–1). This splendid slab roof, brick-and-plaster house is superbly situated beside Lake Michigan. A lively interplay exists between cantilevered slabs, piers, and chimney masses, while the projecting porch and porte-cochère emphasize a union with the surrounding space. The floor level is elevated to improve the view, so that steps from the entrance lead up to a reception hall from which one has a screened panorama across the dining room to the lake beyond. The major rooms – dining room, living room, and porch – all are orientated toward the lake.

Before turning to the work of Barry Byrne, a further word should be said concerning Tallmadge and Watson, and Maher. Both firms remained active, but Maher's production was typified by increasing variety, whereas Tallmadge and Watson were more consistent; their work bore the inevitable hallmark of engaged piers or pilasters rising through two storeys

46 This, as all the renderings done in Van Bergen's office, was delineated by Charles S. Elwood.

47 The design is closest to Drummond's Gordon C. Abbott house in Hinsdale, Illinois, of uncertain date.

48 When the Skillin house was first published there was an accompanying description of the materials and color scheme. Such records are useful but rare; this one is quoted here:

The color schemes in and out were chosen with care that the light, cheerful appearance might prevail. A rich cream colored cement plastering covers the entire exterior of the building. The trim is a rough sawed cypress, stained yellow-brown with sash tinging on the bronze. The roofing is of plastic shingles covered with ground yellow red tile.

Inside, the entry, library, living and dining rooms are treated in the same colors. The walls to the height of the continuous head casing are a light buff, with cream color ceilings. Throughout these rooms a rough sand finish plaster has been used. ... All the woodwork, including doors, is enameled ivory white treated to remove the high gloss. [*Western Architect, 21, 1915, 32*]

Drummond's Baker house of the same year also had light interiors, indicating a trend away from the darker interiors typified in Wright's work.

FIG. 198 John S. Van Bergen. William M. Webster house, 5730 Sheridan Road, Chicago, 1913 (demolished). *Western Architect* 1915

FIG. 199 John S. Van Bergen. C.P. Skillin house, 714 Ashland Avenue, Wilmette, Illinois, 1914. Photo by H.A. Brooks

combined with a pattern in wood trim that was pointed at the top (see
H.H. Rockwell house, 1910, fig. 127). The massing of these houses, however, was never repetitive, and a fine example from the period is the H.A.
Golbeck house of 1914 at 636 Linden Avenue, Oak Park (fig. 202). The
building is compact, except for the broad low porch, and on the interior
there is no spatial flow; the rooms are quite separate and connected only
by a hall.

Maher's work, by contrast, was showing more variety, a variety which

FIG. 200 John S. Van Bergen. Alfred Bersbach house, 1120 Michigan Avenue, Wilmette, Illinois, 1914. Photo by Peter Weil, courtesy Carl W. Condit

indicated lack of direction rather than richness of invention. Among his commercial designs there had long existed a common denominator, as seen in the Watkins Buildings and Savings Bank in Winona, his university and commercial building in Evanston, and even in the brick-faced Joseph Sears Elementary School in Kenilworth (1911). Perhaps this represented his main thrust, with even his A.D. Sheridan house in Evanston (310 Church Street, 1910–11) recalling the commercial style with its aggressive 'Chicago windows' and I-shape; its patterned brickwork is similar to the Sears

FIG. 201 John S. Van Bergen. Alfred Bersbach house. Perspective and plan. *Western Architect* 1915

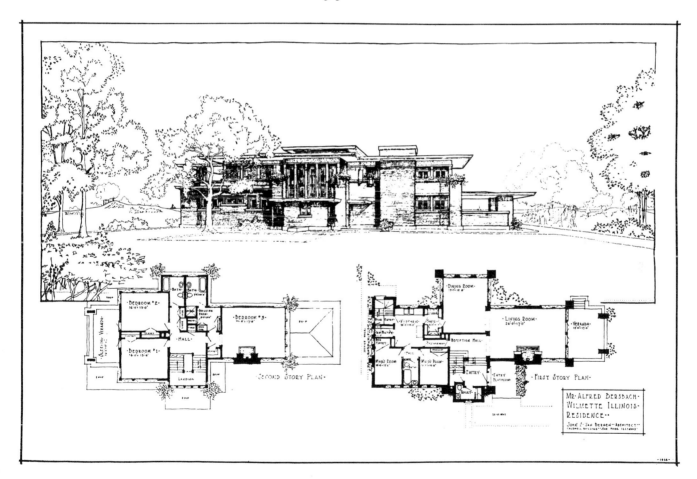

School.[49] Yet other residences ranged from the 1913 revival of the Farson house tradition for the Mills house at 107 Aberdeen Avenue, Hamilton, Ontario, to the Claude Seymour house at 817 W. Hutchinson Street, Chicago, of the same year (fig. 203). The latter was more akin to Parker and Unwin in England than to the midwest tradition. English red-brick Palladianism also gained favor with Maher. By the nineteen-tens of the new century Maher had largely relinquished his spirit of independence, and decisiveness was less often found in his work.

Byrne entered practice in the Midwest in 1914, twelve years after beginning his architectural training. He had worked successively for Wright and Griffin and then gone into partnership with Andrew Willatzen in Seattle. This partnership terminated early in 1913 and he then went to California, where he met Irving Gill and Alfonzo Iannelli. But attempts to find work in the Los Angeles area proved unrewarding, so Byrne set off for northern California and Oregon where he was intercepted by Griffin's request, in January 1914, that he return to Chicago and assume responsibility for Griffin's office.

For three years Byrne agreed to manage Griffin's affairs, the assumption

49   Illustrations of the A.D. Sheridan house and Joseph Sears Elementary School may be found in Condit, *The Chicago School*, plates 161 and 162.

FIG. 202 Tallmadge and Watson. H.A. Golbeck house, 636 Linden Avenue, Oak Park, Illinois, 1914. Photo by H.A. Brooks

being that Griffin would by then have returned to America or have discontinued his American practice. Architectural drawings were usually labeled 'Walter Burley Griffin, Francis Barry Byrne, Associates,' a title suggesting greater latitude for independent action than a formal partnership would permit. With Byrne installed in the 1600 Monroe Building office, Griffin departed for Europe where, among others, he met Otto Wagner, who he hoped would serve as a juror for the planned international competition to design a capital building for Canberra; the project, due to the war, came to naught. Early in March Griffin was back in Chicago; in May he departed, with his wife, for Australia. Return trips to cope with his practice never materialized, although in later years he did revisit America.

After Griffin's departure Byrne assumed responsibility for all work at Mason City and for commissions in Fort Wayne, Indiana, and Ithaca, New

FIG. 203 George W. Maher. Claude Seymour house, 817 W. Hutchinson Street, Chicago, Illinois, 1913. Chicago Architectural Club *Catalogue* 1913

York. In each instance he redesigned the buildings, but whether from necessity or not is difficult to ascertain. A large concrete house projected for F.L. Morse in Ithaca was completely redesigned but never built.[50] At Mason City the Sam Schneider house was perhaps already, or nearly, under construction, and here only minor changes were made. However, the two adjoining houses were redesigned (see fig. 181 for Griffin's proposal). The

50 Griffin's perspective drawing of the Morse house is in the collection of Northwestern University, while a plot plan dated 11 April 1914, is at the Burnham Library. Information concerning this redesigned project was obtained from Barry Byrne. Corre-

FIG. 204 Barry Byrne. Hugh Gilmore house, 511 S. State Street, Mason City, Iowa, c. 1915. Courtesy *Prairie School Review*

spondence from Byrne to Griffin dated 22 May 1915, says that bids on the house ran to $47,000 and that work was temporarily delayed; a letter dated 5 June 1915, says that the Morse job was dropped. I believe that these remarks pertain to Byrne's project, but have no documentary evidence on this point.

Hugh Gilmore house, built for James Blythe's son-in-law at 511 S. State Street, was a rather stark, forbidding, and somewhat awkward design which indicates that the architect was still not master of his medium (fig. 204). But the characteristics of his mature years were already present in the broad, heavy wall surfaces and severe, often austere, forms – he had learned a lesson in elimination from Louis Sullivan and Gill. The materials were those favored by Griffin – quarry-face ashlar below, smooth cement-plaster above, materials repeated next door in the somewhat larger but less distinctive Edward V. Franke house at 507 S. State Street.

After the State Street houses were completed work at Rock Glen–Rock Crest came to its premature end. There was, of course, the war, and in 1915 the death of Minnie Spencer Melson, for whom Byrne designed a mausoleum in Elmwood Cemetery. Strong and simple, and with an almost Richardsonian dignity, the monument was constructed of rough-faced ashlar (fig. 205). Two spur walls flank the mausoleum proper, which is visible only from the side. The word Melson was embossed on a bar of polished stone.

Less notable, but indicative of the period, is the little Orth house at 127 Bertling Lane, Winnetka, which may have resulted from a Griffin contact. This severe, block-shaped house has been much remodeled.

Two large commissions of 1914–15 brought Byrne's work to maturity.

FIG. 205 Barry Byrne. Melson Mausoleum, Elmwood Cemetery, Mason City, Iowa, 1915. Photo by H.A. Brooks

The first was still an unhappy compromise between the lingering influence of Wright and the more expressionistic forces then shaping Byrne's personality as a designer, that is, the simplifying tendencies of Louis Sullivan and Gill and the boldness of Griffin. This conflict is evident in the J.B. Franke house at 2131 Forest Park Boulevard, Fort Wayne, Indiana, where an earlier Griffin design inevitably affected the final result. Griffin planned a three-storey cruciform with tall vertical windows wrapping around the corners, rising from the high masonry base to the low-hipped roof. The plan was ingenious, with its carefully zoned areas and with the high ceilinged living room located half way between the first and second floors. This scheme reached the blueprint stage but it was ultimately rejected and a larger house was designed by Byrne (figs. 206–8). A modified version of the earlier plan was retained, but the living room was lowered to the ground level while preserving its two-storey height; an organ loft was built along one side. The verticality of this room found expression on the exterior in the post and lintel frame for the windows – a last vestige of the tall mullions envisioned by Griffin. Yet the union between high, compact forms and the low, Wrightian wings is far from satisfactory.

The interior is the most memorable aspect of the Franke design with its dining and living rooms on axis, separated only by a dramatic change in

FIG. 206 Barry Byrne. J.B. Franke house, 2131 Forest Park Boulevard, Fort Wayne, Indiana, 1914. Courtesy Barry Byrne

51 *Western Architect*, *33*, March 1924, caption of plate 2

ceiling height and by four space-defining piers under the balcony. Alfonzo Iannelli, in this the first of his numerous collaborations with Byrne, assisted with both the color scheme and decorations. The fireplace mural was by Iannelli; many of the furnishings were a joint undertaking; and the rich, lively colors were a far cry from the sombre interiors of earlier, more arts and crafts inspired, prairie houses. The description in the *Western Architect* is illuminating: 'The wood banding is of natural walnut with the rough plastered walls gilded. The area of gilt is sufficient to make it the controlling tone. In the lower part of the room are panels of vermilion, and in the ceiling bands of ivory. The rugs and hangings are of green blue and the upholstering material of pale gold.'[51] The architectural drawings for

FIG. 207 Barry Byrne. J.B. Franke house. Plan. *Western Architect* 1924

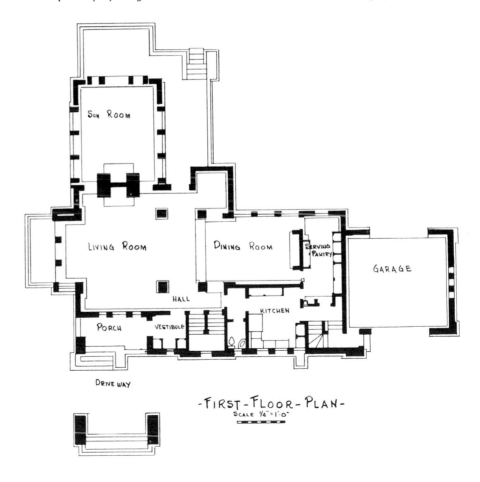

this house are dated 28 August 1914, with both Griffin and Byrne listed as the 'Architects.'

With the brilliant design for the Dr James Frederic Clarke house at 500 S. Main Street, Fairfield, Iowa, of 1915, Byrne's work reached full maturity (figs. 209–11). Bold and heavy massing, precise geometric shapes, broad, unbroken surfaces, and crisp, clean edges typify this most important of all his early works. The shape of the house, determined by two interlocking rectangles, is clearly expressed in the massing and the tight, precise gables of the roof; it is also evident in the plan. The living and dining rooms form one rectangle, overlapped by the secondary rectangle containing sub- sidiary services – hall, stairs, kitchen, and garage. Only the low, one-storey sun porch fails to fit this scheme.

Common brick, a deep rich red, is the material of the broad, knife-edge

FIG. 208 Barry Byrne. J.B. Franke house. Living room. Mural by Alfonzo Iannelli. *Western Architect* 1924

walls into which precisely incised semi-circular or rectangular windows are cut. The emphatic triangularity of the closed-end gable roof is emphasized by the color – black and white. The small balcony and front door are painted blue, giving an exterior color theme of black, white, red and blue.

The interior walls are white, the hangings yellow, the rug red, and the upholstery blue – almost de Stijl except that the primaries lack full strength. These colors were selected by Iannelli, who designed the rug. The furniture was by Byrne.[52]

As the circumstances of this commission are recorded, we have further documentation of the emerging picture of client attitudes. According to the architect, Dr Clarke knew and liked Griffin's work in Mason City, but on learning that Griffin was gone asked Byrne to design his house. Mrs

FIG. 209 Barry Byrne. Dr J.F. Clarke house, 500 S. Main Street, Fairfield, Iowa, 1915. Barry Byrne Archives, courtesy *Prairie School Review*

Clarke, however, wanted a colonial design. But the doctor circumvented her wish by pretending that a colonial house would cost more than they could afford, and built Byrne's design with day labor to conceal the true expense from his wife. Fortunately Mrs Clarke was delighted when the house was finished.[53]

Dr Clarke thwarted his wife; Messrs Salzer and Brown had managed a compromise; and Mr Scott, as we shall learn in the following chapter, capitulated and built a colonial house (fig. 233). These were signs of the times; sympathetic clients were becoming increasingly hard to find.

The Prairie School had become strong, vital, and independent. From a

FIG. 210 Barry Byrne. Dr J.F. Clarke house. Interior: living room seen from dining room. *Western Architect* 1924

52 The above information was supplied by Barry Byrne (letter dated 6 February 1963).

53 Information furnished in conversation by Barry Byrne (26 March 1965). The blueprints list only Byrne as architect; they are dated 18 September 1915.

54 Louis H. Sullivan, 'Wherefore the Poet?' *Poetry*, 7, 1916, 305–7
55 Bernard Duffey, *The Chicago Renaissance in American Letters*, Michigan State University Press, East Lansing, 1954, p. 190

small close-knit group it came to embrace many men, and from a few designs, mostly remaining as projects, its achievements expanded to scores of executed works. Quality was never higher and the best designs of this period are monuments in the history of architecture.

Personal design maturity was attained by numerous architects at this time. Griffin, Byrne, Drummond, Purcell and Elmslie, Francis Sullivan, Tallmadge and Watson all developed distinct, individualistic expressions of their own, while remaining faithful to the broader limits of the school itself. An interwoven pattern of influences became increasingly apparent and Wright's work became less seminal as the architects widened their perspectives and nurtured their own ideas.

Diversity was increasingly apparent in stylistic expression and in the number of participants – also in the type of buildings built; no longer were houses to dominate the list of new commissions. Geographic diversity, or

FIG. 211 Barry Byrne. Dr J.F. Clarke house. Plan. *Western Architect* 1924

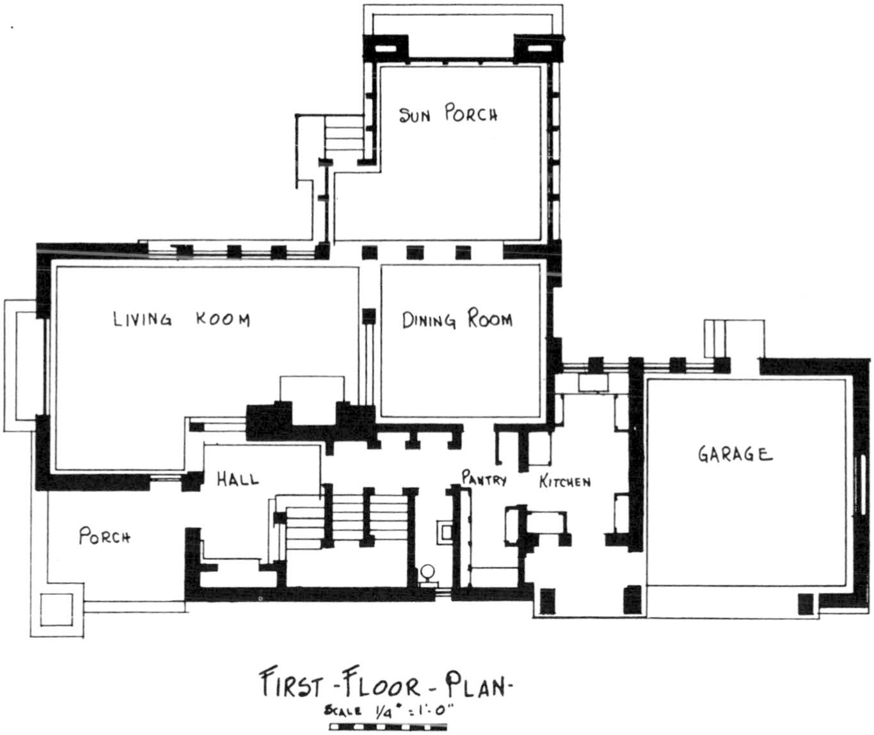

FIRST-FLOOR-PLAN-
SCALE 1/4" = 1'-0"

decentralization, was becoming increasingly important; no longer was activity focused on suburban Chicago, but extended to the less affluent, rural Midwest. But the very time-lag that resulted in the belated westward flow of cultural expressions meant that the attitudes which supplanted them were similarly retarded in transmission, so that after suburban Chicago had largely rejected the principles of the Prairie School, the prairie towns continued, for some years, to accept them. Gradually, however, the intuitive values of the Midwest were being displaced by acquired learning, and individuality was giving way to conformity – with its accompanying inferiority complex toward things 'back east.'

Conflicting values were becoming increasingly apparent at this time, as can be seen in various areas of creative activity. And inevitably they were resolved in favor of the East. In the Chicago literary world 1912 witnessed the founding by Harriet Monroe of the internationally renowned *Poetry* magazine (for which Sullivan wrote in 1916);[54] in 1914 Margaret Anderson founded the *Little Review* (to which Wright contributed $100);[55] and in 1915 Carl Sandburg published his *Chicago Poems*. Bernard Duffy in his book *The Chicago Renaissance in American Letters* cites 1912 as the beginning of 'Chicago's second golden age of letters,' yet before 1920 Hamlin Garland, Edgar Lee Masters, and Sherwood Anderson had all moved east, Margaret Anderson found nothing worth publishing in the *Little Review* so left its pages blank, and *The Dial* moved to New York, while *Poetry* lost its local identity.

Architectural publications were also undergoing change – to the detriment of the Prairie School. The *House Beautiful* moved east in 1910 and withdrew its recognition of the school in 1914, while the *Craftsman*, now out of tune with public taste and beset with financial woes, ceased publication in 1916. Support from the eastern-based *Brickbuilder* diminished; it began systematically to publicize colonial architecture in 1913. Only the *Architectural Record*, and belatedly the *Western Architect*, continued to demonstrate an active interest in the Prairie School. Meanwhile that marvelous barometer of architectural currents, the Chicago Architectural Club, held its last self-sponsored exhibition in 1914; thereafter it lacked sufficient vitality to carry on alone.

These indications of changing values in taste were not obvious to the casual observer; one was impressed rather by the vitality of the architectural movement, the quality and variety of work being produced, and the sense that the Prairie School had truly come into its own. In three years, from 1912 to 1914, much had been achieved.

When the annual architectural exhibition opened at the Art Institute of Chicago in April 1917, Thomas Tallmadge expressed the lament: 'What is ... to be regretted is the absence of any evidence that the [Prairie School] as a potent style of architecture any longer exists. ... Where are Sullivan, Wright, Griffin and the others? The absence of the work of these men has removed from the show the last vestige of local color.'[1] Three years before, in 1914, the Prairie School had been a vital, driving force, and the Chicago Architectural Club had exhibited much of their work. With amazing rapidity the situation had changed. By 1915 the architectural club was seeking co-sponsors to help finance the exhibition, and the prairie architects were having difficulty obtaining commissions, despite the fact that the quality of their work remained steadfastly high, and the building industry continued active. Non-residential commissions became an increasingly

FIG. 212 Purcell and Elmslie (for William L. Steele). Woodbury County Court-house, Sioux City, Iowa, 1915–17. *Pencil Points,* 1941

FIG. 213 Purcell and Elmslie (for William L. Steele) . Woodbury County Courthouse. Lobby. Murals by John W. Norton. P&E Archives, courtesy David Gebhard

significant source of new work, while the movement itself was rapidly decentralizing. The reasons, largely sociological, for this situation will be discussed in the following chapter, but first the architecture post-dating 1914 deserves our attention.

In 1914–15 Purcell and Elmslie were at the height of their activity and renown, and during the latter year two issues of the *Western Architect* (January and July) were devoted to their work. That same year they also undertook their largest commission, one typical of the times in being non-residential and located far from a metropolitan center. The Woodbury County Courthouse at Sioux City, Iowa, was the only major civic building built by the architects of the Prairie School;[2] it got built only because the design was substituted for the one selected by the building committee. William L. Steele, a local architect who had worked for Sullivan during Elmslie's time,[3] had won the closed competition. But after obtaining this important work he lacked sufficient confidence to execute

FIG. 214 Purcell and Elmslie (for William L. Steele). Woodbury County Courthouse. Courtroom. P&E Archives, courtesy David Gebhard

1 Thomas E. Tallmadge, 'The Chicago Architectural Club Exhibition: 1917,' *Western Architect*, 25, 1917, 27

2 Other, relatively insignificant, civic structures were built by Purcell and Elmslie such as the small Jump River, Wisconsin, Town Hall (1915) and the Municipal Building at Kasson, Minnesota (1917).

3 Steele (1875–1949) was a native of Illinois, being born at Springfield and graduating with a BS degree in architecture and engineering from the University of Illinois in 1896. Until 1904, when he moved to Iowa, he worked in Chicago, where he spent some three years in Sullivan's office. At Sioux City, after a brief partnership, he entered private practice, his work only vaguely recalling his training under Sullivan.

4 For a complete photographic record of the Woodbury County Courthouse see the *Western Architect*, *30*, February 1921. For examples of Elmslie's sensitive rendering technique see: David Gebhard, *Drawings for Architectural Ornament by George Grant Elmslie 1902–1936*, Santa Barbara, 1968. This limited edition folio contains twelve plates, three relating to the Woodbury County Courthouse, and one each to various other projects.

it and therefore asked Elmslie for assistance. Elmslie moved to Sioux City and prepared the final design; Purcell served as general consultant and also supervised the work of decoration, including sculpture by Iannelli and murals by John Norton. Although Steele was officially the architect, with Purcell and Elmslie as his associates, the design was largely Elmslie's.

The Woodbury County Courthouse is a superb building which covers nearly a city block (figs. 212–14).[4] Its public and private functions are clearly differentiated. The nearly square, four-storey structure, with a large domed lobby, contains the various public services – tax, registration, and licensing offices – as well as courtrooms on the upper floors. The non-public areas – administrative offices and secretariat – are housed in the prow-shaped tower (intended to have been several stories higher) which contains dining facilities and meeting rooms on the upmost floors.

The exterior material is a light tan brick (the horizontal joints are raked), with stone or earth-colored terra cotta for the trim and capitals. The main façade is topped by a massive lintel, below which a lively rhythm is established between the narrow piers and broad recessed spandrels. The effect is that of an open screen of piers hung from a great frame, a screen behind which the interior space can be freely arranged. The side walls, however, are articulated in a different way. They are clearly of

FIG. 215 Purcell and Elmslie. O.L. Branson and Company Building, Mitchell, South Dakota, 1916. P&E drawing, courtesy David Gebhard

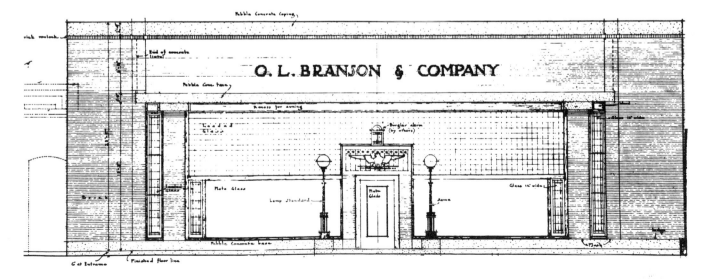

FIG. 216 Purcell and Elmslie. First National Bank, Adams, Minnesota, 1917–24. P&E Archives, courtesy David Gebhard

FIG. 217 Purcell and Elmslie. Farmers and Merchants State Bank, Hector, Minnesota, 1916. P&E Archives, courtesy David Gebhard

5 These heavy, rich forms create an impression not unlike Wright's interiors at the Imperial Hotel.

secondary importance and take as their theme the large, rectangular courtroom windows of mottled glass – windows protected by thin, cantilevered slabs. The entrances are accentuated by Iannelli's sculpture, which is unfortunately not too happily integrated with the architectural design.

The clarity and precision of this splendid exterior is not echoed in the more boldly articulated, richly embellished, and heavily scaled interior lobby.[5] With a lushness approaching that of Mayan architecture, these terra cotta surfaces contrast sharply with other parts of the interior such as the almost austere courtrooms with their tinted plaster walls and precise wood trim. A light, spacious dome crowns this lobby, its prominent ribs sheathed with terra cotta and the intervals filled with colored glass set in geometric patterns. Illumination, natural by day and artificial by night, floods through the dome which, however, finds no exterior expression. It rises beneath the tower, from whose lower windows it receives its light.

The Woodbury County Courthouse is a landmark which has never – due to its geographic isolation – received the notice it so richly deserves. In many respects it summarizes the best in midwest architecture of the previous quarter century, harking back to Sullivan's Wainwright Building in St Louis (1890), Wright's project for the Smith Bank (1904), and Purcell and Elmslie's own masterpiece, the Merchants Bank of Winona (1911–12).

Another Purcell and Elmslie essay on the post and lintel theme is the one-storey bank for O.L. Branson and Company (1916) at Mitchell, South Dakota (fig. 215). Here the volume of space enclosed is clearly expressed by the structural frame which frees most of the long front from intermediary supports. This support system made possible the installation of a glass screen consisting of small leaded squares of mottled glass, under which are located the long plate glass windows.

Smaller and somewhat less satisfactory as a design is the First National Bank (1917–24), Adams, Minnesota (fig. 216). Emphatically rectangular in form, and constructed of dark brick and patterned terra cotta (for the coping and window casements), this corner-sited building is articulated by a long window along its side and by block-like windows and a rectangular door on the more narrow front façade. The disposition of these features, however, lacks harmony. The commission came to Purcell and Elmslie in 1917, but construction was delayed until long after the war, when the partnership was dissolved and Fred Strauel was assisting Elmslie. The building now serves as the community liquor store.

The two-storey Farmers and Merchants State Bank Building (1916), Main Street, Hector, Minnesota, also housed a printing press and rentable office space. The design differs sharply from earlier Purcell and Elmslie banks in its use of a white plaster surface, which stretches like a skin over the building frame above the brick-faced ground storey (fig. 217). Windows are precisely cut into this surface and the cornice has all but disappeared. As a design it is a significant step toward the aesthetic of the International Style, one which was first essayed by these architects in the 1915 parish house project for the First Congregational Church in Eau Claire, Wisconsin. There smooth white plaster was also intended for the walls – between the brick of the corner piers (fig. 218). Directness and simplicity are strikingly apparent in both designs; they are almost free of the romanticism that often touched the work of the Prairie School.

FIG. 218 Purcell and Elmslie. Project: Parish House, First Congregational Church, Eau Claire, Wisconsin, 1913. P&E Archives, courtesy David Gebhard

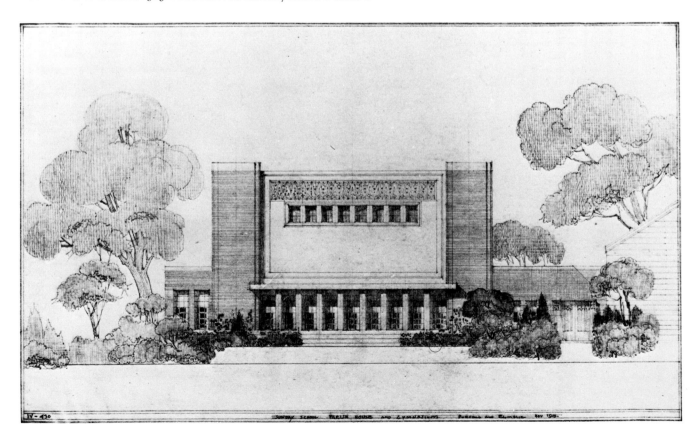

6 The two verticals seen at the side of the building in this photograph are rain drains, not structural lally columns.

Industrial architecture, except for administrative offices, was seldom commissioned of the Prairie School. There were notable exceptions, however, such as the International Leather and Belting Corporation manufacturing plants built by Purcell and Elmslie at Chicago and at New Haven, Connecticut, in 1917–18 (fig. 219). These identical factories were the first of an intended three-unit group, never completed, and both buildings have now all but disappeared. To these simple, utilitarian structures was imparted a real sense of dignity. The long window-walls, among the earliest in the United States, continued uninterrupted for 130 feet along the side.[6] The ends of the building were simple screens – battered brick walls which broke into a regular rhythm of piers and windows near the center. They were crowned by smooth white plaster pediments that echoed the shape of the roof.

Banks, public buildings, and industrial designs, rather than residences, had become the mainstay of Purcell and Elmslie's work. Yet the firm continued to build homes, such as the splendid little C.T. Bachus house (fig. 147) in 1915, and the larger Louis Heitman house of 1916 in far-off Helena, Montana. In 1916–17 the A.H. Hunter house, with its broad gable roofs and wood and plaster siding, was built at 1441 Braeburn Road, Flossmoor, Illinois, while the service buildings for Henry Babson at Riverside constituted the largest semi-residential commission of the period. These one-storey buildings of 1915–16 consisted of housing for the gardener and

FIG. 219 Purcell and Elmslie. International Leather and Belting Corporation, Chicago, 1917–18. P&E Archives, courtesy David Gebhard

chauffeur, a green house, stables, workshops, and a three-car garage (fig. 220). All were disposed around a courtyard with a central reflecting pool. Brick, wood, and plaster were the materials, and the windows were of leaded glass with casements painted white. The light and playful character of the entire complex was captured in the decorative details, such as the delicate constructivist sculptures silhouetted against the white of the garage gable, the fanciful lamp standards and stable spire, or the carved beam ends (ducks and rabbits) by Iannelli. The focal point of the u-shaped grouping was the garage gable, the other buildings, terminating with the

FIG. 220 Purcell and Elmslie. Service Buildings for Henry Babson, Riverside, Illinois, 1915–16. P&E Archives, courtesy David Gebhard

two houses, were arranged contiguously along the sides. In the 1930s the entire group was converted into residences.

During the war Purcell moved to Philadelphia to become advertising manager for Alexander Brothers, and in nearby Moylan-Rose Valley he built a summer home distinguished for its impressive sliding glass doors. By 1919, however, Alexander Brothers went bankrupt and Purcell returned to the Midwest. Because of deteriorating health, he entered semi-retirement and by 1920 moved to Portland, Oregon, where he built a gable roof home surfaced with smooth plaster (fig. 221). He carried on an extremely limited practice which included such works for himself as a house in Palm Springs (1933) and in Banning, California (1939), both in association with Evera Van Bailey. Ultimately he retired in Pasadena. As a bachelor who invested wisely in west coast real estate, Purcell was not caught in the financial pinch faced by many of his former colleagues.

Purcell and Elmslie's partnership dissolved quietly after the war but will

FIG. 221 William G. Purcell. William G. Purcell house, 2649 Georgian Place, Portland, Oregon, 1920. P&E Archives, courtesy David Gebhard

long be remembered for such successive triumphs as the Bradley, Decker, Hoyt, and Purcell houses, the Babson Buildings and the Edison Shop, the Winona Bank and the Sioux City courthouse. As a team they worked splendidly together and their designs always showed an exemplary concern for problems of how a building worked. By judicious planning and subtle manipulation of interior space they created an environment which was efficient and pleasant in which to be, and they enclosed this with forms that were at once lively and expressive of the building's use. Often their designs emphasized surface and thin-edged shapes. This, and their particular use of materials, distinguished their work from Wright's, while sharp, triangular silhouettes, sometimes evocative of a cottage, co-existed with a predilection for an abstract interplay of horizontals and verticals within the building mass. Their abandonment of decorative wood trim over exterior stucco walls, a legacy from Wright, in favor of smooth, unadorned surfaces with incisively cut window voids (figs. 217–19) was to forecast the aesthetic of the International Style, yet without dematerializing the surface to the same degree.

Elmslie remained far more active during the 1920s and 1930s than his former partner, but once on his own his designs lost some of the conviction they had once expressed. They became more conservative reflections of what had been done before. The partnership continued officially until 1922 with the last major commission being the Capitol Building and Loan Association Building in Topeka, Kansas, for which Elmslie prepared the plans, with construction undertaken only after the dissolution of the firm (fig. 222). The design lacks the decisiveness and clear relation between parts which distinguished Purcell and Elmslie's best work, suggesting, instead, a curious eclecticism of the firm's own banks (for the ground storey) and of the early work of Sullivan – specifically his St Nicholas Hotel in St Louis of 1892–3 (for the upper storeys with the gable roof). A stronger design was The Old Second National Bank Building (1924) on River Street in Aurora, Illinois, with its staccato-like effect of window-dividing piers. The Healy Chapel (1927), also in Aurora (5 E. Downer Place) was one of his least effective designs, yet in comparison with its conventional neighbors it has considerable merit. Elmslie prepared a campus plan for Yankton College, Yankton, South Dakota, in 1927 and during the next few years built there a science building (Forbes Hall of Science, 1929) and dormitory (Look Hall, 1931). It is obvious that residential work had now become the exception and not the rule, with one of the rare houses for which Elmslie received a commission being the James B. Montgomery house

7 The most complete record of Elmslie's late architectural career will be found in the Burnham Library–University of Illinois Microfilm Project, Roll #7, July 1952, where working drawings for 12 buildings, dating from 1922 to 1931, are recorded.

(1922), Bennett and Grant Streets in Evanston, with its gable roofs and plan based on 'A Fireproof House for $5000.'[7]

FIG. 222 George G. Elmslie. Capitol Building and Loan Association Building, Topeka, Kansas, 1918, and 1921–2. *Western Architect* 1924

The depression further undercut Elmslie's already reduced activity and he sought employment with William S. Hutton, for whom he helped design the Oliver Morton School in Hammond, Indiana (1935) and the Thornton Township High School at Calumet City, Illinois, of 1934–5. The

FIG. 223 William S. Hutton Architect, George G. Elmslie Associate Architect. Thornton Township High School, 755 Pulaski Road, Calumet City, Illinois, 1934. P&E Archives, courtesy David Gebhard

latter, particularly in its monumental entrance, vividly recalls the sliding horizontals and verticals of earlier years which, however, are now somewhat less robust in their treatment (fig. 223). The central piers and spandrels were sheathed in polished marble while a snowflake ornament, in metal, adorned the intervening windows. The light, delicate terra cotta decoration unobtrusively adheres to the brick walls without creating rich accents of highly plastic ornament. The sculptured figures were by Emil Zettler.

By this time Elmslie was nearly 65 and his last years were spent in relative retirement; he wrote a few articles and occasionally gave an informal talk. His long professional career had lasted more than 50 years, nearly half of which was spent with Silsbee and Sullivan. Then followed the richly productive, but relatively brief, partnership with Purcell, and an almost equal time in private practice. Finally he returned to serving others, which seemed to imbue new vitality and freshness in his work.

Louis Sullivan, during the war years, produced one of the finest works of his entire career – the People's Savings and Loan Association Bank (1917–18) in Sidney, Ohio (figs. 224–5). Never had he achieved such splendid unity between exterior and interior design, or such a complete integration between building and ornament. The precise, rectangular structure is emphasized by a great multi-colored glass window which, like a precious painting, is richly framed with a sculptural terra cotta ornament. The small office windows – below the foliated corbels – have a subtle relation to the building, which they lacked in the earlier banks at Owatonna and Grinnell. Front and side elevations are carefully integrated by a common belt-course, a polished marble base, and a patterned terra cotta coping, while the deep red tapestry brickwork and black marble are repeated on the interior as partition walls and counter tops. The wickets are of burnished bronze with carved oak beams, or lintels, resting overhead. The walls and ceiling are tinted in sympathy with the whole, while through the skylight and great west window filters a soft green light. Overt decoration is nowhere to be found.

After the splendid results achieved at Sidney, the Farmers and Merchants Union Bank (1919) at Columbus, Wisconsin, seems like an anticlimax. It lacks the unity and balance of the Sidney bank and has less dignity than the little Adams Building in Algona. The external features owe much to its immediate predecessor, yet the battered wall – from which spring piers that divide the windows – perhaps recalls Wright's project for 'A Village Bank' more than any previous Sullivan, or Purcell and Elmslie, design. The interior is plain and severe to the point of austerity, thus appropriately ending the series that began twelve years before with the highly ornate banking chamber of the National Farmers' Bank at Owatonna.

With the completion of the Columbus bank Sullivan's career was nearly at an end. He might have built the Oakland Township High School, Owatonna, in 1918 except he lost the commission when his irascible temperament offended a member of the board.[8] In 1922 a former assistant asked him to design a façade for the combination music shop and residence of William P. Krause at 4611 N. Lincoln Avenue in Chicago. This was his last architectural work. That same year he began writing *The Autobiography of an Idea* and sketched the nineteen plates which com-

8 Willard Connely, *Louis Sullivan as He Lived*, New York, 1960, p. 270

FIG. 224 Louis H. Sullivan. People's Savings and Loan Association Bank, Sidney, Ohio, 1917–18. Photo by H.A. Brooks

9 Ibid., pp. 271–2

10 Parker N. Berry (1888–1918) was
born in Nebraska but raised in Princeton, Illinois, where his father had a
planing mill and construction business.
He graduated from the local high
school in 1906 as valedictorian and class
president. In 1907–8 he studied architecture at the University of Illinois and
then moved to Chicago where, in the
autumn of 1909, and just prior to
Elmslie's departure, he obtained work
with Sullivan.

For an excellent short biography see
Donald L. Hoffmann, 'The brief career
of a Sullivan apprentice: Parker N.
Berry,' *Prairie School Review, 4*, 1,
1967, 7–15.

prised *A System of Architectural Ornament*. Both were published in 1924,
the year of his tragic death.

In 1918 Sullivan closed his office at 1600 The Auditorium Tower; the
last of his staff had already left. Homer Sailor and Frank Elbert had withdrawn early in 1917, soon after completing the drawings for the Sidney
bank. Parker N. Berry left that May following a disagreement over free-
lance work – the same reason that precipitated Wright's departure in 1893
In July 1917 Adolph Budina resigned and Sullivan was alone.[9]

Of Sullivan's last employees, only Berry[10] actively pursued his master's
course. But Berry, always frail and sickly, had only nineteen war-time
months to live before influenza, complicated by pneumonia, claimed his
life in December 1918. He had joined Sullivan in 1909 and soon assumed
Elmslie's former role as chief assistant, helping with such designs as the
Adams Building in Algona. This participation should not be over-esti-
mated, however, as is evidenced by the First State Bank of Manlius, Illinois,

FIG. 225 Louis H. Sullivan. People's Savings and Loan Association Bank. Interior.
Photo by Richard Nickel

which he built about 1915.[11] It owed much to the Algona building yet was awkward and immature, as might be expected at this time.

The presentation drawing of the Adeline Prouty Old Ladies Home, Park Avenue, Princeton, Illinois, prepared by Berry early in 1917, lists the architect's address is 1600 The Auditorium Tower – that is, in Sullivan's office. The design was to have three parts, two flanking dormitory wings with a living and dining room building in between. Of these only the west dormitory was built (fig. 226). Its porch, steep roof, and dormers impart a non-institutional, home-like character to the design while a strong, assertive quality exists in the clean, crisp horizontals and the sharp, triangular forms.

The Interstate National Bank (1917–18) which Berry built at Hegewisch (now part of Chicago) has since been demolished (fig. 227). Here again the Adams Building set the theme, but this time the solution was more per-

11 An illustration of the Manlius bank will be found in Hoffmann, ibid., p. 9.

FIG. 226 Parker N. Berry. Adeline Prouty Old Ladies Home, Park Avenue, Princeton, Illinois, 1917. Photo by Donald Hoffmann

sonal and direct. It is a strongly unified design except that the terra cotta
ornament and heavy stone trim are so assertive as to detract from the

FIG. 227 Parker N. Berry. Interstate National Bank (demolished), Hegewisch (Chicago), Illinois, 1917–18. *Western Architect* 1918, courtesy Donald Hoffmann

FIG. 228 Tallmadge and Watson. William V. Carroll house, 611 Fair Oaks Avenue, Illinois, 1916. Photo by H.A. Brooks

FIG. 229 Percy D. Bentley and Charles Alford Hausler. Emil T. Mueller house, 128 S. 14th Street, La Crosse, Wisconsin, 1914. Photo by H.A. Brooks

FIG. 230 Percy D. Bentley and
Charles Alford Hausler. Emil T.
Mueller house. Hall and staircase.
Photo by H.A. Brooks

simplicity of the whole. Nevertheless it is impressive as an early work.

Unfortunately, Berry never had time to reach design maturity. He died at the age of 30, in the midst of preparing drawings for his next commission, the Julia Rackley Perry Memorial Hospital in Princeton, Illinois.

Tallmadge and Watson, meanwhile, were building fewer homes. Yet the William V. Carroll house (1916) at 611 Fair Oaks Avenue, Oak Park, is so typical as to be easily identified as one of the firm's designs (fig. 228). Its emphasis is vertical rather than horizontal and the dark (but subsequently white-painted) wood trim over light stucco assumes a point under the gable roof. In plan the house is cruciform, the living and dining rooms being on axis from front to rear; there is a sun porch on one side and an entry, stairs, and kitchen on the other.

Tallmadge and Watson increasingly specialized in ecclesiastical work during the 1920s, and in this field became widely known. This programmatic change also resulted in a change in design. Their churches would never pass for creations of the Prairie School, rather they tended toward a simplified Gothic mode. Their residences, often blocky but articulated with light, delicate vertical elements, had always been distinctive and fre-

FIG. 231 Percy D. Bentley and Charles Alford Hausler. Emil T. Mueller house. Plan. By James Acland

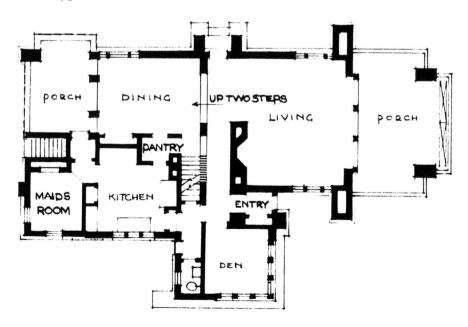

quently were the conception of Watson rather than his partner.

Percy Bentley, meanwhile, was less active in La Crosse due to a partnership with Charles Alford Hausler in St Paul. Hausler was an excellent public relations man and was particularly persuasive with school boards; Bentley was the chief designer for the team, although the character of his Minnesota work became increasingly conservative. They did, however, build a few more houses in La Crosse, including that for the brewer Emil T. Mueller, constructed at 128 S. 14th Street in 1915 (figs. 229–31). The plan is rectangular with an unobstructed view throughout the length of the house; it is entered at the side through an open hallway. This hall divides the living room (partly screened by the chimney mass) from the dining room and stairs, both of which are raised two steps above the main floor. The interior is finished in smooth plaster and quartered oak, the latter being superbly matched and crafted, and rubbed to a rich natural finish. Particularly handsome are the balusters (massive oak planks set on end and trimmed with oak strips), the beamed ceiling in the dining room, and the special light fixtures in leaded glass. A small library located near the entrance (and just visible in the illustration) is outstanding in its detail, especially the glazing of windows and cabinet doors.

The exterior of the Mueller house faithfully reiterates the plan. The two-storey, rectangular building (its right side recalls the Salzer house) has a porch (originally open) at the front and a single-storey library at the side. The broad chimney mass rests at right angles to the hip of the roof. The dark trim of the window casements, cornices, and belt course originally contrasted with the tinted plaster walls in a color combination destroyed by repainting.

In nearby Fountain City, Wisconsin, perched high above the Mississippi, is the brick and wood trim M.L. Fugina house (1916) at 348 Main Street. Smaller than the Mueller house, it is closer to the Wakefield house in design. Still inhabited by its original owner, its interior is in perfect condition (fig. 232), All the woodwork is of hand-polished quartered oak, the plaster walls are tinted tan, and the windows are glazed with leaded glass set in abstract, rectangular patterns. The warm gray Roman brick of the fireplace is laid with raked horizontal joints and the andirons, alone among the furnishings, are perhaps designed by the architect.

Mrs Fugina informed the author that her husband had made the choice of architect; he had admired the La Crosse houses by Bentley and had taken her to see them. She thought they were rather unusual, yet not without appeal; nevertheless she left the decision to her husband. Such feminine passivity, however, did not characterize Mrs Argyle Scott of La Crosse who insisted – according to Bentley[12] – that she have a colonial house. Mr Scott, being a complaisant husband, left such decisions to his wife. Bentley acquiesced and in 1920 built their home at 1721 King Street (fig. 233). Its plan is typically colonial with a central hall and stairs, a living room on the right and a dining room and kitchen on the left. The exterior, while following the traditional scheme, is, nevertheless, anti-archaeological in detail. The clapboards are not lapped boards but flush planks separated by deep grooves while the columns, entablature, and pediment at the entry are a highly personal variant on the classical theme.

The Scott house began a new phase in Bentley's career, one detached from La Crosse and the type of designs that he had created there. Otto Merman, his former assistant, assumed Bentley's local practice and briefly maintained the old tradition, as did certain speculative builders, but their designs, lacking vigor, were but a shadow of what had been done before.

FIG. 232 Percy D. Bentley. M.L. Fugina house, 348 Main Street, Fountain City, Wisconsin, 1916. Living room fireplace. Photo by H.A. Brooks

12 : As interviewed, on behalf of the author, by Marion Card Donnelly (18 April 1967)

Bentley typified the dispersement of the movement which occurred at the time he began his practice. He had never personally known Sullivan, Wright, or the others, yet he absorbed their message and preached it where it had not been heard before. His short but brilliant La Crosse career altered the course of architecture in that area and demonstrated what might have been done in almost any midwest town.

For Byrne the years 1916–17 were also a time of transition, but of a different kind. The brilliant synthesis achieved at the J.F. Clarke house of 1915 (figs. 209–11) heralded no series of related designs. Instead, it initiated a trend toward greater simplicity and increasing independence from Wright. Characteristic was the severity of the Kenna Apartments at 2214 E. 69th Street, Chicago, of 1916 where the precise, emphatic massing was relieved only by the texture of the brickwork and by the terra cotta window moldings designed by Iannelli (fig. 234). Had the exterior been of white plaster, instead of brick, the building might pass as a work of the International Style in the late 1920s.

FIG. 233 Percy D. Bentley. Argyle Scott house, 1721 King Street, La Crosse, Wisconsin, 1920. Photo by H.A. Brooks

Simplification, as the controlling concept of the design, reached an extreme in Byrne's work at the University of New Mexico, a project originally awarded to Griffin as the renowned planner of Canberra. The proposal was to plan the entire campus and then construct the various buildings, beginning with a Chemistry Building that would temporarily serve as a general Science Hall.[13] Griffin's design, dated 14 December 1915 and prepared in Australia, proposed a two-storey building with the second floor classrooms and labs lit by skylights and courtyard windows (fig. 235). Second-storey exterior windows being therefore unnecessary, this area was treated as a high attic devoid of decoration – not even a molding defined the cornice. The attic was separated by a strong horizontal projection, below which the windows were regularly placed, a concept found in pre-Columbian architecture such as the so-called Palace of the Governor, Uxmal, Yucatan, which may have been Griffin's source.[14] This helps to confirm our previous inference that the Blythe house and Stinson Memorial Library owe something to pre-Columbian design. Griffin's project also bears comparison to Wright's Aline Barnsdall house of 1916–20, although the possibility that Wright arrived at his solution via the little known Griffin design seems remote. It is significant that Griffin apparently reached his conclusion first.

13 The chronology of the University of New Mexico commission is as follows: Griffin visited the site during the summer of 1913 and, before commencing the design, departed for Australia from Vancouver in the spring of 1914. He intended to return within three months and visit Albuquerque. The university officials patiently attended his arrival, continued to acquire additional lands, and gradually grew impatient – while rejecting Griffin's suggestion that another visit was not necessary. On 25 July 1915, the president of the Board of Regents, George L. Brooks, wrote Griffin that 'We do not expect to place an order for the work until after you have been on the ground again.'

Griffin responded by submitting a general design for the campus (dated August 1915) and in the same letter suggested it might be expedient if his American partner, Byrne, visited the site. On 17 November 1915, Brooks notified Griffin that they could not await his arrival much longer and would, meanwhile, contact Byrne who was asked (17 November 1915) 'Have you any suggestions to make as to the size and general appearance of the Science Hall building which is to cost 80,000 ...' Thus Byrne was brought directly into the negotiations.

On receipt of the Brooks letter Griffin prepared a design, dated 14 December 1915, for the Chemistry Building (fig. 235) and sent it to Byrne who, meanwhile, had prepared his own design for the building. Byrne submitted only his own project to Brooks (the working drawings, revised, were prepared later and dated 15 April 1916, fig. 236) without immediately forwarding Griffin's design. Because Byrne's drawings bore only his name, and because Byrne had not forwarded Griffin's project to Brooks (Griffin later – 11 March 1916 – sent a duplicate copy of his design directly to Brooks), Griffin was furious and an already strained relationship nearly reached the breaking point. Griffin approached (letter of 13 September 1916) Purcell and Elmslie pursuant to their becoming his American partner, but Purcell (25 October 1916) rejected the suggestion on the grounds that a three-way partnership split the commissions too thin.

The minutes of the Regents meeting on 21 March 1917 reveal that the bids for the Science Hall (Byrne's design) were too high and that the architects were to be notified. Apparently more modifications were undertaken before construction was begun.

(The author is indebted to David Gebhard for making available the above-mentioned correspondence.)

14 Griffin, in his correspondence, described the design of the Chemistry Building as of the 'pueblo type' in obvious reference to the traditional architecture of the region.

FIG. 234 Barry Byrne. Kenna Apartments, 2214 E. 69th Street, Chicago, 1916. *Western Architect* 1924

FIG. 235 Walter Burley Griffin. Project: Chemistry Building, University of New Mexico, Albuquerque, New Mexico, 1915. Courtesy Northwestern University

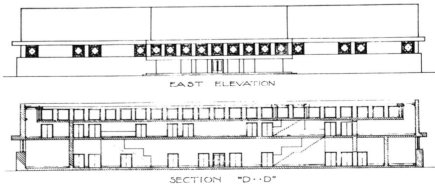

Byrne's design for the Chemistry Building envisioned a one-storey building topped by a narrow coping of ornamental cast stone (fig. 236). Wall predominated, with the deeply incised windows accentuating the thick, heavy character of the masonry. The symmetrically grouped windows were divided by strips of ornamental cast stone; the walls were of tile covered with cement plaster. The 162-foot long east elevation projected forward at the center to emphasize the simply framed double doors of the main entrance. Additional light for labs and lecture rooms came from angled (saw-tooth) factory-type skylights, the silhouettes of which were

FIG. 236 Barry Byrne. Chemistry Building, University of New Mexico, Albuquerque, New Mexico, 1916. Elevations. University of New Mexico

SOUTH ELEVATION

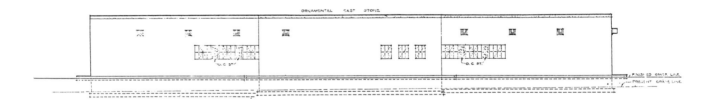

WEST ELEVATION

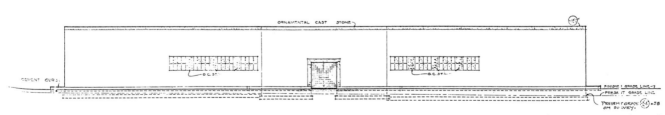

EAST ELEVATION

15 Among Wright's Taliesin drawings there is an unpublished project for a Municipal Art Gallery which is variously (post-) dated from 1907 to 1916 – the latter date being stylistically more probable than the former. In certain respects it is similar to the Byrne Chemistry Building – the long, low proportions are nearly the same, there is a curb along the bottom and, most significant of all, there is a narrow, decorative coping at the top. Whether Byrne knew the Wright drawing, or vice versa, it is difficult, if not impossible, to say.

held below the cornice.

The simplifying tendencies which Byrne inherited from Sullivan, Gill, and the Southwest are here represented at an extreme never to be exceeded in his work again – and in the executed building the severity was intensified for reasons of economy. The ornamental coping (a visual device for softening, yet accentuating, the skyline) was eliminated, as well as the door frame and the ornamental panels between the windows. The original working drawings (fig. 236), prepared prior to the modifications, are dated 15 April 1916.[15]

A third Byrne commission in 1916 was a large house for C.M. Rich at 1229 Grand Avenue, Keokuk, Iowa, which, though typified by broad plaster walls and sharply defined windows, was not decisive in its massing and, in truth, lacked distinction as a design. More conclusive was the John Valentine house at 707 Riverside Avenue, Muncie, Indiana (now the Sigma Tau Gamma fraternity house at Ball State University, the blue prints for which are dated 28 September 1917) with its incisive, clean-cut rows of windows in the plain walls (fig. 237). Yet the tube-like copper gutter, ironwork, and oriel windows impart to the design an elegance – in spite of the texture of the brickwork – more akin to Josef Hoffmann in Europe (Stoclet Palace) than to the work of the Prairie School. The elegance recalls certain

FIG. 237 Barry Byrne. John Valentine house, 707 Riverside Avenue, Muncie, Indiana, 1917. Photo by H.A. Brooks

FIG. 238 Barry Byrne. Immaculate High School, 640 W. Irving Park Road, Chicago, 1921–2. Historic American Building Survey photo by Harold Allen

FIG. 239 Barry Byrne. St Patrick's Church, Racine, Wisconsin, 1923. Photo courtesy Barry Byrne

interiors by Byrne and Iannelli, such as their remodelling work for William F. Tempel in Kenilworth or the earlier J.F. Clarke interiors at Fairfield (fig. 210).

The 1920s saw Byrne become a specialist in ecclesiastical and educational architecture while virtually abandoning residential design. His work tended increasingly toward expressionistic forms constructed in brick, and demonstrated a continued predilection for broad, unadorned expanses of

FIG. 240 Barry Byrne. Church of Christ the King, Tulsa, Oklahoma, 1926. Photo courtesy Barry Byrne

wall – accentuated with rich, plastic areas of intense decoration. This sensibility was a parallel to the so-called Spanish colonial which, after the San Diego fair, enjoyed such a vogue. But in Byrne's mind lingered the recollection of Sullivan's relation between surface and ornament, an idea best expressed in Sullivan's banks. Iannelli was responsible for the sculpture and much of the decoration for these buildings, although the two men worked closely on all such matters. In the early 1920s Byrne entered into partnership with John Ryan, who acted as the business manager and contributed little to the designs.

This new phase in Byrne's career opened with the Immaculata High School at 640 W. Irving Park Road, at Marine Drive, Chicago, of 1921–2 (although the Convent of St Thomas Apostle dates from the preceding year). The strong massing, relieved by tall arches which vertically unify three storeys (a favorite Richardson and Sullivan device) is executed in brick and set off by Iannelli's sculpture (fig. 238). Probably the best known of all Byrne's Chicago buildings, the Immaculata High School commands a prominent site near the north end of Lake Shore Drive.

With St Francis Xavier High School, 808 Linden Avenue, Wilmette, designed in 1922, the pointed arches of the previous year give way to stylized triangular indentations. Constructed of brick, these are corbelled to create a rich pattern of light and shade. Iannelli's sculptured figures adorn the corners and the zig-zag of the coping is also of his design. A more elaborate variation on this theme was prepared in 1923 for St Catherine's High School in Racine.

In 1922 Byrne built his first church, the first of many he built during the next 40 years. In character they recall the high schools, except that the churches are richer and more elaborate in their ornament, especially in their silhouette against the sky. The plastic, sculptural cornice coping at the Church of St Thomas the Apostle (5472 Kimbark Avenue, corner of 55th Street, Chicago, built in 1922) is almost overbearing, yet effectively emphasizes the plain surfaces of the broad brick walls. Paired windows, joined by sculptured niches, establish a rhythm along the walls while the corners of the building are blunted by the setting back of successive rows of bricks in a serrated fashion, this having the effect of fluting. The entrance portal, as constructed, is not according to Iannelli's intended design.[16]

More personal, and more restrained in ornament, is St Patrick's Church in Racine, designed in 1923 and constructed the following year. Here the façade is divided by brick shafts set at 45° to the wall surface, an angle

16 For illustrations of St Francis Xavier High School and Church of St Thomas the Apostle, see the *Prairie School Review*, 3, 4, 1966, 21 and 23.

reiterated by the blunted corners that rise as caped pinnacles above the roof (fig. 239). A coping, saw-tooth in silhouette, repeats the angular motif as do the pointed windows and glass insets of the doors. The church, situated on a commanding hilltop site, is approached by a broad staircase. The bold and simple interior, nearly square in plan, recalls at modest scale the dignified monumentality achieved at St Thomas the Apostle, where the emphasis was also upon the volume of space enclosed.

A larger and more complex variant of the Racine church was built in 1926 at Tulsa, Oklahoma, a commission received from Bishop Kelly, who was transferred to Tulsa from St Thomas' in Chicago. At the Church of Christ the King the corner motif of the earlier churches was further developed and consummated; also introduced was a prow-shaped cluster of serrated shafts rising through the center of the façade (fig. 240). The ornament, done with the collaboration of Iannelli, was less robust in detail and somewhat smaller in scale. The bold rectangular massing – as emphatic as a Sullivan bank, which is here recalled – clearly reflects the enclosure of a

FIG. 241 Barry Byrne. Church of Christ the King, Cork, Ireland, 1928. First sketch. Courtesy Barry Byrne

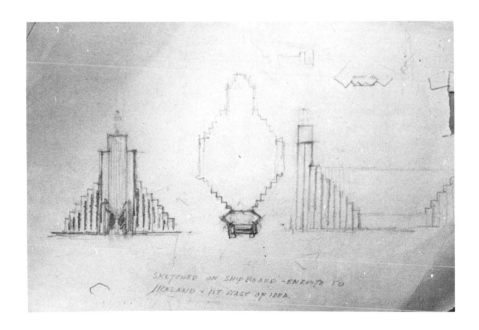

cubic volume of space and, with equal clarity, reiterates the basis of the plan.

Byrne's next church, coming after another interval of two years, was the Church of Christ the King at Cork, Ireland, probably the first European Catholic church to be built by an American architect. The design departed radically from its predecessors. The Sullivanesque space enclosing cubic form constructed of brick and ornamented with richly molded terra cotta, which typified the earlier churches, gave way to an even more expressionistic form where the roof and walls were combined in a single unity (fig. 241). The purely decorative shafts of the earlier churches here became an integral part of the walls – indeed they are the walls – and their height coincided with the slope of the roof. An outline of the front elevation, if revolved around the ground line as an axis, described almost exactly the plan of the church; thus the elevation was a true expression of the plan. Light penetrated through narrow slits between the shafts (really piers) which stepped up, and forward, toward the tower, which was the most prominent 'pier' of all. Exterior decoration was limited to the stylized figure of Christ, a relief sculpted by John Storrs, which stood between the portals. The building was constructed of concrete, a departure from Byrne's previous preference for brick.

This intensified expressionism, and general abandonment of ornament, probably resulted from Byrne's two-month trip, with Iannelli, to Germany, Holland, and France in 1925. The Bauhaus was visited, where Byrne met Meyer, Feininger (a life-long friend), Kandinski, and Klee (Gropius was away at the time), and in Holland they met Wijdeveld and Kramer and also looked at the work of de Klerk and Oud. Poelzig's work was studied and a warm friendship developed with Eric Mendelsohn – with Byrne making many arrangements for Mendelsohn's American lecture tour that resulted in the publication of *Amerika* in 1928.[17]

By this time it seems fair to say that Byrne was moving beyond the formal expression, but not the ideals, of the prairie architects and into a more personal approach of his own, one which was less akin to the American Midwest than to the emerging avant-garde of Europe. His predilection for expressionistic forms, typified already in the J.F. Clarke house of 1915 (fig. 209), and his preference for brick, created within him a natural sympathy for his overseas counterparts. Although Byrne built a few houses during the late 1920s, his ecclesiastical work was sharply curtailed, first because Cardinal Mundelein of Chicago apparently disapproved of his designs, and then because of the depression. These factors led Byrne to

17 Information obtained in conversation with Byrne (26 March 1965)

18 These two churches, with plans, are well illustrated in the *Architectural Record, 109,* 1951, 87–95.

19 The Rogers project is illustrated in the *Western Architect, 21,* April 1915.

20 For a daughter, Miss Barbara Erwin, Van Bergen designed a house (1927) at 621 Warwick Road which, being less Wrightian, was intrinsically less interesting. Erwin, twenty years earlier, had built a home in Oak Park designed by Maher (fig. 48).

leave the diocese for New York, returning to Chicago only after the war in 1945. The seeds for his later work, nevertheless, lay in his designs of the 1920s, with such hallmarks as the fish-shaped church plan (for St Columba Church, St Paul, Minnesota, and St Francis Xavier, Kansas City, Missouri, of 1948)[18] being a refinement on the plan for Cork. Perhaps, too, the wall piers of the Cork church, with narrow windows between, was the basis for St Benedict's Abbey at Atchison, Kansas, designed in 1955.

Byrne, although trained under Wright, had responded primarily to Sullivan's sense of form, a preference which was reinforced by his contact with Irving Gill, the architecture of the Southwest, and his association with Griffin. Severe, space-enclosing cubic shapes, rather than space-defining intersecting verticals and horizontals, typified his work. Where ornament existed (and it was used only for major non-residential works) it emphasized edges or changes in plane; it framed wall surfaces but did not adorn them. Over the years – significantly – his vocabulary of form evolved and grew; it always retained its freshness. This was a real achievement. His was a strong personality in design; he learned from his mentors but left their stylisms behind – while continuing a life-long pursuit of his early ideals. In this he exemplified the best in the Prairie School.

Van Bergen, like Byrne, had trained under both Griffin and Wright but, unlike Byrne, he never successfully synthesized that experience. Too often he accepted the letter for the law. He did have a saving grace, however, which was his superior sense of proportions that imparted to his work a finesse rare to the profession.

One of his more inventive works was Alfred Bersbach's house of 1914, which was outstanding for its plan as well as exterior design (see p. 280 and figs. 200–1). It failed, however, to initiate a less literal phase in his career, as is exemplified by the W.R. Rogers project of 1915, which combined various Wrightian features and accepted the Coonley house as the basis for the plan.[19] Not until 1926, a rather late date, did Van Bergen produce his masterpiece in the C.R. Erwin house at 615 Warwick Road, Kenilworth (fig. 242).[20] Even this recalls Wright's Oak Park houses, but reinterpreted on Van Bergen's terms. Rough limestone and cement plaster are the materials, the window-to-wall relation is well studied, and the entire building has a pleasant feeling of breadth and repose. The interior, climaxed by a two-storey living room, is almost ceremonial in its layout; it is an impressive space in which to be.

Van Bergen's problems as a designer are interesting to compare with those of Maher. The latter was constantly concerned with invention, yet lacked a refined sense of proportions. He eschewed the work of the Prairie School but, like them, sought inspiration both from the vernacular and from contemporary British design; he dreamt of creating an American style. His determination, however, was not matched by his ability and he was unable to consistently synthesize his borrowed forms. Instead, he jumped from type to type and as time passed these became less original, tending increasingly toward the prevailing name-styles, particularly Georgian. For a highly dedicated man, his was a frustrating career, one which led, in 1926, to his suicide.

Maher, in spite of his shortcomings, cannot be dismissed lightly. His influence on the Midwest was profound and prolonged and, in its time, was certainly as great as was Wright's. Compared with the conventional architecture of the day, his work showed considerable freedom and originality, and his interiors were notable for their open and flowing, if not sophisticated, space. His designs, like Mies van der Rohe's in more recent years,

FIG. 242 John S. Van Bergen. C.R. Erwin house, 615 Warwick Road, Kenilworth, Illinois, 1926. Photo by H.A. Brooks

were easily emulated; they also embodied the ideals cherished by the client.

Drummond was more typical of the prairie architects, both in his training and his subsequent career. In 1915, when the *Western Architect* devoted an entire issue to his work, he had reached the peak of his renown. That year he designed a recreational building for Shedd Park, a design notable for its careful attention to detail and effective juxtaposition of materials (fig. 243). Built for the West Chicago Park Commission, and still admirably serving its intended multifarious functions, the building (be-

FIG. 243 William E. Drummond. Park Building. Shedd Park, Chicago, Illinois, 1915. Courtesy *Prairie School Review*

cause of its sculpturally enriched gable roof and slab-like trellis) is much less severe than his earlier work.

The John A. Klesert house on Keystone Avenue in River Forest dates from the same year (figs. 244–5). It also has a broad gable roof with flaring eaves, a roof-type more traditional than the slabs that Drummond's own house showed him to prefer. Yet the design remains clear, angular, and precise, a quality emphasized by the contrast between wood and plaster and by the thin-edged roof.

With the post-war years there was a significant change in Drummond's

FIG. 244 William E. Drummond. John A. Klesert house, Keystone Avenue, River Forest, Illinois, 1915. Photo by Thomas M. Slade

FIG. 245 William E. Drummond. John A. Klesert house. Plan. *Architectural Record* 1916

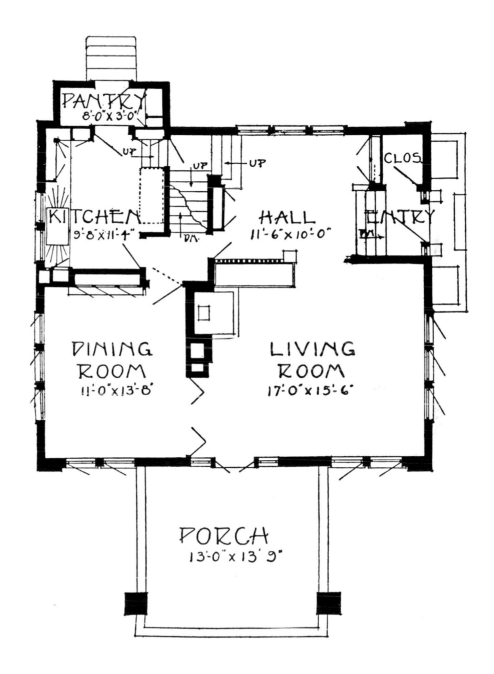

FIG. 246 William E. Drummond. O.B. Higgins house, 535 Edgewood Place, River Forest, 1926. Photo by H.A. Brooks

FIG. 247 William E. Drummond. River Forest Public Library, 735 Lathrop Avenue, River Forest, Illinois, 1928. Courtesy *Prairie School Review*

career. No longer were residential commissions available as before; rather, he found it necessary to depart from his training and offer the client something more obviously traditional. At first he tried compromise, as at the Benjamin Badenoch house (1925) built beside his own in River Forest (house on the right, fig. 67). Here he emphasized geometry, as he had always done, but now with triangular forms suggesting picturesque roofs, rather than the right angle and flat roof preferred in his youth. But this was evidently not the answer and the following year he built the O.B. Higgins house at 535 Edgewood Place, River Forest, which emulated the Tudor Gothic so popular in that decade (fig. 246). Although the materials are well handled, the architect was apparently not at home in his adopted style; the design is somewhat disorganized and the transitions are often weak.

At the River Forest Public Library, built on the eve of the depression (1928–9), Tudor Gothic was frankly used (except for the multi-sided corner piers) and although this ordered, symmetrical design is of considerable merit, it is far removed from the ideals of the Prairie School (fig. 247). In any event, Drummond's private practice was all but over. The depression ruined him and what employment he received was in other offices; after the second war he was too old to begin again.

Perhaps Griffin and Wright were right. They, by happy coincidence, had obtained major commissions outside the United States. But for those left behind the alternatives left much to be desired. One could build what the client wanted (which Drummond rather unsuccessfully tried to do), or try to change one's specialty to non-residential work (which Elmslie did), or abandon domestic practice while simultaneously evolving a new vocabulary of form more in keeping with the times (which Byrne did). Into these categories most of the prairie architects were to fit. Other, less satisfactory, alternatives were to go without work and starve (which Sullivan did), or to commit suicide (which Maher did).

It is evident, therefore, that in the post-war years the group which had constituted the Prairie School no longer existed as a cohesive force or even as a diverse collection of individuals united by common ideals. Any semblance of a school had well-nigh vanished – although independently several of the architects struggled through the boom years by either modifying their kind of practice or compromising their ideals as designers.

What, then, brought this once vigorous movement so abruptly to an end after 1914/16? Although some reasons have already been suggested this question warrants further consideration.

Why the Prairie School came to an end, and especially why the ending was so abrupt, is a question which has long baffled the historian. Yet the answer is not hard to find thanks to the many clues left by contemporary architects, clients, critics, and novelists. Their testimony is underscored by a consistent theme: that the midwesterner increasingly rejected individuality in favor of conformity, that the client rather than the architect stipulated the change, and that the housewife, sooner and more readily than her husband, renounced the work of the Prairie School.

The client's concern with individuality – and our interest is with that minority of clients who might patronize the Prairie School – was noted by Drummond: 'fortunately for art's sake the ordinary layman of the [Mid] West does not yet recognize his own "ignorance" – instead he instinctively feels an individual need, not related to former time or place. He wants

1 *Western Architect*, *21*, 1915, 11 (reprinted in the *Prairie School Review*, *1*, *2*, 1964, 8–11). Another section (pp. 11–12) of Drummond's article is worth quoting for its insight into the midwesterner's attitude toward style:

'The typical "Westerner" may request of his architect a building, "a little out of the ordinary." In other words, by way of protest against the present tendency toward "style" mongering, he is saying that he does not care for templesque or cathedralesque or for any expression of "style" intended to recall these by the use of derived forms. The architect may assure him that style may well take care of itself, provided he wants his buildings so designed as to be suitable to the limitations of actual conditions and to nicety of use, and is willing that the architect may have free opportunity to work within the scope of these restrictions.'

2 *Architectural Record*, *23*, 1908, 158. For a discussion of Wright's clients see Leonard K. Eaton, *Two Chicago Architects and Their Clients: Frank Lloyd Wright and Howard Van Doren Shaw*, Cambridge, Mass., 1969.

3 John Szarkowski, *The Idea of Louis Sullivan*, Minneapolis, 1956, p. 3. It is worth noting that Mrs Wheeler was fond of Wright's and Sullivan's work and encouraged her husband in this direction; also, she was a student of the Froebel kindergarten method.

4 *Architectural Record*, *15*, 1904, 363

5 Ibid., *38*, 1915, 386

6 Ibid., *56*, 1924, 32

"individuality" and a harmonious disposition of the elements [in his buildings].'[1] Wright expressed a similar point of view, saying of his clients: 'I found them chiefly among American men of business with unspoiled instincts and untainted ideals. A man of this type usually has the faculty of judging for himself. He has rather liked the "idea" and much of the encouragement this work receives comes straight from him because the "common sense" of the thing appeals to him.'[2] J.R. Wheeler, Sullivan's client for the Farmers and Merchants Union Bank at Columbus, Wisconsin, was a man such as Drummond and Wright described. He expressed himself as follows: 'all that I knew was that I wanted a good bank building, a place to carry on my business efficiently. Of course I wanted it to look well, but I had no deep-seated prejudices about what that meant.'[3]

Similar reactions were obtained by the author while interviewing Prairie School clients. Their choice of architect was often made because they had seen other buildings (sometimes only in magazine illustrations), either by the same architect or of similar design. These were found appealing (called 'good looking,' 'sensible,' or 'appropriate'), and so the architect was commissioned.

Clients' attitudes, however, did not remain consistent over the years. The change is documented by the architectural critic. In 1904 Arthur C. David said of the midwest architects, 'their clients ... do not seem to demand the use of European styles and remnants to the same extent as do the eastern owners of expensive dwellings,'[4] while eleven years later, in 1915, Peter B. Wight observed, 'in the course of the collecting of material for illustrating this article I have learned that a large part of the "Colonial" buildings recently erected [in the Midwest] are the result of instructions of clients rather than the recommendation of the architects.'[5] Thus a different attitude prevailed in 1904 and in 1915 and, according to Peter B. Wight, it was the client and not the architect who stipulated this change, a conclusion corroborated by Bentley's experiences in La Crosse as specifically noted at the Argyle Scott house (fig. 233) and the plan for the earlier Salzer house.

To avoid the historical styles, yet win acceptance, became increasingly difficult. To this Sullivan attested, as Wright recorded in the Masters' obituary of 1924: 'Not long ago ... Louis [Sullivan] said to me ... that it would be far more difficult now to do the radical work he did – more difficult to get accepted than when he worked.'[6] Times had changed, and with them attitudes affecting public taste.

The residential client was a single individual, or perhaps a man and wife. Wright mentioned only men when describing his clients in 1908: 'I found them chiefly among American men of business,'[7] he said. But nine years later, in 1917, Tallmadge felt compelled to include women in his discussion: 'Clients, the wives of whom at least, [having] received their architectural education in magazines edited in Boston and New York, now have turned back to pretty Colonial or the fashionable Italian.'[8]

Tallmadge's statement introduces two points of special significance. First, the wife had assumed a critical role in architect-client relations and, second, her taste in matters architectural frequently varied from that of her husband – she was less sympathetic than he to the work of the Prairie School. This view is supported by Byrne, who had a rule of thumb on entering private practice in 1914: if the initial interview indicated that decisions were made by the husband, Byrne felt sure of the commission. If, however, the wife made the family decisions, then Byrne considered the job as good as lost. Whereas the husband would accept Byrne's designs as logical and apparently sound, the wife would reject them as being out of fashion.[9] The J.F. Clarke house, for example, was built only after Mrs Clarke's attempt to get a colonial design was thwarted (see chapter 7, p. 292). In this vein Byrne noted: 'I recall Mr Richard E. Schmidt once saying to me that it wasn't the clients who were a problem in this connection; it was their wives and daughters.'[10]

The testimony is consistent and corroborated by contemporary literature. Sinclair Lewis' *Main Street*, with its brilliant characterization of rural midwestern life, relates precisely to our theme. The time is between 1912 and the end of the war; the locale is a typical, though fictitious, town called Gopher Prairie, Minnesota. Carol, as the heroine and wife of Dr Will Kennicott, represents the liberated female who seeks to reshape her world according to her own ideas – to reform Gopher Prairie, her household, and her husband. Her single-mindedness on matters architectural – she wants a colonial house but her husband does not – is a primary factor in the disruption of their marriage. For Carol a colonial house becomes a symbol of culture and only when, after a prolonged separation, Will feigns fondness for colonial designs – 'I see how you mean. They make me think of those pictures of an old-fashioned Christmas'[11] – does reconciliation seem at hand.

Such schisms between man and wife existed and were occasionally incarnated in the design of a house. At the Salzer house (1912), as mentioned above (p. 265, fig. 185), Bentley's exterior conformed to Mr Salzer's preferences while his interior incorporated the colonial plan stipulated by Mrs

7 Ibid., *23*, 1908, 158

8 *Western Architect*, 25, 1917, 27

9 Told to the author in interview, July 1961. Byrne's midwestern practice began in 1914, just as the client problem was becoming acute.

10 Barry Byrne, 'The Chicago Movement,' paper delivered before the Illinois Society of Architects, 28 November 1939. Manuscript at the Ricker Library, University of Illinois

11 Sinclair Lewis, *Main Street* (Signet Classics editions), New York, 1963, pp. 419–20. Among American literary works *Main Street* is uniquely appropriate for comparison with the situation facing the prairie architects. The time is 1912–18, the setting a rural midwestern town, and the characters represent the upper middle class. Most other Chicago literature was portraying the social extremes, abject poverty or incredible wealth, as in Theodore Dreiser's *Sister Carrie* and *The Titan*. Sister Carrie, of course, had more pressing financial needs than the luxury of building a house; Cowperwood, the titan, had more money than he could spend. Yet when he built his Chicago mansion about 1880 this social-climbing financier from Philadelphia selected – without seeking his wife's advice – both the architect and the style (French château) for his house; he had no need to contend with an emancipated wife.

12 Letter to the author dated 13 November 1956

13 This parallels the concurrent situation in Germany where Peter Behrens, Walter Gropius, Eric Mendelsohn, and others found acceptance largely outside the realm of the single family house.

Salzer. A similar situation developed with the D.S. Browns of Peoria, Illinois (see above, p. 265). Mr Brown approached Wright but his wife rejected the architect's ideas of interior design. A compromise architect was therefore hired who built the split-personality house of which Mrs Brown later said: 'The outside is a Frank Lloyd Wright design – the inside is English and furnished with antiques.'[12]

Other evidence confirming that women were less sympathetic toward the Prairie School than men (who were subject to many of the same cultural influences) is evident in the post-war period. At that time commissions were still available if the prairie architect abandoned residential work, with its dual clients, in favor of other types of buildings. Byrne remained active by specializing in ecclesiastical and education work; Elmslie designed schools, universities, banks, churches, and funeral homes (often classified as conservative among building types), though for him, as for Byrne, house design had been a specialty prior to 1914–18. The residential client, quite obviously, no longer wanted their designs.[13]

The weight of evidence, therefore, including the buildings themselves, indicates that clients more than architects, and women more than men, were receptive to the change in ideals which led to the demise of the Prairie School. Yet these propositions, and the general cultural milieu, require further consideration.

While the pressure for conformity was continuous, patronage of the Prairie School abruptly diminished after 1914. This date coincides with the European war, but it was a combination of events, not a single factor, that brought about the change. Women's rights had long been increasing, while interest in the Arts and Crafts Movement, bungalows, Craftsman furnishing (all discussed in chapter 1), and the like, had long been on the wane. Women gained the suffrage in 1920; the last prairie houses appeared in the *House Beautiful* in 1914 – and in 1916 the *Craftsman* ceased publication because it was no longer attuned to public taste (the readers were discontented with Stickley's designs and demanded more examples of colonial work). Thus the paradox: when women exerted less influence (c. 1900) in matters architectural they were more sympathetic toward the work of the Prairie School; by 1914, when their authority had increased, they were not in sympathy with the work of the Prairie School. The concurrence of these factors does much to explain why the reaction was so sudden. By the time the post-war building boom got underway, patronage had been withdrawn from the Prairie School.

Increasingly the orientation of the midwesterner had been eastward.

The tale of 'The Russells in Chicago, the experiences of a young Boston couple who moved to the West' (see chapter 1, p. 15), lost much of its validity between 1901 (when published) and 1914. Social attitudes were becoming less distinct and the frontier concept of Chicago (previously called the 'West' rather than the 'Midwest') was fast breaking down. These changes affected women more directly than men. Indicative perhaps is the fact that until about 1910 Rockford College, Rockford, Illinois, was the proper place to send one's daughter; thereafter only Smith or Vassar would do. The homemaker magazine (which owed its very existence to the new role of the housewife) followed suit. In 1910 the *House Beautiful*, longtime friend of the Arts and Crafts Movement and the Prairie School, abandoned Chicago and moved east – and after 1914 ceased to support the Prairie School. In New York it joined its younger competitors, the *House and Garden* (founded New York 1901) and *American Homes and Gardens* (founded New York 1905), in expressing an eastern point of view. Eastward also went several among the literary group. Hamlin Garland moved to New York in 1915, and by 1920 both Edgar Lee Masters and Sherwood Anderson had left Chicago. Travel, whether for pleasure or because of the war, heightened the midwesterner's awareness of other regions and different standards of taste. This, combined with wartime nationalism and a patriotic sympathy for the mother country – England – added impetus to the prevailing revival of colonial and Tudor Gothic forms.

By the 1920s the interior decorator came into his own and, backed by the authority of the homemaker magazines, these self-styled mentors of public taste concentrated on the lady of the house. The built-in, individualistic, and almost impossible to 'decorate' prairie houses were hardly on their recommended list. Not so, however, with the speculative builder. It is, in fact, surprising how often these men accepted the work of the Prairie School as their example, debased and inept as the result might be. But the lack of character and quality in their homemade, often ill-conceived designs did more to discredit than enhance the prestige of the movement. Rarely does the speculative builder seek out the established architect. A notable exception was Arthur L. Richards of Milwaukee, for whom Wright designed the American System-Built houses, few of which, however, were actually built.

'Americanism' and 'democracy' were bywords among architects, and might be used in reference to traditional or to highly original designs. Sullivan preferred the word democracy; Wright later adopted the word Usonian, meaning United Statesian. An article entitled 'A Plea for Americanism in

14 The author was Van Bergen, and the article was published in the *Western Architect*, 21, 1915, 24–31.

15 Robert Wendell, 'Colonial Architecture,' *House Beautiful*, 2, 1897, 53

Our Architecture' could as easily allude to the colonial revival as to the work of the prairie architects (it was, actually, written to support the latter).[14] Robert Wendell, in 1897, said that 'Colonial Architecture ... still remains the only distinctly American style which has arisen since the first settlement of our country,'[15] a belief which inevitably gained force during the 1914–18 war. In the year of Wendell's remark Maher called his Farson house (fig. 4) 'colonial,' not because it revived colonial forms but because of its so-called simplicity. Confusion existed between forms and ideals and the border line between revival and invention was very close. Thus when Prairie School architecture is observed out of context it seems radical, but in reference to time and place it seems less daring.

This delicate balance between revivalism and the prairie house, usually unnoticed, is important to understand. It explains much about the architecture as well as about the school itself. The James R. Chapman house by Nimmons and Fellows at Kenilworth, 1910 (fig. 129), can be analyzed from two points of view – as a prairie house or as a revival of Tudor Gothic. All the external characteristics of a prairie house are here – an interplay between verticals and horizontals, with the long, low-pitched gable roofs accentuating the horizontal, a horizontality which is emphasized by bands of windows, continuous sills, multiple string courses, strong divisions between the storeys, brickwork with raked joints and, finally, the lower roofs spread laterally across the landscape. This description fits a prairie house, yet the design is decidedly English – and for many of the same reasons. Wood strips on stucco suggest half-timbering, multiple gables – although severely ordered – recall medieval, while the combination of brick and stucco intensifies the English effect. And the Tudor arched doorway, cruciform window mullions, central hall plan, and panelled interior confirm what was foremost in the architects' minds. Lest this design be dismissed too readily as mere revival, however, a comparison, full of significance and highly provocative, should be made between the Chapman house (fig. 129) and the William Emery house by Griffin (fig. 29). This comparison speaks for itself.

Such comparisons need not be limited to dwellings. Banks were second only to houses among Prairie School designs and here again a parallel existed with the prevailing mode. Wright's pace-setting project for the First National Bank of Dwight, Illinois (fig. 74) combined two temple-like piers in antis with the high attic of a triumphal arch. True, this combined form does not look like a classical building because of the precise rectangular shapes, unorthodox materials, and absence of classical ornament.

Yet the relation is there. At this time most banks sported free-standing columns and a pediment, yet during the war and post-war years the two columns in antis, flat roof, and severely rectangular (safety deposit box) shape became prevalent – perhaps influenced by the Prairie School. An example is the Detroit Savings Bank (1916) on Woodward Avenue at Milwaukee Avenue E. in Detroit.[16] Designed by Albert Kahn, whose early work was occasionally influenced by the prairie architects, this bank is as severely rectilinear as Sullivan's Merchants' National Bank at Grinnell, which is perhaps recalled in the column-screened window along the side. Two columns in antis repeat the motif in Wright's unpublished project, a motif more familiar in the work of Purcell and Elmslie (the Merchants Bank of Winona, fig. 130, or the Edison Shop in Chicago, fig. 155).

An affinity in form (but not in plan or ornament) existed between prairie architecture and the current revival styles. Though different, they were related, and this relation was one reason for the existence, and for the acceptance, of the Prairie School. And in like manner the prairie house, bank, or courthouse could undergo certain mutations and return to the guise of a historical style. This did happen, especially among the less central or peripheral members of the group, men like Spencer, Garden, Perkins, Tallmadge and Watson, Maher, Dean, Tomlinson, and White. These men began their careers in the prevailing modes, but evolved toward a freer and more independent expression. Later, however, they ebbed back into the tradition from which they had grown. The distinction, often, was not great. Charles White, Jr's work (see the J.F. Skinner house, fig. 55) seldom crossed that line. Spencer's gardener's lodge on the Stevens estate of c. 1901 (fig. 17) evolved something substantially new from a recognizable type, as did Wright in his *Ladies' Home Journal* project 'A Fireproof House for $5000' of 1906 (fig. 62). The Chapman house, however, epitomized that moment when the prairie house was apparently fusing back into the main stream of development (fig. 129). Some prairie architects, Sullivan, Byrne, Griffin, Mahony, Purcell and Elmslie, and Wright (except for his bootleg houses and the N.G. Moore house) forever avoided historicism – although the small gabled houses by Purcell and Elmslie occasionally recall English design. Drummond and Bentley, by contrast, were initially independent but later turned to eclecticism (see figs. 247 and 233). Among the various architects, therefore, the entire range of possibilities was accounted for.

This affinity between prairie architecture and the prevailing norm was significant for several reasons. It helps explain why prairie architecture

16 For an illustration see: *Architectural Record, 43*, 1918, 84.

17 The sponsors were the Illinois Society of Architects, the Illinois Chapter of the American Institute of Architects, the Art Institute of Chicago, as well as the Chicago Architectural Club.

In spite of the apathy which existed, or perhaps because of it, the Prairie School was well represented at the last few Chicago Architectural Club exhibitions, where these architects, and their sympathizers, regularly served on the jury of admissions. The most notable instance was that of 1914 when, among others, Wright entered 32 items.

came to exist, and why it passed into oblivion. It also suggests why some architects apparently teetered between two alternatives, alternatives not as distinct as they may seem. And because the *basic* external distinctions were not always obvious to the uninitiated (only the superficial ones) some clients more readily accepted the work of the Prairie School. Actually the real design distinction is to be found in the plan but, alas, few potential clients appreciated this fact. Or perhaps they did understand it, and it was because of the plan, not exterior design, that this architecture was rejected. We noted (at the Salzer and Brown houses) that when one thing was sacrificed, it was the unconventional interior, not the exterior design. Thus the truly significant contribution of Wright and his contemporaries (a new concept of interior space) was ill-understood and often not accepted.

Our discussion thus far has dealt with the client, the general cultural milieu, and the relation between the Prairie School and prevailing eclecticism. Next we must speak of the architects, and the school itself, for here also are to be found poignant reasons for the demise of the prairie movement. The ease with which some men (such as Spencer) crossed historical bounds has already been discussed. Significant also was the inability to attract strong, new blood after 1903 – the date that Sullivan hired Purcell. Later recruits, such as Bentley, Van Bergen, Willatzen, Francis Sullivan, and Berry, were not the equal of Purcell, Elmslie, Griffin, Byrne, or, obviously, Louis Sullivan and Wright. And of singular importance is the fact that the years of greatest achievement (1909–1914/16) saw the fewest newcomers – only Bentley and Berry. The maturing generation more willingly accepted the status quo; for example, the Chicago Architectural Club was unable to arouse sufficient interest among its members to continue its famous exhibitions. Its last Annual Exhibition was held in the spring of 1914; thereafter an Annual Chicago Architectural Exhibition, sponsored jointly by several organizations, took its place.[17]

Personal factors, not unique to the group, also took their toll. Some members of the group, such as Sullivan, Drummond, and Elmslie, worked less well alone than when in partnership. Others, such as Schmidt and Garden, were distracted by an expanding business, and accepted a more expedient course. Still others, trained as residential architects, were unable or unwilling to seek new specialties when their residential market failed. A house designer, for example, was ill-equipped to design skyscrapers – as was made evident by the Chicago Tribune Tower competition of 1922. Griffin, Drummond, and Spencer made submissions, but their designs left much to be desired.

The movement's accelerated growth, rapid though it was, was inevitably affected by the departures of Wright, Griffin, and Purcell. But in spite of the impact which Wright's personal life and travels had upon his own career – and they were profound – there is no concrete evidence, contrary to general opinion, that this jeopardized the movement as a whole. One point is absolutely clear: the school without Wright survived, and enjoyed greater prosperity and prestige than ever before.

A misfortune was its inability to win approbation from families of great wealth, which would have added commissions and prestige but probably would not have extended, appreciably, the movement's life. Only two immensely important social commissions came to the Prairie School and both were of early date and went to Wright. For Harold McCormick, heir to the reaper fortune, Wright planned a sprawling lakeshore home in 1908. But this brilliant design was rejected by Mrs Edith Rockefeller McCormick and an Italianate mansion by the eastern architect C.A. Platt was built instead. Equally regrettable was the loss of the commission for the Henry Ford estate which, in effect, was forfeited when Wright, in 1909, left his practice in the hands of von Holst.

The midwest architect-client situation of 1914–16 contrasts sharply with that in the east of some 25 years before, when McKim, Mead and White, without specific instructions from their clients, abandoned the precedent of their earlier work and submitted academic designs for the Villard houses and the Boston Public Library. Yet the midwest conditions were similar to concurrent ones in California. After 1908 the highly personal work of Greene and Greene and of Gill enjoyed considerable local prestige and nationwide publicity; their continued success seemed assured.[18] But as suddenly as in the Midwest these architects found themselves without clients. For this reason, in 1916, the Greene brothers went into semi-retirement and Gill closed his San Diego office; at Los Angeles he had little but remodeling work to do.[19] The Panama-Pacific exposition at San Diego (1915) had firmly established Bertram Goodhue's Spanish colonial as the reigning mode.

The cultural, sociological changes that culminated with the 1914–18 war were prodigious, far too broad and complex to be examined in this limited survey. Involved was the entire western world; England, Austria, and Australia were as profoundly affected as was the American Midwest – and all in a similar way. To understand why the Arts and Crafts Movement ended in England – or the Secession in Austria, or the commercial work in Chicago, or the residential developments in southern California – is to

18 The work of Greene and Greene first appeared in the *Inland Architect and News Record* and the *Western Architect* in 1908, and the latter magazine first illustrated Gill's buildings in 1909. Stickley gave the California architects more publicity than he did the Prairie School, with the first Greene and Greene houses illustrated in the *Craftsman* of 1909 followed by a major article in 1912; Gill wrote an article, illustrated with his own work, which appeared in 1916.

19 Concerning the closing of the Greene brothers office, see L. Morgan Yost, 'Greene and Greene of Pasadena,' *Journal of the American Institute of Architects*, *14*, 1950, 125; and regarding Irving Gill's office see Esther McCoy, *Five California Architects*, New York, 1960, p. 87.

20 D.H. Burnham is usually criticized for permitting eastern architects to establish the design character of the World's Columbian Exposition in 1893, rather than presenting this opportunity to the architects of the Chicago School. Yet what would they have done? Unless they constructed skyscrapers on the fairgrounds they had little else to offer. As Dimitri Tselos has rightly observed (*Journal of the Society of Architectural Historians*, 26, 1967, 259–68), Sullivan's Transportation Building was not structurally remarkable nor, except for the splendid Golden Doorway, was it a brilliant architectural design. And Root's unexecuted project, or Cobb's Fisheries Building, were intrinsically even less rewarding.

21 Vincent J. Scully, Jr, *The Shingle Style*, New Haven, 1955, pp. 157–8

reach toward an understanding of what happened in the other areas. The Prairie School was not an isolated phenomenon, but rather a regional manifestation of the international reform or revolt that occurred during the late nineteenth and early twentieth centuries. Our discussion has touched only on the local factors relevant to the Midwest – how, for example, the homemaker magazines influenced the client – and has not dealt with the broader question of why the magazines, their editors, and their New York publishers advocated the designs which they did. Such would constitute a study in itself.

Among the other turn-of-the-century movements, none compares more closely to the Prairie School than the Viennese Secession. Each was inspired by an older man – Louis Sullivan in Chicago and Otto Wagner in Vienna – and each occurred at virtually the same time. Both owed much to locally prevailing modes, as well as to England, and both phased back into a more conservative expression once their impetus was spent. The Vienna group, however, was smaller and less productive; only Wagner, Olbrich, Hoffmann, and Loos were principal participants. Although highly publicized, their best work seldom equalled, and rarely if ever surpassed, the finest designs produced in the American Midwest. They did, nevertheless, have a more direct influence on the architecture of the 1920s.

Earlier in date was the sensuous Art Nouveau, with its attempt to break with the past and self-consciously create something new, rather than just to seek reform. In this it enjoyed a marked success, particularly in the decorative arts, but its ultimate architectural influence was less profound than that of the Austrian or American groups.

During the late nineteenth century in Chicago (where William Le Barron Jenney perhaps came closest to being father of the group in which Adler and Sullivan played the most distinguished role) the true character of a school hardly existed, nor did these architects develop a universally expressive style – one that was applicable to all building types, and not limited only to tall commercial structures.[20] This lack posed severe limitations on their effectiveness, and inevitably reduced their influence.

In California, home of the ubiquitous bungalow, highly personal expression by several men – notably Maybeck, Gill, and Greene and Greene – were characteristic rather than a cohesive school. Of these individuals only the Greene brothers developed a following, although no strong personalities emerged. Their work, as Vincent Scully has observed,[21] represented the last phase of the Shingle Style rather than something vital and new. Their houses typified an Arts and Crafts craftsmanship at its best, and were strongly influenced by Japan. Gill, by contrast, achieved his formal expression by ordering and simplifying the so-called Mission Style, the effect of which was close in spirit to the somewhat later work of Loos and Oud in Europe. Maybeck's architecture expressed a romantic world, charming but aloof.

The Sullivan phase, the preliminary one in the history of the Prairie School, is clearly represented among the first 30 illustrations of this book: Garden at the Herrick and Madlener houses (figs. 5 and 9), Spencer at the McCready house (fig. 38), Dean in the Alpha Delta Phi Fraternity (fig. 22), Nimmons and Fellows at the Rosenwald house (fig. 13), Maher for John Farson (fig. 4), and Wright at the Charnley house or Francis Apartments – all of these (except the Rosenwald house [1903] and the McCready house [1907]), designed in or before 1902. Sullivan's message was that of elimination and simplification, of accepting the building mass and transforming it by ordering and simplifying the individual forms, the mass, and the openings, and then integrating a structured ornament. This is what he had done at the Auditorium Building and the Wainwright Building, with their echoes of the Marshall Field Warehouse and the palazzo form. This process of design was mirrored by the younger architects, as is so evident in Garden's Madlener house or Spencer's McCready house (figs. 9 and 38), and in Wright's more complete and personalized transformation of building forms, as in his Thomas house (1901) or project for 'A Fireproof House for $5000.' The intent was to reform, but through reform to create something substantially new – an architecture of democracy as Sullivan called it – a uniquely American architecture which had been sought so long.

Sullivan, as teacher, offered a manner of thinking, a means to achieve an end; Wright, while advocating an organic architecture, communicated formal solutions – stylisms – more effectively than a means of design. Organic architecture, vital as a concept, had little to do with creating expressive forms. The road to independence lay not in separating Wright's concept from his vocabulary of form (as he had hoped), but in accepting his forms as a consequence of his process, and then applying Sullivan's manner of thinking to gain independence and a more individual, personal expression. This final stage was epitomized in such remarkable designs as the Clarke house by Byrne (1915, fig. 209), the Stinson Memorial Library or Blythe house by Griffin (1913, figs. 179, 183), and the River Forest Women's Club by Drummond (1913, fig. 187), all by Wright's former apprentices. But the simplifying tendencies were also apparent in work that

22 *Architectural Record*, 65, 1929, 434
23 See Vincent J. Scully, Jr, 'Wright vs. the International Style,' *Art News*, 53, 1954, 32–5, 64–6, and also Scully's 'The Heritage of Wright,' *Zodiac 8*, 1961, 8–13.

stemmed from entirely non-Wrightian sources, such as the pre-1902 examples already mentioned, or later examples, such as the Golbeck and Carroll houses by Tallmadge and Watson (1914, 1916, figs. 202, 228), or the Powers and Beebe houses by Purcell and Elmslie (1910, 1912, figs. 125, 149).

The second phase of the Prairie School, therefore, was dominated by Wright's contribution – his own work, the earlier work of his former apprentices, and the work of those subject to his direct influence. All who trained at Wright's Studio naturally began their independent careers reflecting his personal style; the true test of his creativity came only after years of searching. Thus Griffin's work from 1906 to 1911 was largely Wrightian; thereafter he evolved his own more individual expression. For some, such as Van Bergen, true independence was not forthcoming. This second phase, commencing after 1902 with Wright's maturity, began to wane by 1909, the year of Wright's departure and of the founding of the firm of Purcell, Feick and Elmslie.

In its third phase, with the various influences assimilated, the Prairie School reached full maturity and found fulfilment in creating the often brilliant designs that crowned the period from 1909 to 1914/16. Self-supporting, vital, and strong, the school seemed destined to continue, until deprived of its clientele. Yet over the preceding months and years these architects had proved their skill, and created a significant body of intrinsically superior work – their legacy to the future.

Post-war America turned its back on this more inventive aspect of her architectural past, thus completing the trend commenced years before. There was no immediate sequel to the Prairie School; America was not ready to support one, any more than she was prepared to extend the life of the school itself. Yet buildings are their own best testimony and the work of the Prairie School inevitably tempered the derivative designs of successive years, 'quieting the skyline, broadening and strengthening the mass, ordering the openings, reducing the "fancy-feathers," [and] marrying all of them to the ground,' as Wright was wont to phrase it.[22] This, however, was small consolation; a marvelous opportunity had been lost.

The immediate line of continuity lay elsewhere, especially in Europe through Wright's publications, and in Australia through the personal influence of Griffin. On both continents the impact was profound, but for America's future the European branch was the more significant; it fed back into the American stream.[23] Wright's work became well known in Europe through major publications in Germany and in Holland; he also held an exhibition in Berlin. To a limited extent other members of the Prairie School were also known in Europe. Griffin exhibited in Paris in 1914, the year of his visit to Europe, and as early as 1910 his work (as well as that of Tallmadge and Watson, White, and Schmidt and Garden) was published in Alexander Koch's *Academy Architecture. Architectur des* xx *Jahrhunderts* published Griffin's Carter house in 1914 and F.R. Vogel's *Das Amerikanishe Haus* (Berlin, 1910) recognized the midwest contribution years before similar recognition was accorded in an American book.

When American architecture sought regeneration it turned to Europe and elsewhere rather than to its own native soil. The indigenous quality of the Prairie School held little appeal during the interval between the wars. Only after 1945 was it rediscovered, when public taste again favored a low, small-scale, anti-monumental architecture, an architecture rooted in the earth. By then, however, continuity was broken, principles were forgotten, and the architects dead or dispersed. The features of the prairie house, often ill-understood and debased, were incorporated into the promoter-built split-level or ranch-style houses of mid-century. Only in California, and more recently in the Midwest, has the work of the early century inspired a younger generation in the direction of a new, vital course for American architecture.

The prairies of the Midwest are dotted with buildings that nestle quietly into the broad, flat landscape where they seem to belong. Silently they pay homage to the Prairie School. For here remains the record of one of the most native, original, and dynamic developments in the history of American architecture.

BIBLIO GRAPHICAL NOTE

The footnotes have dealt extensively with matters of bibliography, providing information not to be repeated here. Nor is it intended to list a definitive bibliography for the more than twenty architects discussed, that objective being more appropriate to a monograph. This note, therefore, will primarily consider the major sources for Prairie School research and, presumably, offer guidance to those seeking additional background or wishing to pursue the subject further. The specialist must ultimately use the footnotes.

Three types of material will be considered: primary source material, secondary sources of more recent publication date, and background information. The latter – chiefly a knowledge of Wright's early work – may prove helpful in approaching this study, with Grant C. Manson's *Frank Lloyd Wright to 1910* (New York, 1958) and Henry-Russell Hitchcock's *In the Nature of Materials* (New York, 1942) being particularly appropriate, although several shorter accounts exist. Among the group, only Wright was to publish an autobiography (Frank Lloyd Wright, *An Autobiography*, New York, 1932 and 1943). Hopefully my introduction, which chronicles the Prairie School in history, will also help to furnish background.

The primary sources are of two types – original documents and contemporary publications (with the latter especially useful in preparing this book). The *Western Architect*, but only after 1911, contains the best illustrative material, most of which appeared in special issues devoted to a single architect. These were on Purcell, Feick and Elmslie (Volume *19*, Number 1, January 1913); Griffin as planner and architect (*19*, 8, August 1913); Maher (*20*, 3, March 1914); Spencer and Powers (*20*, 4, April 1914); Purcell and Elmslie (*21*, 1, January 1915); Guenzel and Drummond (*21*, 2, February 1915); Van Bergen (*21*, 4, April 1915); Purcell and Elmslie (*22*, 1, July 1915); Tallmadge and Watson (*22*, 6, December 1915); Byrne (*34*, 2, February 1925, with additional work in *33*, 3, March 1924). The three special issues devoted to Purcell and Elmslie have been republished, with an introduction by David Gebhard, as *The Work of Purcell and Elmslie, Architects* (Prairie School Press, Park Forest, 1965). A reprinting of other monograph issues would be most welcome.

No journal gave the Prairie School more consistent coverage over the years than the *Architectural Record* and, in a more restricted sense, the *House Beautiful*; both are indispensable for research. The Chicago-based *Inland Architect and News Record* is less helpful, being useful only for the pre-1900 years and for Maher's work after that date. *The Brickbuilder* (which after 1916 became the *Architectural Forum*) gave some coverage, especially in the earlier years, as did the *Architectural Review* of Boston. The role of these magazines has been discussed at length in the text. The illustrated *Catalogue* of the annual Chicago Architectural Club exhibition is the rarest of all bibliographical items. It began publication in 1894, its title varies, and in some years the list of exhibits and exhibitors was printed separately from the illustrated booklet. These lists furnish indispensable information concerning architects' addresses, where they were employed, and what were their most recent commissions (terminal dates on designs).

Personal archives happily exist for four of the principal architects. Wright's drawings (but few other records from the early days) are held by the Frank Lloyd Wright Foundation at Phoenix, Arizona, while other items, primarily from the John Lloyd Wright Collection, are in the Avery Library, Columbia University. The Purcell and Elmslie archives, surely one of the most systematically preserved and complete in America, were assembled and catalogued under Purcell's personal direction. The collection is presently on deposit at the University of Minnesota. Griffin's work, mostly as renderings prepared by Marion Mahony Griffin, is at the Art Department, Northwestern University, the Burnham Library at the Art Institute of Chicago, and the Avery Library. Final disposition of Byrne's remarkable collection of drawings and office records has not been made. Maher's life work was destroyed some ten years ago – at a time when libraries were unwilling or ill-prepared to accept such collections. Of the other architects' work only occasional drawings remain.

One of the richest sources of architectural drawings remains uncatalogued and virtually untouched; these are the blueprints possessed by the buildings owners. These are every bit as useful for research and documentation as the working drawings (ink on tracing paper or linen) from which they were printed, yet because of the collector's mania for 'originals' these have been largely overlooked. The situation also reflects a curious quirk among preservationists, who prepare costly measured drawings of significant buildings while paying little heed to blueprints. It seems to me that the first (and cheaper) priority should be to preserve a record of blueprints; they show the architect's real intention rather than the client's modifications. In this respect much praise is due the exemplary 'Burnham Library–University of Illinois Architectural Microfilming Project' of 1950–2 which, under the chairmanship of Earl Reed, recorded nearly 6,000 architectural drawings – mostly work of the Chicago and Prairie Schools. This project, which has been continued by the Burnham Library at a slow pace (2,700 drawings), deserves encouragement.

Original correspondence from the architects to their clients and colleagues is scarce, with the result that most quotations used in this book are from letters written to the author by surviving members of the Prairie School – now all dead.

Last but not least are the buildings themselves. Fortunately most survive because they are located far from large city centers. And they have withstood the temptation of clients to remodel or 'modernize' because this has not been necessary; the buildings have proven satisfactory in terms of contemporary needs. The most common mistreatment has been a coat of white paint and the removal of leaded glass or wood-mullioned windows. Happily the HABS (Historic American Buildings Survey, National Park Service, Department of the Interior) is recording increasing numbers of these buildings, and their drawings, photographs, and data sheets are being preserved at the Library of Congress.

The revival of interest in Prairie School architecture beginning late in the 1950s has led to ever increasing research and publication. David Gebhard is the undisputed authority on Purcell and Elmslie with his doctoral dissertation ('William Gray Purcell and George Grant Elmslie and the Early Progressive Movement in American Architecture from 1900 to 1920,' University of Minnesota, 1957) containing a wealth of information; he has also written numerous articles and his book should soon appear. Griffin has had more researchers, the first being Mark L. Peisch, whose 1959 dissertation was published under the title *The Chicago School of*

Architecture (London, 1964; New York, 1965); it is studded with factual inaccuracies. James Birrell's *Walter Burley Griffin* (Brisbane, 1964) emphasizes the planner-architect's Australian career and is rather weak on Griffin in America. David T. Van Zanten has edited *Walter Burley Griffin: Selected Drawings* (Palos Park, 1970), which presents some 50 splendid renderings mostly prepared by Marion Griffin of her husband's work. Carl W. Condit, in a special chapter of his *The Chicago School of Architecture* (Chicago and London, 1964), discusses early twentieth-century developments; and Sherman Paul in *Louis Sullivan, An Architect in American Thought* (Englewood Cliffs, 1962) investigates the intellectual milieu surrounding Sullivan and his younger colleagues during much the same period. Hugh Morrison's *Louis Sullivan* (New York, 1935) remains the classic Sullivan monograph; it deals at some length with the architect's post-1900 career. Willard Connely's biography, *Louis Sullivan as He Lived* (New York, 1960) is particularly helpful for understanding the man. The most pertinent early-Wright material has already been discussed.

Articles increasingly are appearing in American and foreign journals, especially since the founding of the *Prairie School Review* in 1964. This quarterly, profusely illustrated with high quality photographs, drawings, and plans, is publishing numerous studies among which some of the most exemplary are those by Joseph Griggs on Iannelli (2, 4, 1965), David T. Van Zanten on Mahony (3, 2, 1966), Donald L. Hoffmann on Berry (4, 1, 1967), and Robert E. McCoy on Griffin's work at Mason City (5, 3, 1968). The publisher, the Prairie School Press, has also made available reprints and new books pertaining to the Prairie School.

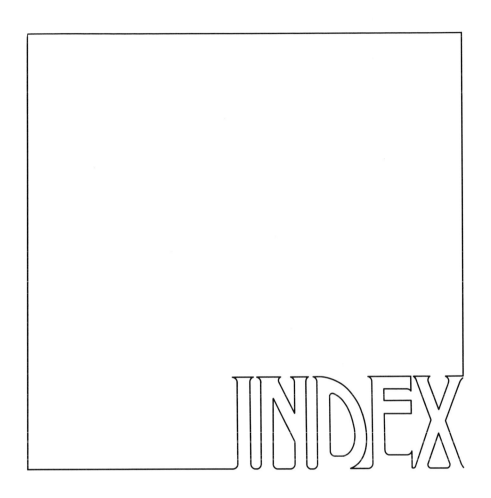

INDEX

The main biographical entry for each architect, as well as the principal discussion of each building, is designated in boldface type. Buildings are indexed according to architect (thereby establishing a check list of work discussed), and by location (thereby serving as a guide to Prairie School architecture).

This book

was designed by

WILLIAM RUETER

under the direction of

ALLAN FLEMING

of the

University of

Toronto

Press